# Michael Engle and Mario Monti

STACKPOLE
BOOKS

Published by
STACKPOLE BOOKS
5067 Ritter Road
Mechanicsburg, PA 17055
www.stackpolebooks.com

Printed in the United States of America

10 9 8 7 6 5 4 3 2 1

FIRST EDITION

*Cover design by Tessa J. Sweigart and Caroline Stover*

**Library of Congress Cataloging-in-Publication Data**

Engle, Michael.
    Diners of New York / Michael Engle and Mario Monti. — 1st ed.
      p.    cm.
    Includes bibliographical references and index.
    ISBN 978-0-8117-3525-4 (pbk.)
    1. Diners (Restaurants)—New York (State)—Guidebooks.  2. Diners
(Restaurants)—New York (State)—History.  I. Monti, Mario, 1929–  II. Title.
TX907.3.N7155E54   2008
647.95747—dc22
                                        2008026551

FOR LUCILLE

# Contents

# A Word about
# Diner Manufacturers

As you read this book, you'll notice many references to diner manufacturers. This section offers a crash course on the companies that made the diners and provides some pointers for identifying a diner's make. Several of the following descriptions are excerpted from *Diners of Pennsylvania*, by Brian Butko and Kevin Patrick. We have added some regional variations.

**DeRaffele.** 1933–present, New Rochelle, New York. Vertical fluting in the 1940s, fluted corners combined with streamline style in the 1950s, angular vestibule overhang starting around 1960, zigzag rooflines in the 1960s, arched windows with orange tile mansard roofs in the 1970s. Newer diners and remodels have many 90-degree lines and exaggerated exteriors.

**Fodero.** 1933–81, Bloomfield, New Jersey. Either horizontal stainless or flat vertical porcelain fluting in the 1940s, both having rounded corners with stainless sunbursts. The company used the name **National** from 1940 to 1945 and thereafter referred to those models as Foderos. Vertical stainless ribs below roofline in the 1950s.

**Kullman.** 1927–present, Avenel, New Jersey. Vertical fluting in the 1940s, picture windows beginning in the 1950s, five-foot-wide canopy starting in 1955. The company began making other structures in 1969, and by 1990 only 7 percent of its output was diners.

**Mountain View.** 1939–57, Singac, New Jersey. Distinctive rolling roofline and glass block corners after World War II, cowcatcher corners in the late 1940s to early 1950s, square roof corners in the early 1950s, and thin scrolls at roofline in the late 1950s.

**O'Mahony.** 1913–56, Bayonne, New Jersey. Barrel roofs up to 1930s, monitor roofs in mid-1930s with transom windows up to about 1940. Formica ceiling work in early 1940s. Flat porcelain panels on the outside until the early 1940s, rounded end windows from the late 1930s through 1950s. Stainless steel exterior from mid-1940s.

**Paramount/PMC.** 1932–present, Oakland, New Jersey. Completely stainless with burnished circles or vertical fluting in the 1940s, balls on wedding-cake or waterfall corner tops in late 1940s, zigzag rooflines in the 1960s.

**Silk City.** 1927–64, Paterson, New Jersey. This is the only make that was not custom built. Old-style monitor roofs until about 1952. Siding look until the mid-1950s with porcelain enamel horizontal metal area. Corners in the 1950s were slim with stainless early, glass later. Zigzag stainless pattern with large windows in the 1960s.

**Sterling.** 1936–42, Merrimac, Massachusetts. This company constructed barrel-roof sectional diners with porcelain enamel panels on the inside and outside, usually cream colored.

**Swingle.** 1957–88, Middlesex, New Jersey. Vertical stainless fluting along roofline on early models.

**Tierney.** 1905–33, New Rochelle. Patrick Tierney founded this company in New Rochelle. After his death in 1917, his sons, Edward and Edgar, took over the business and manufactured up to a diner a day by 1925. Their barrel-roof diners included indoor toilets and interior tiling.

**Ward & Dickinson.** 1924–circa 1940, Silver Creek. Charles Ward, previously a hotel manager, and Lee Dickinson, a prominent businessman, came together in Silver Creek to build lunch cars. Their business produced the most diners of any manufacturer in western New York. Their standard model, for which Ward received a design patent, was known as the Ward Dining Car. Their diners are best known for their green stained glass on the upper sash of the diners' windows.

Another way to identify a diner is to look for tags. The usual location for tags is inside or outside the main door. In later models, tags can be found inside above the doors to the vestibule or above the doors to the bathrooms. O'Mahony identification numbers can be found on the back of the removable interior transom windows on older diners and on the outside doors of later diners, such as the Skylark Diner in Vestal.

There are a few diners in New York built by other manufacturers: **Bixler,** Norwalk, Ohio (1931–36); **Comac,** Irvington, New Jersey (1947–51); **Manno,** Fairfield, New Jersey (1949–78); **Master,** Pequannock, New Jersey (1947–57); **Valentine,** Wichita, Kansas (1938–74); and **Worcester,** Worcester, Massachusetts (1906–61).

New York was home to many lunch wagon and diner manufacturers. The following are some of the older, more obscure ones.

**Bramson Engineering.** 1958, Oyster Bay. Two stainless steel diners were constructed by the company in Oyster Bay, Long Island.

**Closson Lunch Wagon Company.** 1903–17, Glens Falls, Westfield. Albert Closson built lunch wagons with monitor roofs (similar to trolley cars) in Glens Falls, New York, before his company was bought by Dr. Charles Welch and moved to Westfield, New York.

**General Diner Co.** 1939–42, Watertown, Oswego. Founded by Arthur Halladay and Morris Whitehouse in Watertown, the company quickly moved to Oswego, where it manufactured sectional diners. Whitehouse made one more go of it in Syracuse in 1942, but was unsuccessful. General diners were covered with vinyl siding.

**Goodell Hardware.** 1926–? Silver Creek. This Silver Creek company built diners. A resident of the town noted that for a brief period they built four diners a year.

**Liberty Dining Car.** 1927–31, Clarence. When Charles Ward left Ward & Dickinson, he started his own company, with a factory in Clarence and offices in Buffalo. Liberty diners were similar in style to his former company's cars.

**Modern Dining Car.** Circa 1929. This company may have been located in Dunkirk. Estes Pickup Sr. was one of the investors. When the other investors bailed out, Estes was left with three diners. One went to Batavia and another to East Aurora. The third diner went to Brooklyn, but Estes later moved it to Olean and ran it himself.

**Mulholland.** Circa 1925–circa 1934. At its factory in Dunkirk, Mulholland built truck and ambulance bodies. An independent company called Dunkirk Dining Car Company was formed to sell the diners, which were similar in style to Ward & Dickinson models.

**Orleans.** 1947–48, Albion. This company built two or three diners in Albion, Orleans County. The Highland Park Diner in Rochester is the only one that survives.

**Richardson.** 1921–26, Silver Creek. Earl Richardson moved to Silver Creek in 1909 and opened a homemade lunch wagon. It proved so successful that he started to build lunch cars to sell in 1921. Richardson passed away in 1925. His son Raymond took over the business briefly, moving it to Dayton, Ohio, in 1926.

**Rochester Grills.** 1936–40, Rochester. Similar to Bixler, the company built sectional diners in Rochester. Their diners were built at the factory and assembled on site.

**Guy Russell.** 1930, Ripley. Only one diner is known to have been built by Russell in Ripley. It was later moved to North East, Pennsylvania.

**Peter Schneider.** 1922. Built at least one diner in Gowanda, which was operated by his daughter and son-in-law.

**Dr. J. J. Sharpe/National.** 1923–circa 1931, Silver Creek. A dentist by trade, J. J. Sharpe apparently built a dozen lunch wagons and diners in Silver Creek. His later diners featured barrel roofs.

**Sorge.** Circa 1946–circa 1950, Silver Creek. The Sorge brothers built three to five diners and remodeled at least one other. They were also located in Silver Creek. Sorge diners were very similar to Ward & Dickinson models, with the exception of stainless steel on the ceilings.

Some manufacturers including Mountain View, O'Mahony, Silk City, Sterling, Swingle, and Worcester used serial numbers.

Mountain View diners were numbered consecutively, apparently indicating when an order was placed. By the 1940s, their numbers had reached the 200s, and by the time the company folded in 1957, they were up to the 520s. The Mineola Diner, built in 1946, is #236; the Jackson Hole Diner, built in 1952, is #441.

On most Silk City tags, the first two digits are the year built, followed by the job number. Betty's Diner in Marcy is #45125, the 125th diner built in 1945 and Rocco's Pizza in Patterson is #5804, or the 4th diner built in 1958. But a few numbers don't fit that pattern: Johnny B's Diner in Glenmont (#3671), Coach Ali's Millerton Diner in Millerton (#5871), and the former Sautter's Diner (#1271) are examples of this. Though they seem like random numbers, the last two digits of these diners are all 71. The numbers could indicate a reconditioned car or, more likely, a new numbering system that was adopted between 1961 and the factory's closing in 1964. All three diners appear to be of early sixties vintage and are the same style, with angular ceilings and a zigzag pattern in their stainless exteriors.

Swingle uses a serial number that consists of the month and year of delivery and letters that give information about the diner: D=diner, L=L-shape, V=vestibule outside, U=used, K=kitchen, R=reconditioned, and DR=dining room. For example, the Country View Diner in Brunswick is #488DKV, so this means it was shipped April 1988 and was a diner with a kitchen and vestibule.

# A Word about
# Diner Styles

The following are general categories of diner styles developed by Brian Butko and Kevin Patrick, the authors of *Diners of Pennsylvania* (1999). The styles are based on traits typical for the era. Not all features are listed, and some styles overlap periods. Years are also approximate.

**Barrel Roof (1910–35)**

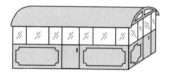

*Exterior:* Wood and porcelain enamel; sliding doors at front center and side.

*Interior:* Marble counter; porcelain enamel ceiling with vents; honeycomb tile floor; walls of two-by-four-inch off-white and green tiles. Booths and restrooms are introduced. Cooking is done behind the counter.

*Note:* This category also includes the few monitor roof diners from the 1930s (usually by Ward & Dickinson).

**Modern Stainless (1935–55)**

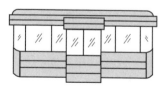

*Exterior:* Large porcelain panels or vertical fluting in early years, stainless facade later; glass block, corners rounded in early years then getting squarer; monitor-style or rounded roof.

*Interior:* Booths at one end; stainless-steel backwall behind counter with sunburst pattern; Formica countertops and ceilings; four-inch square-tile walls of yellow, pale blue, pink, or gray. Cooking is done behind the counter or in an attached kitchen or both.

### Exaggerated Modern (1955–65)

*Exterior:* Stainless steel with colored horizontal bands of flexglas or anodized aluminum; large, canted windows; wide, flared canopies with zigzag shape and recessed lights; flat roof.

*Interior:* Booths at both ends and along front windows; terrazzo floor of pink or green; tiered ceiling with mirror strip. Cooking is seldom done behind the counter.

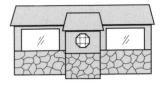

### Environmental (1965–85)

*Exterior:* Stone or brick facade; brown or red mansard roof; colonial traits, such as coach lamps, or Mediterranean traits, such as pillars or arched windows.

*Interior:* Wood grain; curtains and carpeting; brown or avocado upholstery; stools with backrests; wagon-wheel or chimney-flue chandeliers; acoustic tile ceilings with faux wooden beams; copper fixtures. No cooking is done behind the counter.

*Note:* Many older diners were remodeled in this style, some retaining their original interiors.

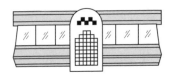

### Postmodern (1985–present)

Reinterpretation of classic diner elements: quilted stainless steel, neon trim, black-and-white-checkered floors, chrome fixtures, glass block, boomerang Formica on tables and counters. No cooking is done behind the counter.

*Note:* This category includes the late modern style, a transition between environmental and postmodern, typified by black or mirrored glass exteriors. Some older diners have been remodeled with postmodern elements.

### ABBREVIATIONS USED ON MAPS

| | |
|---|---|
| BR | Barrel Roof |
| MS | Modern Stainless |
| EM | Exaggerated Modern |
| E | Environmental |
| P | Postmodern |
| R | Remodeled |

# NEW YORK: LAND OF CLASSIC DINERS

L ike other northeastern states, New York has many classic diners. Doc's Little Gem in Syracuse is a 1957 model manufactured by Fodero that retains its original stainless-steel facade. In the Hudson Valley, the West Taghkanic, a 1953 Mountain View on the Taconic Parkway, and the Mill-brook, a 1948 O'Mahony in the town of the same name, are other classic stainless-steel diners in the state. These are the types of buildings most people envision when they think of the great American diner. But diner companies made a variety of styles through the years. In the sixties and seventies, the manufacturers abandoned stainless designs and began making diners with stone and brick facades and mansard roofs, with colonial or Mediterranean features. These are now known as environmental diners, and New York is home to many of these as well, such as the College Diner in New Paltz, which typifies the colonial look, and the Manos Diner in Ithaca, which reflects a Mediterranean design.

What makes New York so unique in the diner world? It's the sheer variety of styles and manufacturers' models in the state. Rare diners exist throughout the state. There are very few Ward & Dickinson diners in existence in other states, and those are mostly remodeled, but New York has some of the best-preserved gems in the country: the Miss Port Henry Diner in Port Henry, Morey's Diner in Oneida, and Steve's Diner in Silver Creek. A beautiful Rochester Grills model is preserved in Bradford, Pennsylvania, but you can't get a bite to eat there; it's now a flower shop. To eat in a Rochester Grills diner you need to go to the JR Diner in Syracuse or Broadway Diner in Endwell.

Before going further, it's important to define the word diner as we will use it in this book. Many restaurants around the country use diner in their names. In this guide we will be referring primarily to prefab diners, those buildings that were built in a factory and moved to the point of operation. We may mention some on-site diners along the way and even some railcar restaurants, but our focus will be on manufactured diners.

Ward & Dickinson diners, shown here at the factory in 1925, were similar in appearance to lunch cars.

Although it is commonly believed that classic diners were converted railroad dining cars, the industry actually evolved from the lunch wagon. The first lunch wagon appeared in 1872, when Walter Scott began selling sandwiches and pies at night from a horse-drawn wagon in Providence, Rhode Island, to newspaper employees who worked through the night. Competitors filtered in and, before long, the lunch wagon business was born. It made perfect sense that the lunch wagons would originate in New England, where the Industrial Revolution was in full swing and factories were running twenty-four hours a day, with shift employees coming in and out around the clock.

A few people in New York State tried to build lunch wagons. The Ellis Omnibus and Cab Co. in Cortland and the Morrisania Wagon Works in New York City built wagons in the 1890s. During this time, the wagons were mostly used as night lunch wagons, so the June 1894, edition of *Hub* reported. The magazine said that the day lunch wagons mostly served milk and sometimes muffins and coffee.

But it was the lunch wagon builders in New England, centered around Worcester, Massachusetts, that established the wagon as a permanent feature in northeastern America. T. H. Buckley, C. H. Palmer, and Ephraim Hamel were all major players in building wagons. Hamel and Buckley placed some of their wagons in upstate New York, though Buckley focused more on northern New York locations.

After the first decade of the twentieth century, only one New England manufacturer, Sterling, was able to make any sort of dent in New York State. From then on, it would be the companies in metropolitan New York and New Jersey that would supply a majority of the lunch wagons to New York State. Tierney (1905) and O'Mahony (1913) were the main builders from this point on. They supplied population centers and factory towns with lunch wagons. Still, the lunch wagon companies only made a very minor dent in western New York and beyond.

Builders centered in Chautauqua County proved that the smaller industrial towns and cities located on the Great Lakes could also support lunch wagons and diners. Closson, followed by Richardson and Ward & Dickinson, sold diners to many locations around the region. This encouraged a few companies like Brill and Bixler to open up in Ohio. Richardson moved

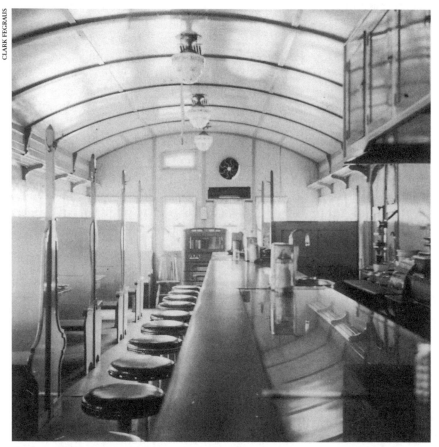

CLARK FEGRAUS

The Route 9W Diner was a Bixler, one of the early companies to have booths inside their diners lengthwise along the outer wall.

*Want your own Business?-*

**VISIT CORTLAND, NEW YORK**
and see our latest dining car. It has just been delivered there.

**Owning and operating a modern diner is good business—**

Profits the year 'round—Good earnings in or out of depression or inflation.

Diner business is the easiest, least costly, least red-tape, least "technical" high-earning business you can get into.

Mr. John Grinwis, Factory Sales Manager, will be at the new Skyliner Diner, 141 Main St., Cortland, from September 23rd to 27th inclusive. Drive over for full information.

**SILK CITY DINERS:**
**PATERSON VEHICLE COMPANY**
E. 27th St. & 19th Avenue
Paterson 3, New Jersey

Phone:
MUlberry 4-2500

An advertisement for Silk City diners that appeared in the *Herald American*, circa 1957.

to Dayton, Ohio, in 1926, believing that New York had already become saturated with diners. It appears that by 1930, there were the same number of diners per capita in western New York as there were on the other side of the state.

By the time the Depression was in full swing, many of these companies were fading or had already closed shop. From 1937 to 1942 western New York saw one last generation of the diner industry with companies like General and Rochester Grills. Sterling still had one of their representatives in Rochester, who brought a good deal of business to the company. But World War II put an end to the industry in western New York. From this point on, if someone wanted to buy a new diner, they looked in the metropolitan New York and New Jersey area.

In New Rochelle, Tierney had been building lunch wagons since 1905. By 1925, they were building a diner a day, but by 1933 they had closed shop due to the Depression and bad financial deals. Tierney spun off other companies with its former employees. DeRaffele also called New Rochelle home, and was started by Tierney carpenter Angelo DeRaffele. Samuel Kullman was an accountant for Tierney. The Paramount Company was started in 1932 when Arthur Sieber left Silk City, which had started making diners in 1927. The Depression, which hurt the western New York diner industry so badly, actually helped the industry downstate.

New Jersey always seemed to have the latest in diners, and in New England you're likely to see a Worcester lunch car. While these are interesting to any diner fan, in New York, you never really know what you might find. The variety of styles crisscrosses the state. In one region, you might see a classic 1920s diner, followed by an environmental or retro diner. If you throw in a classic stainless-steel diner in between, you experience the variety that only New York can offer. Kingston is the perfect example. Of the ten diners brought into town between 1925 and 1957, Kingston had at least nine different manufacturers. Unless Michael's Diner was built by DeRaffele, amazingly the New Rochelle company did not send one diner to Kingston. Paramount is the only company to send more than one diner to the city, with four: both Deitz Stadium Diners (1960 and 1978), the Texas Lunch, and the Park Diner.

The period after World War II is often called the golden age of the diner. But, more appropriately, it should be called the silver age of the diner. There were many reasons for the move from porcelain enamel, tile, and painted steel to stainless steel. Besides the fact that it looked attractive and different on the outside of diners, it was also easier to maintain. For interiors, a piece of stainless steel was easier to install than placing tiles one by one. It was also much more durable than wood.

Diner flooring was also being changed, and terrazzo floors were the wave of the future. Terrazzo is defined as a form of mosaic flooring made by embedding small pieces of marble in mortar and polishing. Terrazzo is used in places where there is a high volume of foot traffic, like schools, and it was also perfect for diners. Tile floors looked great and held up moderately well, but they were no match for terrazzo when it came to cost, durability, and maintenance.

This silver age only lasted until the mid to late fifties. Especially in the fast-paced world of metropolitan New York, everything changed quickly. Exaggerated lines and large windows were the wave of the future, described as Space Age or "Googie." The brevity of this period, along with pressures on the high-volume locations of the diners, seem to explain the scarcity of these types of diners in the state. Placed in highly commercialized areas, many of these diners were butchered in the name of development. In passing years, the exaggerated lines would be softened, and more earthy schemes took over.

For about the next twenty years, diners went about the business of serving food, with very little fanfare. They made money for the owner and gave the locals a place to eat. They were a place to meet and a place to stop at 3 A.M. on a late-night trip home. They also needed to compete with fast food restaurants. They had to serve large numbers of people efficiently, and provide higher-quality food than a fast food joint. To operate successfully—especially in highly populated areas—they needed large buildings. The cozy diner with more stools than booths was going away. Enter the environmental period of diners.

Four things led to the demise of the small diner. They were small. They were cramped. Their age was showing. It took a special owner who was willing to toil long hours and make less money than the larger diners. The more populated the area, the more evident this became to the owners of the smaller diners. It was fight or flight. The smaller diners of the 1940s and 1950s were still profitable in some locations, but in others—especially Long Island and the rest of metropolitan New York—owners were already purchasing the next generation of diners.

As diners began to move to highly commercial settings in the suburbs, they needed more space. They began to build diners in two sections, and then three or more. Sometimes an owner would build an addition onto their old diner like Gibby Wolfe in Quaker Street. Gibby bought a small Mountain View diner in 1953 and set it up in the quiet hamlet on the road between Binghamton and Albany. He built three additions to the diner over a span of thirty years. Other owners bought annex buildings from diner manufacturers. In Lake Ronkonkoma, on Long Island, Jesse and Isabel Maines bought an annex for their diner from Mountain View, and in Bayshore, Long Island, the Island Diner also received a Mountain View annex. Some diner owners stayed with the same company, like Tops Diner in Rotterdam. They bought a Paramount annex for their Paramount diner; both the diner and the annex were leveled in 2006.

By the 1960s, stainless steel on diners all but disappeared. First, the windows became larger. The Syosset Town and Country Diner, a Swingle built with large picture windows, is an example of this movement. Another example was Coach Ali's Millerton Diner, Silk City's attempt to keep up with trends. Their efforts were in vain, as they closed shop in 1964. Silk City was known for mass-producing diners in one distinct style, based on the year. The only choice they gave their customers was the color scheme. Other manufacturers made more dramatic diners. DeRaffele's Space Age diners could be found in Albany with the Gateway Diner and Fodero's Colonie Diner in nearby Colonie. Both diners stand on the main four-lane commercial thoroughfare of the 1960s, though both have been remodeled to remove the exaggerated lines of the Space Age design. But perhaps the most well known

GLENN WELLS

Currently operating as Plain Jane's Diner in Rumney, New Hampshire, this diner was formerly the Bells Pond Diner.

The Croton Colonial Diner is an environmental in colonial style.

Space Age diner in the country is the Market Diner in Manhattan. The Market is the only diner in Manhattan to have its own parking lot, and is the last diner built for the chain of Market Diners that used to dot Manhattan.

Very few new diners are located in downtown areas. The urban diners that survived into the 1960s were more than likely on their last legs. Many long-time owners were retiring, or diners were going through a succession of owners, like the Seneca Diner (1927–53) built by Ward & Dickinson in Ithaca, which had at least nine owners, or the Cayuga Diner (1929–66), also in Ithaca, which had at least twelve owners. The story was the same everywhere upstate. The diners that survived were in the minority.

Downstate, though, there were a few diner owners that bucked the trend, placing environmental diners in downtown locations, or on the edge of the original shopping district. The Greenvale Townhouse Restaurant-Diner sits close to the road in an older commercial district on Long Island. Note that the name "diner" is secondary. Not only did the style of diners need to change, but the name also went out of style. New diners were built to resemble restaurants, not diners. The owners wanted you to think of a building imported straight from Italy or Greece. The Spartan Diner took this one step further when the owners remodeled their 1950s diner. The Greek marble alone ran $23,000.

Along with the environmental period came colonial-style diners. Especially during the Bicentennial, thoughts went to the Revolutionary War and all things colonial. Diners like the Croton Colonial Restaurant & Diner and

Swingle reused diners that they took in for trade. This one is in Schenectady.

the Roscoe Diner of the early 1990s were perfect examples of this movement. Another diner featured in this book, the New College Diner, incorpo-
rates a brick and stone facade with a cross-hatched fence on the roof. The
owner has no intention of changing the look as long as he owns the place.
Other diners look more like houses than diners. The Yorktown Colonial
Diner has a shingled roof on top of a building made entirely of brick and
colonial-style windows that would look more at home on a house.

Other environmental diner materials became popular. Stone facades
began to overtake brick. Some were pebbles glued to plywood, seen at Gilly's
Diner in Mount Pleasant. Swingle took in a 1950s diner in trade and turned
it into an environmental diner in 1979. Others, though, used larger stones
and large windows, usually crescent-shaped windows at the top. Many examples exist today in the Hudson Valley and on Long Island. Manos Diner in
Ithaca fits this bill, and is the farthest west environmental diner in the state.
These diners look more like banquet halls or fancy restaurants and less like
the diners of the past.

Richard Scholem pointed out in a 1999 *New York Times* article, "fast
food forced many diners to go further upscale." This is especially true the
closer to New York City one gets. Diner menus in environmental diners are
mammoth. Practically anything you could want, you can find on the menu.
Unlike restaurants that focus on one cuisine, diners are vast and varied. People often joke that their menus are a novel.

Even with novel-sized menus, many people who eat at diners go for the specials. At lunchtime, diners are favorites of many businesspeople. Some diners, like the Goshen Plaza Diner, benefit from being located in the county seat, and are popular with lawyers and courthouse employees.

With so many baby boomers reaching retirement age and 1950s style becoming popular once again, diners have capitalized on these trends. It didn't hurt that diners faced a new threat from chains like TGI Fridays and Johnny Rockets, which offered food and fun, together. Diner makers brought back the flashy materials from their 1950s diners, like mirror-finished stainless steel and glass block, and installed them on the frames of their current models. These diners signaled a rebirth of stainless-steel diners, with all the modern conveniences of today.

In the eastern half of the state, particularly downstate, many of these diners were built by the three remaining diner companies: Paramount (now known as PMC), Kullman, and DeRaffele. Diners like these can cost 2 to 3 million dollars! Other owners have had their diners remodeled to look like new postmodern diners. If you go to the Gateway Diner in Highland today, you can hardly tell that PMC just remodeled the environmental diner in 2005. The owner saved money, and has himself a shiny "new" diner. Another company, Progressive Designs, has done many diner remodels on Long Island.

Each region of New York offers a different mix of styles and ages of diners. The different regions even demonstrate different remodeling materials

As diners became popular again, they were moved to new homes. The Royal Diner was relocated from Kingston to Springfield, Vermont.

for diners (which seemed to follow the economic prosperity of a region). At one time, there was probably a direct correlation between population and the number of diners in each region, but today diners are definitely clustered on Long Island and along the Hudson Valley. To put it simply, the closer to New York City, the more diners an area is going to have. Along I-90, the number of diners in the cities of Albany, Syracuse, Rochester, and Buffalo declines from east to west.

We have divided the state's diner map into seven regions, each with its own unique set of characteristics that can be described as its "place identity."

New York City consists of the five boroughs: Queens, Brooklyn, Bronx, Manhattan, and Staten Island. Diners are varied in styles from the classic to the environmental and the occasional postmodern. Diner drives can be very difficult due to traffic congestion.

Long Island consists of Nassau and Suffolk Counties. A large majority of diners in this area have been remodeled in the past ten years, ranging from complete makeovers to partial renovations. Most diners fall into the postmodern or environmental categories.

Hudson Valley goes from the Bronx up to the northern end of Columbia and Greene Counties. The diners along this route are more diverse than Long Island, particularly as you move farther from the city. The density is obviously higher closer to New York City, but there are also more likely to be environmental diners in these areas.

Catskills consists of the Catskill Mountains and the southern valley of the Delaware River. This area offers a diverse choice of diners in urban and

The USA Diner in the Rosedale neighborhood of Queens shows off postmodern belly windows along with its environmental stone facade.

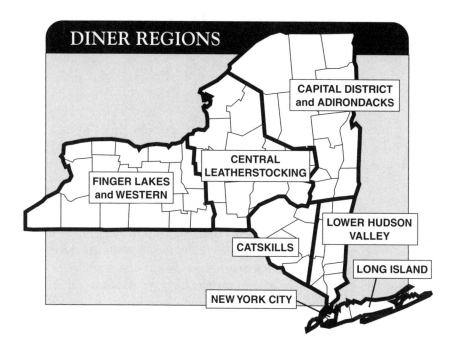

rural settings, both classic and environmental. Of all the regions, the Catskills has the highest percentage of closed diners.

Capital District consists of the greater Albany area and Interstate 87 up to Plattsburgh. This region is just as diverse as the Catskills, and most of the diners are open.

Central Leatherstocking is a wide area that goes from approximately Binghamton to Syracuse to Watertown to Amsterdam and back to Binghamton. There are more vintage diners and diners whose exteriors and interiors have been muddled by non-diner renovations. Diners tend to be located near populated areas and main roads.

Finger Lakes and Western New York has the most unique assortment of pre-war diners in the country. Diners are sparse in this wide region, and the majority of diners are on main roads.

# NEW YORK CITY

A t the beginning of the twenty-first century, New York City had more than 9 million people and over one hundred diners, more than any other city on earth. This diner metropolis is made up of five boroughs or counties: Manhattan, The Bronx, Brooklyn, Queens, and Staten Island. Most people, however, identify themselves more with the smaller neighborhoods within the boroughs. For example, in Queens, people say they live in Astoria. If they did, they might frequent the Neptune Diner in this Greek neighborhood. The Neptune typifies the environmental style that dominates every borough except Manhattan. As important as diners are to communities, land isn't cheap, and owners must get the most out of their business and parcels. So when environmental diners began to be built, they sold well to metropolitan diner owners, who wanted a large size and an up-to-date look.

In Brooklyn, one will find vintage diners in now trendy Williamsburg. The neighborhood grew up as a mix of industrial and residential, populated by traditional Orthodox Jewish families. As the industries closed, the 1950s diners like Relish, Miss Williamsburg, and "Diner" hung on and now thrive as trendy diner-themed restaurants. According to the Relish Web site, "The food at Relish pays tribute to many flavors and endeavors of cuisine, while being respectful of the history of the diner." These diners fit in well with the young crowd moving into Williamsburg today. Many southern neighborhoods like Sheepshead Bay sport environmental diners, although some diners have met their demise recently due to the condo craze near the water.

In Manhattan, the majority of diners would have been found in the southern and lower western reaches of the island. These regions were either commercial or industrial, like the wharf neighborhoods on the west side. Historically, these diners catered to workers and neighborhood residents at different times of the day. The Square Diner in Tribeca is a perfect example of this. Tribeca is full of old factories that have been converted into trendy residential lofts.

On Staten Island (that's right, on, not in) you'll find the most suburban feeling of the five boroughs. The Victory Diner had the most neighborly feeling of any diner on the island until it was moved in 2007. The massive Colonnade Diner better represents the overall feeling of what a neighborhood diner means to residents of Staten Island.

Diners emerged from the working-class streets of New York. With the dawn of the Industrial Revolution, factories needed workers twenty-four hours a day. Not only the factory workers, but hack drivers, cabbies, and railway employees all needed some place to eat during the brief breaks in their work shifts. Many bars offered quick, affordable meals, but they also provided the temptation to drink.

In stepped the Woman's Temperance League. They thought that if they offered the opportunity for a good meal without alcohol to these workers (and all citizens), they could promote their vision of a sober society. The women began selling meals from wagons. The manager, Miss H. K. Graham, stated that "if a man got a hot meal in a convenient place, he would be less likely to patronize the saloon." In 1894, the league reported selling 67,000 10-cent meals at a profit of $1,100.

The league's first wagon was named Good Cheer, and was bought with money donated by Cornelius Vanderbilt. Other wagons followed, such as The Owl and The Firefly, names appropriate for night businesses. By 1922, the wagons were closing at 6 P.M., because The Firefly had been robbed overnight, and the league did not want to endanger their employees.

At that time, a few lunch wagons were open at all times of the night. Around the turn of the century, all wagons were forced off public roads, except for the temperance wagons. But even in 1922, these wagons could still be found on public thoroughfares near public squares or, like the one at 34th and 4th Avenues, set up for conductors and drivers at the entrance to the Holland Tunnel.

An environmental remodel hides a 1943 Kullman at the Fresh Pond Diner in the Ridgewood neighborhood of Queens. In 2005, the diner succumbed to the wrecking ball to make way for a bank.

Mike's Diner, a remodeled 1948 Paramount in New Dorp on Staten Island.

The Temperance League was not the only organization to use lunch wagons for their cause. The Woman Suffrage Party bought a lunch wagon in Fordham Square and invited people to "have a Suffrage Sandwich."

Many people made money by speculating on land in New York City, buying a piece of land and waiting for its value to soar. Renting the land to diners was a way of putting their land to profitable use before selling it off for development. There were also plenty of odd slices of land near elevated trains, sometimes even under the trestles, that were perfectly suited for diners. The Ridgewood Diner was such an example, having been placed under the elevated tracks at 5455 Myrtle in Bushwick in 1964. It was later torn down during an MTA expansion.

Owners could rent space until they had accumulated enough money to buy the land. By 1922, people were advertising in *The New York Times* that they had vacant land suitable for lunch cars. The city itself was leasing out odd parcels of land to diner owners. In 1935, the city leased out 25 Grand Street. The activity was not without its detractors. Some people wanted to discontinue giving leases to "objectionable businesses" (lunch wagons) on city-owned land around Madison Avenue and Union Square.

The New York Central Railroad leased land at 10th Avenue at the corner of 33rd Street, 586 Manhattan, and the northwest corner of Bethune and Washington to diners. Kennedy Properties operated nine diners at the time, all on the west side of Manhattan. Beacon Oil Co. and Milage Gas Corp. also leased land for diners on the same small parcels they were buying for gas stations.

New York's diner business expanded rapidly during the 1920s. In 1925, the Bronx Exposition of Industries included a lunch wagon builder, but no name was given of the builder. In 1929, a publisher for the *Red Book* buyers' guide was surprised that no one made, displayed, or sold lunch wagons in New York City. They reported that they got a phone call a day for information on diners. This probably prompted Ward & Dickinson, diner manufacturers in western New York, to make a sales agreement with the Dining Car Sales Corporation of New York City that same year. But there actually were companies that were serving the potential diner owners in New York City, including Bixler of Ohio, and the little-known Dinette Diner Corporation of North Tonawanda, New York. But of greater significance were the companies located just outside of the city. O'Mahony of Bayonne, New Jersey, and Tierney Bros of New Rochelle dominated the sales of lunch cars up to about 1927. Tierney closed in 1932, but O'Mahony would continue to have a huge share of the diner trade. Other companies were started within a stone's throw of New York City, in an attempt to share the market. This included the short-lived Pioneer Lunch Car Co. of New Rochelle and other companies like Kullman, DeRaffele, and Silk City that enjoyed long prosperous years of selling diners.

New York City diners not only survived the Depression, they thrived. After all, everyone had to eat. In the early 1930s, you could get a lease on a property suitable for a diner in Manhattan for $1,500 to $2,000 a year. Diners tended to be placed on street corners, but could be placed anywhere. In 1925, the Williams chain of lunch wagons planned to erect a lunch wagon encased in the footprint of a three-story building at the west corner of 12th and Hudson.

To succeed during the Depression, diner operators had to do what they could to cut costs. A 1934 *New York Times* article reported on a wealthy clubman who found silverware with the name of his club at a diner. He also found names of a 5th Avenue hotel on the plates and the mark of an expensive Madison Avenue restaurant on his coffee cup. While he thought he had found stolen goods, it turns out he found seconds. A company bought imperfect dinnerware and sold it at low prices to diner owners, "who are anxious to make a name for themselves—even if the name belongs to someone else."

Soon after the enactment of Prohibition in 1920, the Woman's Temperance League discontinued their wagons. In 1933, following Repeal, the newly formed Association of Dining Car Owners estimated there were 5,000 wagons within a ninety-mile radius of New York City. *The New York Times* reported, "One of the first actions of the new organization will be to make arrangements for the sale of beer in the small restaurants that are found scattered on vacant lots in the large cities."

Diner operators expanded their clientele in New York City through the 1950s, drawing patrons from other socioeconomic groups besides the working class. In 1944, the American Meat Institute announced there was a "tremendous rush" among the upper class for hamburger meals, which had previously been a meal considered primarily for the working class.

Diners were small enough to be placed on any piece of land, and they could be easily moved when that piece of land became valuable enough to be developed. Some proprietors actually owned the land their diners sat on, but they were in the minority. There always seemed to be enough odd pieces of land on which to place diners. Even the push to the suburbs after World War II did not seem to slow down the opening of new diners. *Diner Magazine* counted fifty-two new diners in the five boroughs from 1948 to 1957. Of those, thirteen were DeRaffele, nine were Kullman, and twenty were Mountain View. However, Mountain View was about to go out of business, so DeRaffele started to gain a greater share of New York City's diner industry.

## THE GREEK CONNECTION

Most people who visit diners in the northeastern United States connect diners with Greek-American ownership. There is a tradition of new Greek immigrants getting work in diners, starting out as dishwashers or busboys and working their way up to diner manager and later ownership. It is mostly a family affair, with sons and daughters, nieces and nephews, and siblings all working for the 24/7 icon, the diner.

Publisher Peter Makrias was born on the island of Chios, Greece, in 1932 and developed an interest in journalism in high school. He worked for two local newspapers and later for newspapers in Athens and for the weekly *Naftiliaki* as editor-in-chief. Makrias came to the United States in 1960 and worked for sixteen years as editor-in-chief of the Greek daily *The National Herald*, in New York City. In 1970 he took over *H Nea Yorkh*, a monthly publication that he renamed the *Greek-American Review*. Today, it is the nation's oldest monthly publication for the Greek-American community.

In 1988 Makrias launched *Estiator* (Restaurateur), a monthly trade publication for Greek-American restaurant owners, the only publication of its kind. *Estiator* recently celebrated its twentieth anniversary. Makrias says, "Men of my age usually are retired. But I love my work."

According to a recent *New York Times* article, *Estiator* has over 24,000 subscribers. The staff of nine produces a spicy mix of gossip and news with up-to-date information about current happenings in the restaurant world. His

Most food is cooked in sight of patrons at City Island Diner in the Bronx.

subscribers make up more than one-third of the 6000-plus Greek-Americans who own restaurants, coffee shops, and diners across the country. Most of these are family-owned businesses, often run by second-generation Greek-Americans. *Estiator* champions the immigrants who made good. A recent article profiled a Greek immigrant who came to the United States at eighteen, worked in doughnut and coffee shops for years, and now owns three restaurants. At least four times a year, during Christmas, Greek Easter, and other special Greek holidays, the magazine is heavy with diner and restaurant advertisements.

Makrias has some words of advice for diner owners. "Change, adapt, limit the menu, offer daily specials and especially, put signs in the windows that say, 'No Junk Food.' 'Fresh Quality Food.' 'Family-owned and Operated.' The future success of diners lies in offering something different to the public." An article in *New York* magazine recently lamented "The Death of the Diner." In it, author Greg Donaldson affirms Makrias's contention that because diners have an extensive menu in order to appeal to a wider range of customers, they need to maintain a vast inventory of foodstuffs and enormous storage facilities.

*Estiator* is the monthly magazine of the Greek-American food industry and is published in a combination of Greek and English. Their offices are located at 427 7th Avenue, Suite 810, New York, NY 10001; phone (212) 643-1642; www.estiator.com; and by e-mail at estiator@estiator.com.

# DINER ENTREPRENEUR HARRY ZELIN

In 1921, Harry Zelin (born Samuel Zelinsky in Poland, in 1893) and his partner, Irving Greenman, rented space at 106 East 14th Street in Manhattan under the name Munson Lunch Company and started a quick lunch restaurant. After twenty-one years, Zelin opened his first restaurant at Greenwich and West Houston Streets, in the old Union Freight Terminal. In 1944, Zelin, under the name Delano Realty, acquired an existing old-style diner built in 1930 on the southwest corner of 49th Street and 11th Avenue. The following year he opened the Munson Diner, a new Kullman model with streamlined stainless steel and blue porcelain enamel flutes. He gradually added other diners and, by 1959, had at least five, including four on 11th Avenue: at 24th, 37th, 42nd Streets, and the aforementioned Munson Diner at 49th Street. Under the Delano Realty moniker, he brought a 1958 Silk City diner to 375 West Street, which was recently the Rib Restaurant, a now-closed barbecue joint.

Zelin had several brothers who also ran diners, including the Market Diner. The family of Irving Greenman also bought several diners, including the Empire Diner at 22nd Street and 10th Avenue. The Market Diner at 572 11th Avenue, was the sixth and last of the Zelin diners to open. Built by DeRaffele in 1964, it is a stainless steel and glass diner in the Space Age style. Its zigzag roofline, vintage blue and ivory interior, green-fluted porcelain, and fine food make it a must visit. In the 1980s there were only three Market Diners, on West and Laight Streets, on 33rd Street and 9th Avenue, and the Market Diner on 11th Avenue. The aforementioned Munson Diner at 11th Avenue and 49th Street, (the fourth or fifth named Munson Diner in New York City), was recently sold and transported to Liberty, Sullivan County, where it is intended to become part of that city's tourist attractions.

During its time in Manhattan, the Munson Diner was located in Hell's Kitchen at 681 11th Avenue at 49th Street. It was built by the Kullman Dining Car Company in 1940. It is an exquisite example of streamlined stainless steel and glass, with a base of blue vertical steel holding up bright blue enamel panels, glass blocks at various points along the window level, and horizontal blue and stainless steel striping along the top. It had earned a reputation as a crossroads where working people, reporters, commuters, lawyers, tough waitresses, artists, city police, and theater-goers all mingled—a gathering place where the nightclubs meet the night shift—a classic diner. It had been delivered on a flatbed truck and was moved in much the same way when the property that the diner sat on was purchased. The American Diner Museum was instrumental both in selling the diner and getting it transported to the Catskills. The diner was the location for a *Seinfeld* episode, scenes from *Law and Order*, a segment of *Al Roker's Diner Destinations* on the Food Network, and numerous television commercials.

Diners had become commonplace in New York. Over time, however, older diners were closing at a faster rate than new ones were opening. New fast-food restaurants were often built to replace them. In addition, diners were now being built bigger, which favored spacious suburban locations over cramped and expensive city sites.

Although a standard in the suburbs during the 1960s and 1970s, few environmental diners were sent to Manhattan. Yet as you travel from Manhattan into the outer boroughs, environmental becomes the dominant style of diner architecture. Brooklyn has several pristine environmental diners, such as the Americana and the Del Rio. The outer boroughs also have diners with postmodern elements, such as the Galaxy Diner in Brooklyn and the Crosstown Diner in the Bronx.

Today, many of the diners still doing business in New York City don't just serve standard diner food. Many have turned to upscale food like the hip, trendy diners in the Williamsburg section of Brooklyn. At the Empire Diner in Manhattan, you can get a meal with real turkey and mashed potatoes or a lamb burger and sweet potato fries while you listen to a pianist playing popular songs. At some diners you can try Caribbean or Chinese food. The good news to many fans of diners is that the architecture they look for is still there.

Driving to diners in Manhattan, the Bronx, or even Brooklyn can be challenging, and parking presents its own set of problems. Taking public transportation may be a better option. Queens and Staten Island, however, lend themselves more readily to conventional diner drives.

# MANHATTAN

Manhattan is the smallest of the five boroughs, at only twenty-three square miles, and nearly 1.6 million people call it home. Most of the diners are south of Central Park on the west side between Broadway and the Hudson River, with a few located downtown, also south of 14th Street. Seeking out an authentic or vintage diner in Manhattan is a challenging delight. Eating establishments calling themselves "diners" may be lunch counters in department stores, luncheonettes, cafes, storefront eateries, cafe-

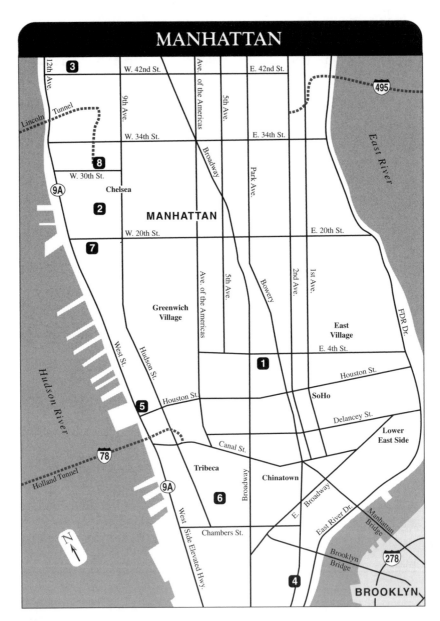

# MANHATTAN

1 Cafeteria: NoHo (R)
2 Empire Diner: Chelsea (MS)
3 Market Diner: Hell's Kitchen (EM)
4 Pearl Street Diner: Tribeca (R)

5 Rib: West Village (MS)
6 Square Diner: Tribeca (MS)
7 Star on 18 Diner Café: Chelsea (R)
8 West Market Diner: Chelsea (R)

terias, or coffee shops. Although not factory built, these restaurants can function as diners, having counters with stools, some booths, traditional diner decor, and similar menus.

Factory built diners were congregated on the western side of the city. Diners of both the Market and Munson chains were predominantly located on 9th, 10th, and 11th Avenues. Varick Street, also located on the west side, was another popular location for diners. There were at least four diners between 18 and 174 Varick Street in the 1920s. Historically, other diners tended to favor the west side of Manhattan as well. Lou's Diner was at 12th Avenue and 43rd, the Bermuda Diner operated at 637 West 55th Street, and Dan-Man Diner was at 9th Avenue and 31st. Kennedy Properties also ran at least ten diners on the west side of Manhattan.

The majority of the diners still left in Manhattan were once part of the Empire, Munson, or Market Diner chains. William Lolis owned the West Market Diner for thirty-eight years in the center of the city's meat packing industry. The diner also served waterfront workers on the west side. The Munson Diner offered meals to cops, cabbies, and construction workers before it was moved to Liberty in the Catskills.

There are only two diner drives in Manhattan. But unlike most places in the country, public transportation is a near must. You could also walk or take a taxi to the diners. The diner directory for Manhattan is arranged by area name. This arrangement enables diner aficionados to find a diner in a

The Moonrock Diner is not a classic diner, meaning it was built on-site rather than in a factory. Many diners of this sort can be found throughout Manhattan.

way that is comparable to taking a diner drive. The diners in a specific area are often close enough that you can walk from one to the next, or you can take the subway or hail a cab.

The Star Diner is one of many corner diners built on-site found in Manhattan.

The Brooklyn Diner was also built on-site, but was fashioned to look like a factory built model.

# DINER DRIVES

These drives can be referenced using the diner directory listings under borough and neighborhood names. Using your vehicle can be difficult. It is highly recommended that you use public transportation or taxis.

**WEST SIDE 1**

At one time, vintage diners were more plentiful on the west side of Manhattan. Now there are only three. Begin with the West Market Diner, a 1940s Mountain View with a 1920s Tierney kitchen, located at 659 West 131st Street. This diner, now closed, is owned by Columbia University. From there, head northwest on 131st Street, turn left onto Marginal Street, and merge onto Route 9A south; turn left onto West 44th Street; then turn right onto 9th Avenue. Go southwest on 9th Avenue; turn right onto West 43rd Street; turn right onto 11th Avenue. The Market Diner is a 1964 DeRaffele in all its exaggerated modern splendor, incorporating a zigzag roofline and extended overhang. Market is the

The Market Diner on West 31st Street in Manhattan.

Now an upscale gourmet eatery, the Empire Diner in Manhattan was once one of the Market Diners.

last of the eight diners once owned and operated by Harry Zelin. Next go southwest on 11th Avenue; turn left onto West 34th Street; turn right onto 9th Avenue and pass the former site of the Cheyenne Diner, a 1949 Paramount that closed in 2008. To reach the Empire Diner at 210 10th Avenue, go southwest on 9th Avenue; turn right onto West 21st Street; turn right onto 10th Avenue. This classy, updated 1946 Fodero, brought to town by Nat Heller, is more like a night club with diner overtones. The interior has a counter, booths, and a great winged clock. On the roof is a stylized model of the Empire State Building. Excellent cuisine, candlelight, and a piano player at night are some of the reasons the *Time Out New York* called the Empire a "Best Bet" in their April 2006 issue.

### WEST SIDE 2

Broadway is probably the most famous street in New York City. This diner drive begins at Broadway's northern reaches and goes south to Tribeca. The West Market Diner is our starting point, as it was for Diner Drive 1. Go southwest on West 131st Street; turn right onto Broadway; and end at Tom's Restaurant on 112th Street, the diner made famous by *Seinfeld*. Though not a vintage diner, Tom's offers the usual diner fare and setting. The next stop is at Ellen's Stardust Diner at West 51st Street. To get there, head northeast on Broadway and make a U-turn at 113th Street and turn right back onto Broadway. Owner Ellen Hart was Miss Subways in March 1955. This retro-style 1940s and 1950s diner is filled with nostalgia and has an indoor train circling the mezzanine. The diner features a singing waitstaff and nightly variety shows. From Ellen's, the trip south to the Square Diner is just four

LARRY CULTRERA

The Square Diner in Manhattan is a 1945 Kullman.

and a half miles. Go southwest on Broadway; turn right onto West 51st Street; turn left onto Route 9A–12th Avenue–West Side Highway; turn left onto Canal Street; turn right onto Varick Street; make a turn slight left onto Franklin Street; turn right onto Broadway; turn right onto Leonard Street, and you are at the Square Diner, a 1970s Kullman that features Greek specialties and special diet offerings.

# THE BRONX

At forty-two square miles, the Bronx is smaller than any other borough except Manhattan. The population is just over 1.3 million, and the Bronx is largely residential with some industrial and commercial areas in its southeastern section. There are not many diners in the borough compared with Brooklyn or Queens. Of the fifty-seven new diners listed in *Diner Magazine* from 1946 to 1957, only six went to the Bronx. Only one of these six diners exists today.

The Pelham Bay Diner in Baychester, the Bronx, is a massive eatery with a grand banquet hall. The 1965 Kullman has recently been given a late modern renovation, complete with stainless-steel facade and a glass tower foyer.

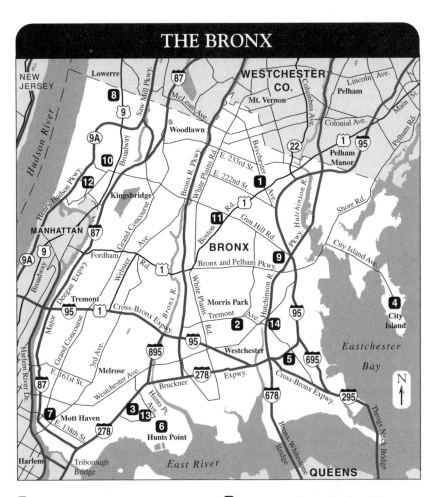

# THE BRONX

1 Baychester Diner: Eastchester (E)
2 Castle Hill Diner: Morris Park (E)
3 Celeste Diner: Hunts Point (MS)
4 City Island Diner: City Island (R)
5 Crosstown Diner: Throggs Neck (P)
6 East Bay Diner: Hunts Point (P)
7 Nick's Blue Diner: Mott Haven (R)

8 Parmel Diner: North Riverdale (R)
9 Pelham Bay Diner: Baychester (P)
10 Riverdale Diner: Kingsbridge (E)
11 Royal Coach Diner: Williamsbridge (P)
12 Tibbett Diner: Kingsbridge (R)
13 Tiffany Restaurant: Hunts Point (R)
14 Tremont Diner: Schuylerville (R)

*The New York Times* periodically mentioned diners in its listing of build-ing permits, or its fire reports between 1925 and 1940. They had ten diners listed in the Bronx, and two still exist today. Those are the Parmel Diner, new in 1939, and Nick's Blue Diner, new in 1938. Obviously there may be some information missing from the research, but all indications point to a dearth of diners compared with the Bronx's population.

Today, there are fourteen diners in the Bronx. No major roads feature more than two diners, but the heavily industrial area of Hunts Point has three. Ten of the diners can be visited on the diner drives, and you can get to another, the Parmel Diner, from the Northern Bronx Diner Drive.

# DINER DRIVES

**NORTHERN BRONX**

This drive starts on Route 9 in the northwestern part of the borough. Two diners are fairly close to each other: the Riverdale Diner on Kingsbridge Avenue at West 238th Street and Broadway; and Tibbett Diner at Tibbett Avenue and 230th Street. The Riverdale, a 1961 Kullman, was remodeled several times, the last time in 1986. It is on a tree-lined corner just south of Van Cortlandt Park. Its bright white roofline edges, blue glass windows, gray stone facing, and huge rooftop sign, all to invite the traveler to visit. All baking is done on premises. Route 9 becomes Broadway as you drive south. Go a short distance west on West 238th Street to the Tibbett Diner. A 1955 Mountain View, it was remodeled by DeRaffele in 1961 in the exaggerated modern style. The exterior has the under-eave, lighted overhang, curtained windows, and a huge sign. The diner has an extensive menu with Greek, Italian, and Irish specialties. Go back to Broadway and turn north onto Van Cortland Park South. Turn east on Van Cortland Park South,

The Riverdale Diner, in the Kingsbridge neighborhood of the Bronx, is a 1961 Kullman reflecting several modern renovations.

The Royal Coach Diner, a 1994 DeRaffele, is on the site of the former Teepee Diner in the Williamsbridge neighborhood of the Bronx.

The environmental facade of the City Island Diner in the Bronx.

which becomes West Gun Hill Road–East Gun Hill Road to U.S. Route 1–Boston Road. A short way south will bring you to the Royal Coach Diner. This splendid structure features blue glass belly windows, great signage, and a red canopied entryway. Open 24/7, they have a huge menu of standard diner fare with daily specials and cocktails. One mile east on East Gun Hill Road is the Pelham Bay Diner, a massive place at the confluence of I-95 and the Hutchinson River Parkway, which has been named Diner of the Year in the Bronx by the *New York Daily News* several times. They have a huge catering hall for banquets and weddings. Kullman built the original diner in 1965, but it has been remodeled into a grand postmodern eatery, with rosy granite and large expanses of glass. They have an extensive menu offering large portions at reasonable prices. A short drive south on I-95, then north on Shore Avenue, then east on City Island Road brings you to the City Island Diner, the last on this drive. This is an old-fashioned 1940s diner. Most cooking is done right out front behind the counter, where the customer can watch the proceedings.

## SOUTHERN BRONX

Starting in Mott Haven at East 138th Street we make our first stop at Nick's Blue Diner. This 1948 Kullman is in almost original condition, with blue fluted siding under the windows, a shingle mansard roof, and a large plywood sign beckoning patrons. They serve standard diner food in vintage surroundings. Travel east on 138th Street, north on Bruckner Boulevard, and east on Leggett Avenue to the Celeste Diner. This 1960 Kullman resembles Nick's Diner, but with an exaggerated modern overhang featuring under-eaves lighting. Turn south on Tiffany Avenue, past the now-closed Tiffany Diner, on the way to the East Bay Diner. Kullman built this diner in 1955. With brick siding under the windows and at the side wall, this blue and white stainless diner has white fluted edging at the roofline. They serve standard diner food. Your next stop is the Crosstown Diner. Once sporting the design of a classic 1950s DeRaffele, it is now remodeled. The Crosstown

Nick's Blue Diner is the oldest diner in the Bronx. Built by Kullman in 1948, it retains its original stainless-steel modern design.

The modern-style East Bay Diner in the Hunts Point section of the Bronx is right out of the 1950s with few alterations, a rarity for New York City diners.

is located at the intersection of Bruckner Boulevard and East Tremont Avenue. Then head north on East Tremont to the Tremont Diner. This diner started out as the Parkway Diner, a 1955 DeRaffele. It is located right next to the Hutchinson River Parkway.

# STATEN ISLAND

The third largest borough at fifty-eight square miles, Staten Island is the least populated with 465,000 people. Historically, the island has had nowhere near the number of diners and lunch wagons as the other boroughs. Of the fifty-two diners reported to have gone to New York City between 1946 and 1957 by *Diner Magazine*, only three of them went to Staten Island, and none of them exist today. There are actually only two classic diners on the island, the Victory Diner built in 1941 by Kullman (now in storage) and Mike's Diner built by Paramount in 1948.

The 1964 opening of the Verrazano–Narrows Bridge stimulated a population boom that led to an explosion of environmental and postmodern diners. When the bridge was completed, the island was still partially rural, especially its southern reaches. Only in the northeast corner were there

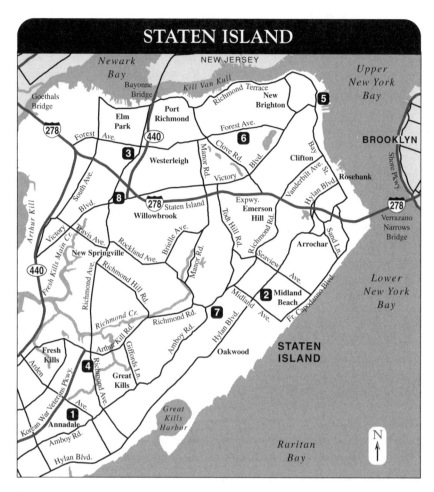

STATEN ISLAND

**1** Annadale Diner: Annadale (E)

**2** Colonnade Diner: Grant City (P)

**3** Dakota Diner: Graniteville (E)

**4** Golden Dove Diner: Greenridge (E)

**5** Karl's Klipper: St. George (R)

**6** King's Arms Diner-Restaurant: West New Brighton (E)

**7** Mike's Diner: New Dorp (E)

**8** Unicorn Restaurant & Diner: Chelsea (E)

densely settled neighborhoods like those in western Long Island. The Verrazano–Narrows Bridge opened the island up to commuters and increased traffic, which attracted entrepreneurs who built diners in the environmental style of the time. The Country Club Diner opened in the 1960s and the Dakota Diner followed in the 1970s. Both the Golden Dove and the Unicorn Diners opened in 1980.

Diners are relatively evenly spaced around the island, with only two major roads possessing more than a few. Richmond Road has three diners and Hylan Boulevard has one. Richmond Road is the main route to the Bayonne Bridge and New Jersey, and Hylan Boulevard parallels the coast from Tottenville to the nearby Verrazano–Narrows Bridge.

# DINER DRIVES

### HYLAN BOULEVARD–RICHMOND ROAD

Travel east on Jefferson Avenue and south on Hylan Boulevard to the Colonnade Diner. This enormous diner sits above its own parking garage. Lots of glass, mirror stainless steel, and gray marble facing mark this custom-built 1995 Paramount diner. The banquet room alone seats 800. The *New York Daily News* named it Diner of the Year in Staten Island in March 2005.

Back on Richmond Road at New Dorp Avenue is Mike's Diner, one of three diners with the same name and ownership. Beneath its Mediterranean-style exterior is a 1948 Paramount. The interior has sunrise stainless-steel paneling behind the counter and a gray and pink decor. Richmond Road forks at Amboy Road. Follow Amboy Road south and take a sharp right onto Annadale Road to the Annadale Diner, about a total of four miles south at Belfield Avenue. Built in 1994, current Annadale owners Steve Bakousis and Magdy Khier bought it in 2001. The diner has one of the most diverse menus on the island. The *Staten Island Advance* has fondly announced, "If diners are as American as apple pie, then the Annadale Diner is the a la mode."

The Colonnade on Staten Island is an enormous 1995 Paramount diner set above its own parking garage.

Above: The Mediterranean facade of Mike's Diner in New Dorp in Staten Island cloaks a 1948 Paramount that is more apparent on the inside. Below: Mike Moudadsos stands behind the counter at Mike's Diner.

## RICHMOND AVENUE

A north to south route from the Bayonne Bridge to Eltingville, this drive passes through the communities of Graniteville, New Springville, and the Richmondtown Restoration before ending at Hylan Boulevard. The three diners along this drive are representative of suburban New York City vintage diners. The Dakota Diner at Forest Avenue is a 1975 Kullman Car A that was renovated in the 1990s. A very long diner, it has a brick facade, modern light

The Dakota Diner in Staten Island is a 1975 Kullman Car A with Mediterranean styling.

The Unicorn Diner in Staten Island from 1980 is Swingle's version of a Mediterranean-style diner.

fixtures between arched windows, and a shingle-style mansard roof. A banner proclaims this as one of the *New York Daily News* best diners in New York City. The Unicorn Diner is said to be the largest diner built by Swingle. Opened in 1980 as #280DKVDR, this Mediterranean-style diner was renovated in 1993, and sits at the intersection of Victory Boulevard. Another Mediterranean, the Golden Dove Diner, is farther down Richmond Avenue at Gurley Avenue. DeRaffele built the Golden Dove in 1980, and today the diner is known for its homemade lemon meringue pie.

# BROOKLYN

The second largest of the five boroughs in terms of land area, Brooklyn is 183 square miles. It is the most populous borough, with more than 2.5 million people. Brooklyn retains a strong separate identity. It has an important central business district and dozens of easily identified neighborhoods, including Bedford-Stuyvesant, the largest black community in the United States, and Williamsburg, Crown Heights, and Borough Park, all of which have large populations of Orthodox Jews. Brooklyn has a strong sense of self, especially when it comes to sports and teams like the old Brooklyn Dodgers.

*Diner Magazine* listed fifty-seven diners in New York City from 1946 to 1957. Only eight of those diners were in Brooklyn. From 1925 to 1945, *The New York Times* would occasionally include diners in lists of building permits issued by the city. Diners also showed up in lists of fires that local fire companies responded to. They listed nineteen different diners. Of these twenty-seven locations, only four exist today.

There are a few classic diners in Brooklyn, but you need to go to the Williamsburg section to find them. Williamsburg is one of the formerly abandoned industrial centers that have been reclaimed by artists who have

Diners undergo many changes over the years. Diner is the fourth name for this classic eatery in the Williamsburg section of Brooklyn. Built by Kullman in 1928, it evolved into the Broadway Diner, Stacey's Diner, Sabrina's Place, and now Diner. Don't be fooled by its unassuming exterior; inside is a stylish diner with an international flair.

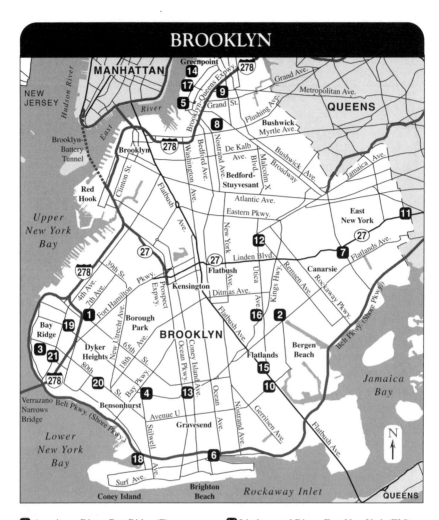

# BROOKLYN

1 Americana Diner: Bay Ridge (E)

2 Arch Diner: Canarsie (E)

3 Bridgeview Diner: Fort Hamilton (E)

4 Del Rio Diner: Bensonhurst (E)

5 Diner: Williamsburg (R)

6 El Greco Diner: Sheepshead Bay (E)

7 Galaxy Diner and Sports Bar:
   East New York (E)

8 Johnny's Restaurant: Williamsburg (R)

9 Kellogg's Diner: Williamsburg (R)

10 King's Plaza Diner: Marine Park (E)

11 Lindenwood Diner: East New York (EM)

12 Mike's Diner: East New York (R)

13 Mirage Diner Restaurant: Gravesend (E)

14 Miss Williamsburg Diner: Williamsburg (MS)

15 New Floridian Diner: Flatlands (E)

16 Paris Diner: Flatlands (MS)

17 Relish: Williamsburg (MS)

18 Retro 50 Diner: Bath Beach (E)

19 Ridge Bay Diner: Bay Ridge (E)

20 Vegas Diner: Bensonhurst (E)

21 Venus II Diner: Bay Ridge (E)

taken over lofts in old industrial buildings. This has turned the area into a trendy neighborhood. The classic diners survived by being located in an industrial area, and they have been reclaimed along with the neighborhood. Relish, Diner, and Miss Williamsburg are renowned for their unique menus that range from classic diner items, zipped up a little, to unique specials like scrambled eggs with grilled trout and homemade pasta.

Above: The original Nebraska Diner from the late 1990s projects a transitional look between the environmental and late modern styles. Below: The former Nebraska Diner in the Bath Beach section of Brooklyn underwent a postmodern remodeling in 2006 and was reincarnated as the Retro 50 Diner.

The majority of diners you see elsewhere in Brooklyn are environmental or postmodern diners. Brooklyn serves as a transition zone between the postmodern diners of Long Island and the stainless-steel classic diners of Manhattan. Some, like the Lindenwood Diner, go outside the box when it comes to diner food. With their motto, "The Spice of Life," they offer Cajun, Caribbean, and Latin food as well as typical diner fare. But there are also places that offer typical diner fare, done just right, like the El Greco Diner.

Brooklyn diners are located throughout the borough, not just in one area. Generally speaking, there are fewer diners in the central portions, with most in southern, eastern, and northern areas. Diner Drives are best accomplished within the individual neighborhoods or towns. Be mindful that many roads are one way and may not be accessed very easily. Carry a local map with you to facilitate your search.

# DINER DRIVES

Brooklyn's diners are scattered around its various neighborhoods. Williamsburg has Relish, Diner, Johnny's Restaurant, Kellogg's Diner, Miss Williamsburg Diner, and the Seasons. Go to Sheepshead Bay for the 3 Star Restaurant, El Greco Diner, and Mirage Diner and Restaurant. You can do the same for Bay Ridge, Bensonhurst, East New York, Flatlands, and all the other villages that make up Brooklyn. At least ten of the diners are in the environmental style, either colonial, with stone or brick facades, mullioned windows, a clock tower, and a white fence around the edge of the roof, or Mediterranean, with round-top windows, white stone facades, and red tile mansard rooflines. These designs were common from 1965 to 1985, with some built in the factories and others remodeled into environmentals from their originally exaggerated modern style.

### KING'S HIGHWAY
King's Highway runs northeast from Bay Parkway and ends at Eastern Parkway. There are six diners along this route. The Del Rio Diner at West 12th Street, is a near-perfect example of the Mediterranean style of diner architecture so common from 1965 to 1975, with red tile roofline, round-top windows, and white stone facade. Make sure you try the warm apple pie with ice cream.

The Mirage Diner-Restaurant near the intersection of Ocean Parkway is a rare Swingle, built in 1981. It exhibits the transition from the environmental to the postmodern, with black glass trimming the roof and a white stone

## CHOKING MAN

Steve Barron is probably most well known for producing television shows and music videos like Dire Straits' "Money for Nothing." A few years ago, he investigated producing a movie set in a diner. As a Long Island resident, he would take the train into Jamaica and sit at different diners, listening to exchanges between staff and customers and observing the dynamics only found in diners. The diner that he would go to the most was the Olympic Diner. The diner became the background for his first independent film, *Choking Man,* a unique movie that looks at one man's attempt for the American dream.

facade. Food portions are huge. One reviewer said his appetizer plate was a meal in itself!

At the intersection of Utica Avenue take Utica north about one-half mile to Glenwood Road. There on the southwest corner is the Paris Diner. This diner opened in March 2006, replacing the Blue Bird Diner, a Mountain View that had stood on this spot since 1950. The Paris is a gleaming, retro diner in blue and silver in the stainless style that brings back memories of diners of the 1950s. Inside are comfortable booths, a long counter, retro floor tiling, and blue globe lights. The present owner is the son of the first owner of the Blue Bird Diner.

Turn north and cross Linden Boulevard to Mike's Diner at Winthrop Street. A DeRaffele from the 1940s, it has been renovated in the Mediterranean style, with a red tile mansard roofline, large windows, and brick siding. Go back south on Utica Avenue to Linden Boulevard. Turn left onto Linden Boulevard to Pennsylvania Avenue. From there you will be going south to the Galaxy Diner and Sports Bar. This postmodern diner has elements of the Mediterranean style, with white stone facade and arched windows. The addition of a sports bar helps to better serve its clientele. Head back north on Pennsylvania Avenue to Linden Boulevard. Turn right to get to the Lindenwood Diner, exaggerated modern in style with a zigzag roofline and large windows. The diner has great signage and the same owners as the POP Diner in Queens.

### BAY RIDGE

This egg-shaped area is enclosed by the Belt Parkway on the west and the Brooklyn–Queens Expressway on the east. Even though these diners are very close to each other mileage wise, you still have to be very careful not to get lost or head in the wrong direction in this highly urban area. Our diner drive starts at the northern end of Bay Ridge, at the Americana Diner just outside the "egg" at 7th Avenue and 65th Street. The diner is a fine example of DeRaffele's 1982 Mediterranean style, with a red tile mansard roofline, large round-top windows, and white stone facade. Take special note of the spinning sign out front. The diner is open 24/7 and has a huge menu. The trip to the next diner is only .7 miles. Go north to and onto 65th Street, south on 6th Avenue, west on 68th Street, and south on 4th Avenue to the former Ridge Diner that has been transformed into Yiannis Restaurant. The new eatery is not very different in terms of the types of foods served. The emphasis, however, has changed somewhat, to brick-oven pizzas, Greek, and other specialties. Their motto is, "We Cook with Love." This former Mediterranean diner has been updated with a tan stucco and stone facade, large square windows, and huge purple awnings.

A little over one mile south is the Bridgeview Diner. Go south on 4th Avenue; turn west on 89th Street, and then south on 3rd Avenue to the diner. The Verrazano–Narrows Bridge is south along the avenue. This 1980–81 Kullman, now updated, has black mirror glass windows, metal mansard awnings, and an attractive sign that features the bridge. The full menu offers Greek classics and Italian specialties. Continue south on 3rd Avenue and take a left on 93rd Street. Take a right onto 4th Avenue to the Venus II Diner. This diner, now closed, is a good example of the colonial style that shared the environmental period of 1965 to 1985 with the more popular Mediterranean style. Located at 9316 4th Avenue, it has a stone facade, large mullioned windows, a clocktower, and a cross-hatch fence around the roof edge. This ends the Bay Ridge diner drive.

# QUEENS

Queens is the largest of the five boroughs, more than 109 square miles. It is overwhelmingly residential and one of the most ethnically diverse communities in the United States. Queens has a population of 2.3 million people, spread over 100 separate communities. People don't usually say they live in Queens—they say they live in Maspeth, Forest Hills, Woodside, or Astoria. Some communities are heavily industrial, others are high-end suburbs.

Diners are mostly concentrated in the northeastern communities of Long Island City, Astoria, and Maspeth. This area is more commercial and industrial and diners serve the workers in these occupations. There were also a number of diners in other sections like Flushing, Jamaica, and Jackson Heights. Many diners are located along the major roads, but most are in

The former Blue Crystal Diner, a 1949 Mountain View in Astoria, is now named the New York Diner. It was the setting for a *TV Guide* photo shoot for *The King of Queens* in 2002.

The Skyline Diner is a 1952 Mountain View located in Long Island City. It has seen many owners and physical changes through the years.

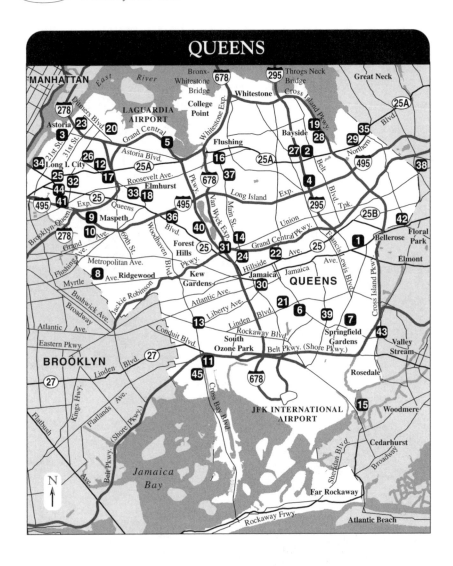

the villages that date back before the borough's 1898 incorporation into New York City.

Of the fifty-seven new diners identified by *Diner Magazine* as having gone to New York from 1946 to 1957, a whopping twenty-seven went to Queens. Flushing and Jamaica were the biggest winners among the neighborhoods mentioned in the trade magazine. The borough has a fair mix of all types and styles of diners. They range from the classic stainless-steel diners like the Jackson Hole on Astoria Boulevard to remodeled diners like the Georgia Diner, a 1962 Kullman updated in 1997.

**1** A.M. Village Diner: Queens Village (R)
**2** Bayside Diner: Bayside (E)
**3** Bel-Aire Diner: Astoria (E)
**4** Blue Bay Diner: Bayside (E)
**5** Buccaneer II Diner: East Elmhurst (MS)
**6** Carmichael's Diner: Jamaica (E)
**7** Caribbean Diner: Springfield Gardens (R)
**8** Castillo Restaurant: Ridgewood (E)
**9** Celeste Diner: Maspeth (E)
**10** Clinton Diner and Bar: Maspeth (E)
**11** Cross Bay Diner: Howard Beach (E)
**12** Diner: Woodside (R)
**13** Esquire Diner: Ozone Park (R)
**14** Fame Diner: Flushing (E)
**15** 5 Town Ceramic Tile: Rosedale (R)
**16** Flushing Diner: Flushing (E)
**17** Free Time Diner: Woodside (R)
**18** Georgia Diner: Elmhurst (E)
**19** Jackson Hole Diner: Bayside (P)
**20** Jackson Hole Diner: East Elmhurst (MS)
**21** JJ Johnson Restaurant: Rochdale (E)
**22** Lucille's Diner: Jamaica (R)
**23** Neptune Diner: Astoria (E)
**24** New Flagship Diner: Briarwood (E)

**25** New Thompson's Diner: Long Island City (MS)
**26** New York Ham N' Eggery: Jackson Heights (MS)
**27** North Shore Diner: Bayside (E)
**28** No. 1 One Chinese Restaurant: Bayside (R)
**29** P & B's Seville Restaurant: Douglaston (E)
**30** Panini's Deli & Grill: Jamaica (R)
**31** Pasta Lovers Trattoria: Kew Gardens (E)
**32** Pete's Grill: Sunnyside (E)
**33** POP Diner: Elmhurst (E)
**34** Punjabi Indian Cuisine: Long Island City (R)
**35** Scobee Little Neck Diner: Little Neck (E)
**36** Shalimar Diner: Rego Park (E)
**37** Silver Pond Seafood Restaurant: Flushing (E)
**38** Skyline Diner: Glen Oaks (E)
**39** Springfield Diner: Jamaica (R)
**40** T-Bone Diner: Forest Hills (R)
**41** Tandori Palace: Long Island City (R)
**42** Triple Crown Diner: Bellerose (P)
**43** USA Diner: Rosedale (E)
**44** Van Dam Diner: Long Island City (E)
**45** Waterview Diner: Howard Beach (E)

# DINER DRIVES

## NORTHERN QUEENS

Astoria Boulevard runs east to west through northern Queens from Northern Boulevard–Route 25A in East Elmhurst to 31st Street and the entrance to the Triborough Bridge in Astoria. Two diners sat side-by-side on this route at 93rd Street. The Buccaneer Diner II is still standing. The Deerhead Diner is now gutted. The survivor, built in 1992 as an adjunct to the Deerhead, shows its late modern styling with rosy granite and polished black stone, a black glass and mirror stainless steel roofline, and lanterns between the pyramidal windows. Their motto is "Where Good Food and Good People Come Together." The original Buccaneer Diner, for which the current diner is named, was across the street and was destroyed in the late 1990s. Buccaneer II has a full menu as well as a full bar.

One of the most famous of all the Queens diners is the Jackson Hole Diner on Astoria Boulevard at 69th Street overlooking the Grand Central Parkway. This Mountain View (#430) began life in 1952 as the Airline Diner because of its proximity to LaGuardia Airport. It is covered in gleaming

The Deerhead Diner in Jackson Heights was a 1963 Paramount in the exaggerated modern style. It was destroyed in the early 2000s.

Buccaneer Diner in East Elmhurst, with its interesting cathedral-shaped windows, is located next to the former site of the old Deerhead Diner.

stainless steel with rounded glass and sports a neon Greek key above the windows and signage showing an airplane about to land. Jackson Hole features burgers along with other diner staples. The 24/7 Neptune Diner at 31st Street is a circa 1952 DeRaffele, built in the classic Mediterranean style, with a red tile mansard roof, lanterns between the big square windows and white stone facing. It lies beneath the IRT elevated line. Voted Diner of the Year by the *New York Daily News* in March 2005, it features a fresh fish case and is known for its exotic egg-lemon soup. The Roman god Neptune is depicted in stained glass on the rear wall.

## CROSS BAY
Running from Cross Bay Boulevard and Beach Channel Drive south to the Rockaways, this drive begins in Ozone Park, the site of the newly renovated Esquire Diner, a postmodern structure trimmed in stainless steel. Blue mirror glass compliments huge belly windows. Your trip south crosses the Jamaica Bay Wildlife Refuge between JFK Airport and Floyd Bennett Field and continues on into Rockaway Park. The small village of Howard Beach boasts two diners differing in their style. The Crossbay Diner is set against the shoreline and is a Mediterranean-style diner with a stone facade, arched windows, and red tile mansard roof. This 24/7 eatery serves standard diner fare, but also specializes in fresh, locally caught seafood.

The Water View Diner-Restaurant is more contemporary, with blue mirror glass edging at the roofline, belly windows, and white stone facing. Here, too, the specialty is fresh seafood.

The Esquire Diner in Ozone Park was remodeled in the late modern style in 2006.

The Water View Diner in Howard Beach is a white rock Mediterranean diner with stainless trim, arched windows, and glass fascia. As its name implies, it offers wonderful views of Jamaica Bay.

## ROUTE 25A (NORTHERN BOULEVARD)

Beginning in Long Island City, Route 25A travels almost the entire length of Long Island. This drive, running west to east, only covers 25A in Queens as it first passes through the heavily industrial western end where many of the older diners are located. Once named the Blue Crystal Diner, the New York

The Blue Crystal Diner (now the New York Diner) is a 1949 Mountain View. The 2001 Queens Diner Tour stopped there for dessert.

DeRaffele completed the late modern remodel of the North Shore Diner in Bayside in 1996.

Beneath the 2006 renovation of the Scobee Diner in Little Neck is a 1965 Kullman.

Ham 'n' Eggery Diner took over the business in 2005. The Blue Crystal Diner, a 1949 Mountain View (#256), was featured in the August 10, 2002 issue of *TV Guide* when the cast of *The King of Queens* appeared there for a photo shoot. It was also the dessert stop for the Queens Diner Tour on September 29, 2001. Of special note are the cowcatcher corners so typical of Mountain View diners. The North Shore Diner at 196th Street is the former Northern Cross Restaurant. The exterior features rosy granite tiles, with a blue glass and mirror stainless-steel canopy. In addition to an extensive menu, baking is done on the premises. The unique Bayside Diner, a 1985–86 DeRaffele, is reminiscent of an Egyptian temple with its slanted brick front wall and tall, massive appearance. The interior features glass block with glowing blue lights. A few miles north of Route 25A on Bell Boulevard in Bayside are the No. 1 Chinese Restaurant, a former diner, and the Jackson Hole Diner (the former Great Bay Diner that was remodeled in 1998). Back onto Route 25A, turn east to the Seville Diner. Originally built in 1972 by Kullman, it has now become P&B's Seville Restaurant. The Scobee Little Neck Diner, also a Kullman, is the last Queens diner on this drive. It was built in 1965, and has recently been renovated by DeRaffele. It is distinguished by its blue glass mansard roof and white stone surrounding the entryway.

## QUEENS BOULEVARD (ROUTE 25)
## AND HILLSIDE AVENUE (ROUTE 25B)

Starting at the Queensborough Bridge in Long Island City, this route first passes the Court Square Diner at 23rd Street. Built around 1955, this 24/7 diner was built over an enclosed creek, and had its exterior covered over with tan stone. After a slight left turn, Queens Boulevard heads southeast. The New Thompson's Diner at 33rd Street, the eatery closest to Museum of Modern Art's two-year temporary relocation to Queens, saw its business improve by changing its menu from strictly Dominican to general diner fare with a Latin twist. Plates of maduro, cabrito, and arroz y habichuelas share

The new stone facing on Long Island City's Court Square Diner is integral to its late-modern styling.

A late-modern roofline capped the Sunlite Diner, a renovated 1974 DeRaffele in Long Island City.

the menu with pastas, avocado sandwiches, lemon chicken, and light fish fillets. The Master Company built the diner in 1950. The original classic streamline styling features red and white striping. However, the interior has been remodeled three times over the years. At 39th Street was the Sunlite Diner and Restaurant. The Harbor City Restaurant at Van Loon Street, in Elmhurst, was once a diner and retains its Mediterranean style despite its conversion to a Chinese Restaurant. The neighborhood also boasts one of the most unique diners in the city, if not the world: the POP Diner, which was inspired by the art of Andy Warhol.

Elmhurst's three-hundred-seat Georgia Diner is a uniquely remodeled 1972 Kullman styled in peach motifs. Open 24/7, it serves specialties in addition to its full diner menu. The interior is startling! Bright lighting enhances the booths and counter areas. Tables are light maple wood in a high-gloss finish. Although not factory built, the Tower Diner, converted from a bank building, stands at the triangular corner of Queens Boulevard, 99th Street, and 66th Road. The T-Bone Diner at the Independent Line subway stop is a 1934 Kullman which replaced a railroad caboose that had been serving as a diner during the Depression. Its location on a major highway and subway stop keeps this 24/7 diner hopping. The Shalimar Diner, a 1987 Kullman that was renovated by DeRaffele in 2000, is one block south of Queens Boulevard on Austin Street. The Pasta Lovers Trattoria is across from the Queens County Court House in Kew Gardens. A remodeled early 1970s Mediterranean-style diner, the building retains its rounded windows

The Shalimar Diner in Rego Park, completed in 2000, is one of several diners that demonstrates the transition between the environmental and late modern styles built by DeRaffele.

The old Bellerose Diner in Queens, a 1947 Paramount shown here, is buried under the parking lot for the new Triple Crown Diner that replaced it in 2001.

and stone facing and features new blue mirror glass. The colonial-style New Flagship Diner is near the end of Queens Boulevard. The former Grand Bay Diner with its classic colonial styling is open 24/7. Be sure to order the popovers for which they are justly famous. Your route takes a left turn onto Hillside Avenue. On the right is Lucille's Diner, a 1960s original. Set back off the street, the diner has a new tan facade, coach lamps, and exaggerated modern overhang with under-eave lighting. In addition to the usual diner fare, they have special vegetarian offerings. A few blocks south returns you to Route 25, now called Jamaica Avenue. Heading east, into Bellerose, you pass the Triple Crown Diner, named for its proximity to Belmont Park Race Track. The previous diner that operated on this spot, the Bellerose, was a small brick-covered diner built by Paramount in 1947. It was demolished and buried in its own parking lot to make room for the present-day Triple Crown. The diner contains a series of etched-glass art panels with racing themes. A tall glass and mirror stainless-steel entryway, blue glass roof trim, and large windows distinguish this diner as a good example of the post-modern style.

## BELL BOULEVARD

This short drive, running north to south through eastern Queens, has only two diners, but they are very different in appearance. The Jackson Hole is part of a chain. Built in the 1940s, this diner was completely changed in 1998 to its present postmodern appearance. Vintage Coke and Pepsi signs and an old jukebox contribute to the retro atmosphere. There is also an outdoor eating area. The No. 1 Chinese Restaurant started as a barrel-roof diner in the 1920s. Over time it was changed into its present incarnation. It is edgewise to the street with a red tile mansard roofline, round top windows, white stone facade, and red brick under the windows. This restaurant is a classic environmental style diner that has been converted to its present use.

## BROADWAY

Broadway begins at 21st Street in Astoria, Queens, and goes southeast to Queens Boulevard in Elmhurst. The Bel-Aire Diner has long been the *New York Daily News* Diner of the Year in Queens. This 24/7 Kullman, built in

The Jackson Hole Diner in Bayside is the former Great Bay Diner, remodeled in postmodern style in 1998.

1965, has undergone some face-lifts over the years, giving it more eye appeal. The metal mansard window awnings have been replaced by green cloth and the roofline edged by a neon design of multi-colored curlicues set between wavy lines. Vegetarian and dairy specials and a catering facility offer more than the usual diner experience. The former Forum Diner in Elmhurst at 79th Street is now the Olympic Garden, a Chinese restaurant, but it has retained its Mediterranean style, with red tile mansard roof edge, rounded windows, and white stone facade.

# CROSSTOWN DINER
## 1950 DERAFFELE, REMODELED 1980s
2280 Bruckner Blvd. at East Tremont Ave., The Bronx • (718) 597-3450

Co-owner Bill Tsibidis describes the Crosstown Diner as a neighborhood diner. It is ten minutes from Yankee Stadium and fifteen minutes from the George Washington Bridge. Most patrons are walk-ins. This stainless diner, shining like a mirror, stands out on well-traveled Bruckner Boulevard. The tall glass vestibule is topped at the roofline with glass brick. One of the windows in the dining room sports a lovely etching on glass of the original 1950s DeRaffele design. The interior has abundant mirror stainless and art deco style etched glass. The indirect lighting around the dining room shines on a marbleized, puffy, blue sky ceiling, similar to an atrium in a Mediterranean villa. There are saucer-like hanging fixtures. The diner is active in the community. It sponsors a local youth soccer team and donates soup to St. Peter's Episcopal Church's Love Kitchen every Thursday.

# RELISH

### MOUNTAIN VIEW #293 1952

225 Wythe Ave. at N. 3rd St., Brooklyn • (718) 963-4546

The former Wythe Diner was a family-operated diner until 1988, when the patriarch of the family died. The diner closed and it remained unused until purchased by Sandy Stillman in 1998. After a faithful restoration, he reopened the diner as Relish in 2000. It has been lovingly renovated with checkered linoleum floors, chrome seats, and spacious booths. A bright blue color scheme adds to the cheery atmosphere. Located in a former commercial industrial area of Williamsburg, the diner is amid a number of buildings that are being converted to loft condos. Construction of private homes is changing the face of the community, which has become trendy enough to have attracted moviemakers. *The Honeymooners*, starring Cedric the Entertainer, was filmed there in November 2004. Relish is a part of Brooklyn's mini-trend of refurbished diners that serve good food at reasonable prices. The menu, featuring such items as brioche French toast with maple ginger sauce and four cheese macaroni, fits the Williamsburg clientele perfectly. The counter functions as a bar and red lighting adds a warm glow to the place. The back room, furnished with tables and chairs instead of booths, is a low-lit plush velvet space with gold-leaf walls, done in a modern art deco style. The atmosphere is lovely. Seasonal dishes are featured along with traditional diner fare. The patio/garden dining area has a statue of the Virgin Mary framed by a lush lawn and trees. An interesting neighbor is the motorcycle shop across the street, operated by "Slick," with rows of cycles as a part of the dining view.

# POP DINER

### 1952–53 DERAFFELE AND 1960s KULLMAN
### RENOVATED BY PROGRESSIVE DESIGNS 2004
80–26 Queens Blvd. (at 51st Ave.), Queens • (718) 426-2229

This is a unique diner where pop art fans can appreciate Warholesque paintings and cartoon-inspired logo designs while downing burgers, shakes, and some fancier diner fare like a Latin-flavored salad entree. The new dining room has been outfitted with eye-popping orange and black vinyl booths, polka-dotted wall partitions, and aqua glass-top tables. Turquoise and beige one-inch square floor tiles, a black granite counter, and a dining room screen made with orange and red circles on an aluminum grid scream out POP ART!

The exterior also sports art elements on an old stone and black glass building. Along the windows and around the roofline are pop art shapes of jutting triangles in bright colors of red, yellow, and turquoise. Elmhurst is the most ethnically diverse town in Queens, which is one of the most ethnically diverse counties in the country. The menu reflects this diversity with a multi-ethnic composition of Latin, Oriental, and Asian delicacies along with traditional American diner favorites. Their specialty is mixing different ethnic tastes to create some of the most unique dishes to be found anywhere. Says co-owner Nick Tsakonas, "We have raised the bar on the diner concept and want to provide our patrons with a totally different and more innovative experience than they might be accustomed to with stereotypical diners. Each day we have ten different specials for lunch and dinner. Our goal is to give our dishes a multi-ethnic flair." Cakes and breads are baked daily on premises and can be customized according to customer specifications.

# DINER DIRECTORY

## THE BRONX

**Baychester Diner**
3771 Boston Rd.
(718) 231-6502
*1990s DeRaffele*

**Castle Hill Diner**
1506 Bronxdale at E. Tremont
(718) 828-3993
*c. 1965 DeRaffele*

**Celeste Diner**
1141 Leggett Ave., Hunts Point
(718) 617-1275
*1960 Kullman*

**City Island Diner**
304 City Island Ave. (at Fordham
and Hawkins Sts.), City Island
(718) 885-0362

**Crosstown Diner**
2980 Bruckner Blvd. (at E.
Tremont Ave.), Throggs Neck
(718) 597-3450
*1950s DeRaffele*
Renovated 1990s.

**East Bay Diner**
1291 E. Bay Ave., Hunts Point
(718) 842-4119
*1955 Kullman*

**Nick's Blue Diner**
217 E. 138th St., Mott Haven
(718) 585-7820
*1948 Kullman*

**Parmel Diner**
6691 Broadway, North Riverdale
(718) 549-9917

**Pelham Bay Diner**
1920 E. Gun Hill Rd.
(near Ely Ave.), Baychester
(718) 892-8171
*1965 Kullman*
Renovated early 1990s.

**Riverdale Diner**
3657 Kingsbridge Ave. (at W. 238th
St. and Broadway), Kingsbridge
(718) 884-6050
*1961 Kullman*
Renovated three times, most recently
in 1986.

**Royal Coach Diner**
3260 Boston Post Rd. (near Gun
Hill Rd.), Williamsbridge
(718) 653-1716
*1994 DeRaffele*

**Tibbett Diner**
3033 Tibbett Ave. (at 230th and 231st
Sts.), Kingsbridge
(718) 549-8893
*1955 Mountain View and 1961 DeRaffele*

**Tremont Diner**
3007 E. Tremont, Schuylerville
(718) 824-3250
*1955 DeRaffele*
Originally the Parkway Diner.

## BROOKLYN

**Americana Diner**
6501 7th Ave. (at 65th St.), Bay Ridge
(718) 748-4614
*1982 DeRaffele*

**Arch Diner**
1866 Ralph Ave., Canarsie
(718) 531-3718
*DeRaffele 1990*

**Bridgeview Diner**
90–11 3rd Ave., Fort Hamilton
(718) 680-9818
*1980–81 Kullman*
Renovated 2006.

**Del Rio Diner**
166 King's Hwy. (at W. 12th St.),
Bensonhurst
(718) 331-3107

**Diner**
85 Broadway (at Berry St.), Williamsburg
(718) 486-3077
*1928 Kullman*
Renovated 1977.

**El Greco Diner**
1821 Emmons Ave. (at Sheepshead Bay
Rd.), Sheepshead Bay
(718) 934-1288
*1974 DeRaffele*

**Galaxy Diner and Sports Bar**
805 Pennsylvania Ave., E. New York
(718) 272-2660

**Johnny's Restaurant**
603 Flushing Ave., Williamsburg
(718) 218-8989
*1945 Kullman*

**Kellogg's Diner**
514 Metropolitan Ave. (at Union Ave.),
Williamsburg
(718) 782-4502
Remodeled by DeRaffele 2008.

**Kings Plaza Diner**
4124 Avenue U, Marine Park
(718) 951-6700
*1975*

**Lindenwood Diner**
2870 Linden Blvd., East New York
(718) 235-6343

**Mike's Diner**
630 Utica Ave. (at Winthrop St.),
East New York
(718) 774-2400
*1940s DeRaffele*
Renovated, possibly by Manno.

**Mirage Diner-Restaurant**
717 King's Hwy. (at E. 7th St.),
Gravesend
(718) 998-3750
*1981 Swingle*

**Miss Williamsburg Diner**
206 Kent Ave. (at Metropolitan Ave.),
Williamsburg
(718) 963-0802
*Silk City 1930s–1954*
Renovated 2000s. Former T and S Diner.

**New Floridian Diner**
2301 Flatbush Ave. (near Utica Ave.),
Flatlands
(718) 377-1895
*1953 Kullman*
Remodeled by Kullman 1983.

**Paris Diner**
4914 Glenwood Rd., Flatlands
(718) 951-2556
*1950–51 Mountain View #295*
Site of the former Blue Bird Diner.

**Relish**
225 Wythe Ave. (at N. 3rd St.),
Williamsburg
(718) 963-4546
*1952–53 Mountain View #293*
Formerly Wythe Diner.

**Retro 50 Diner**
2939 Cropsey Ave. (near Bay, 52nd St.),
Bath Beach
(718) 372-1000
*1975 Kullman*
Renovated by DeRaffele circa 2000.
Formerly Nebraska Diner.

**Ridge Bay Diner**
7404 5th Ave., Bay Ridge
(718) 748-1858
Environmental.

**Vegas Diner**
1618 86th St. (at Bay, 13th Ave.),
Bensonhurst
(718) 331-2221
*Circa 1983 DeRaffele*

**Venus II Diner**
9316 4th Ave., Bay Ridge
Colonial-style diner.
Closed.

## MANHATTAN

**Cafeteria**
371 Lafayette and Great Jones Sts.
(at 119 17th St.), Notto
(212) 414-1717
*1938 DeRaffele*
Renovated 1977. Former Great
Jones Diner.

**Empire Diner**
210 10th Ave. (between W. 22nd
and 23rd Sts.), Chelsea
(212) 243-2736
*1946 Fodero*
Renovated by Kullman 1963.

**Market Diner**
572 11th Ave. (at 43rd St.),
Hell's Kitchen
Closed.
*1964 DeRaffele*

**Pearl Street Diner**
212 Pearl St. (Maiden Lane at
Fletcher St.), Tribecca
(212) 344-6620
*1960s Kullman*

**Rib**
357 West St. (at Clarkson and
Leroy Sts.), West Village
*1958–59 Silk City #5907 and
1990s Kullman*
Renovated 2002.
Closed.

**Square Diner**
33 Leonard St. (at W. Broadway),
Tribecca
(212) 925-7188
*Kullman*

**West Market Diner**
659 W. 131st St. (between Broadway
and 12th Ave.), Chelsea
*1940s Mountain View*
Closed.

## QUEENS

**AM Village Diner**
21812 Village Ave., Queens Village
(718) 217-4091
1940s remodeled.

**Bayside Diner**
207–07 Northern Blvd. (Rt. 25A
at Clearview Expy.), Bayside
(718) 428-8764
*1985–86 DeRaffele*
Former Copper 5 Penny Diner.

**Bel-Aire Diner**
31–91 21st St. (at Broadway), Astoria
(718) 721-3160
*1965 Kullman*

**Blue Bay Diner**
58–50 Francis Lewis Blvd. (at Long
Island Expy.), Bayside
(718) 225-6333
*1985–90 DeRaffele*

**Buccaneer II Diner**
93–01 Astoria Blvd., East Elmhurst
(718) 457-6803

**Carmichael's Diner**
117–08 New York Blvd. (Guy Brewer
Blvd.), Jamaica
(718) 723-6908
*1969 DeRaffele*

**Caribbean Diner**
219–21 Merrick Blvd., Springfield
Gardens
(718) 481-6818
1950s. Formerly Springfield Diner.

**Castillo Restaurant**
54–55 Myrtle Ave. (at St. Nicholas Ave.),
Ridgewood
(718) 386-0387
Exaggerated modern style.

**Celeste Diner**
5561 58th St., Maspeth
(718) 894-7477
*DeRaffele 1956/Kullman 1969*

**Clinton Diner and Bar**
56–26 Maspeth Ave., Maspeth
(718) 446-2308
*1930s DeRaffele*
Renovated in exaggerated modern style.

**Court Square Diner**
4530 23rd St., Long Island City
(718) 392-1222
Circa 1955.

The zigzag roofline and extended eaves on the
Clinton Diner, a 1930s DeRaffele in Maspeth,
resulted from an exaggerated modern remodeling.

**Crossbay Diner**
160–31 Cross Bay Blvd., Howard Beach
(718) 848-9401
Renovated 2002.

**Diner, abandoned**
37th Ave. and 54th St., Woodside
Now used as a church annex.

**Esquire Diner**
105–45 Cross Bay Blvd., Ozone Park
(718) 845-7600
Renovated 2006.

**Fame Diner**
176–19 Union Tpk. (at 176th St.
and Utopia Pkwy.), Flushing
(718) 591-0033
*1980s Kullman*

**Flushing Diner**
44–15 College Point Blvd., Flushing
(718) 463-5787
*1950 DeRaffele*
Renovated 1965. Formerly Kane's Deli.

**Free Time Diner**
61–12 Roosevelt Ave., Woodside
(718) 639-8695
1940s, renovated 1960s.

The Jackson Hole, a 1952 Mountain View, is probably the most famous diner in Queens.

**Georgia Diner**
86–55 Queens Blvd., Elmhurst
(718) 651-9000
*1972 Kullman*
Renovated 1997.

**Harbor City Restaurant**
84–01 Queens Blvd., Elmhurst
(718) 803-3833
Converted.

**Jackson Hole Diner**
35–01 Bell Blvd., Bayside
(718) 281-0330
*DeRaffele*
Rebuilt 1998. Formerly Blue Star Diner and Great Bay Diner.

The Mediterranean facade of the No. 1 Chinese Restaurant in Bayside hides a 1928 barrel roof diner.

**Jackson Hole Diner**
69–35 Astoria Blvd., East Elmhurst
(718) 204-7070
*1952 Mountain View #430*
Formerly the Airline Diner.

**JJ Johnson Restaurant**
Linden Blvd. (at 159th St.), Rochdale Village
*1951 Kullman Princess*
Abandoned.

**Lucille's Diner**
139–32 Hillside Ave., Jamaica
(718) 529-4833
1950s, renovated 2005.

**Neptune Diner**
31–05 Astoria Blvd., Astoria
(718) 278-4853
*Circa 1962 DeRaffele*

**New Flagship Diner**
138–30 Queens Blvd., Briarwood
(718) 261-2899
Colonial style.

**New Thompson's Diner**
32–44 Queens Blvd. (at 33rd St.), Long Island City
(718) 392-0692
*1950 Master*
Renovated three times. Formerly Thompson's Diner.

**New York Ham 'n' Eggery Diner**
49–09 Northern Blvd. (Rt. 25A at 49th St.), Jackson Heights
(718) 626-8857
*1949 Mountain View #256*

**North Shore Diner**
196–52 Northern Blvd. (Rt. 25A
at Francis Lewis Blvd.), Bayside
(718) 225-8000
*DeRaffele 1978–79*
Renovated 1996.

**No. 1 Chinese Restaurant**
42–20 Bell Blvd., Bayside
(718) 279-4912
1920s, converted. Former Bell Diner.

**Olympic Diner**
11733 Myrtle Ave., Jamaica
(718) 847-7500

**P&B's Seville Restaurant**
231–10 Northern Blvd. (Rt. 25A),
Douglaston
(718) 428-3100
*1971–72 Kullman*
Renovated 1990, remodeled 2005–06.

**Palace Diner and Catering**
60–15 Main St. (at Long Island Exp.),
Flushing
(718) 752-8800

**Panini's Deli & Grill**
146–64 Liberty Ave., Jamaica
(718) 883-1100
*1940s Mountain View*

**Pasta Lovers Trattoria**
124–18 Queens Blvd., Kew Gardens
(718) 261-2899
Mediterranean style.

**Pete's Grill**
39–14 Queens Blvd., Sunnyside
(718) 937-2200
*DeRaffele*
Remodeled 2000s.

The Cross Bay in Howard Beach was remodeled in 2002 in the Mediterranean style.

**POP Diner**
80–26 Queens Blvd., Elmhurst
(718) 426-2229
*DeRaffele 1952–53, Kullman 1960s*
Renovated 2004. Formerly Sage Diner.

**Punjabi Indian Cuisine**
13–15 43rd Ave., Long Island City
(718) 784-7444
*1962 Kullman*

**Scobee Little Neck Diner**
252–29 Northern Blvd. (Rt. 25A at
Little Neck Pkwy.), Little Neck
(718) 428-5777
*1965 Kullman*
Renovated 2004.

**Shalimar Diner**
63–68 Austin St., Rego Park
(718) 544-7724
*1987 Kullman*
Renovated by DeRaffele 2000.

**Silver Pond Seafood Restaurant**
56–50 Main St., Flushing
(718) 463-2888
1980s, converted.

**Skyline Diner**
271–27 Union Tpk. (at Lakeville Rd.),
Glen Oaks
(718) 347-1195
*1987 Kullman*
Renovated by DeRaffele 1994. Formerly
Silver Moon Diner.

**Springfield Diner**
12813 Merrick Blvd. (Jamaica)
(718) 525-3540
1950s remodeled.

**T-Bone Diner**
107–48 Queens Blvd., Forest Hills
(718) 261-7744
*1934 Kullman*
Renovated.

**Tandori Palace**
36–10 Greenpoint Ave., Long Island
City
(718) 706-6034
Renovated. Formerly High Class
Greenpoint Diner.

**Triple Crown Diner**
248–27 Jamaica Ave. (Rt. 25), Bellerose
(718) 347-4600
*Paramount 1947*
Renovated 1990 (gone), rebuilt 2001.
Former Bellerose Diner.

**USA Diner**
24303 Merrick Blvd., Rosedale
(718) 949-7933
*DeRaffele*
Renovated 1991. Formerly Cross Island
Diner and Restaurant.

**Van Dam Diner**
45–55 Van Dam St., Long Island City
(718) 392-7037
1944, renovated by DeRaffele 1974
and 1994.

**Waterview Diner-Restaurant**
163–30 Cross Bay Blvd., Howard Beach
(718) 641-7200
Renovated 2002.

## STATEN ISLAND

**Annadale Diner**
813 Annadale Rd. (at Belfield Ave.),
Annadale
(718) 984-3200
1994

**Colonnade Diner**
2001 Hylan Blvd. (at Jefferson Ave.),
Grant City
(718) 351-2900
*1995 Paramount*
Renovated.

**Dakota Diner**
921 Richmond Ave. (at Forest Ave.),
Granitevile
(718) 983-9286
*1975 Kullman Car A*
Renovated late 1990s.

**Golden Dove Diner**
3281 Richmond Ave. (at Gurley Ave.),
Greenridge
(718) 967-1900
*1980 DeRaffele*

**Karl's Klipper**
40 Bay St., St. George
(718) 720-4442
*1962 Kullman*
Formerly St. George's Clipper Diner.

**King's Arms Diner-Restaurant**
500 Forest Ave., West New Brighton
(718) 448-0326
*DeRaffele*
Renovated 1980.

**Mike's Diner**
140 New Dorp Lane (near Hylan Blvd.),
New Dorp
(718) 667-9823
*1948 Paramount*

**Unicorn Restaurant & Diner**
2944 Victory Blvd. (at Richmond Ave.),
Chelsea
(718) 494-2129
*1979–80 Swingle #280DKVDR*
Renovated 1993.

The King's Arms Diner-Restaurant in Staten Island, locally called The Arms, projects a postmodern renovation from the 1980s.

# LONG ISLAND

Diners on Long Island have played a different role in the fabric of society since sprawl has come to dominate the island's lifestyle. In the past, there were lunch wagons and diners in the villages, but their history and significance bears little relationship to what happened to diners after World War II and the establishment of Levittown. Two statistics tell the story of Long Island diners today: more than 50 percent have at least some postmodern touches, and 90 percent were built in the environmental era or later.

Long Island is 120 miles long and 20 miles wide. Brooklyn and Queens share the island, but we will follow the local custom of considering Long Island to be suburban Nassau and Suffolk Counties. Long Island was the receptacle that captured the tidal wave of humanity that relocated to the suburbs of New York City after World War II. Today, each county has a population exceeding 1.5 million people.

Two men laid the foundation for how Long Island suburbanites would live and, ultimately, how they would eat. The first was Robert Moses, officially commissioner of parks for New York City from 1934 to 1960, but widely recognized as a political power broker who built the parkways and expressways linking the city to the beaches, including the popular Jones Beach. The infrastructure he created helped to make the dream of suburban living a reality.

The second man who altered the landscape of Long Island was William Levitt, who plowed up potato fields to grow affordable middle-class housing tracts for the masses. Levittown opened in 1946. The instant and sensational success of Levittown ensured that similar housing developments would not only cover Long Island, but much of suburban America.

In the 1950s, Long Island shopping was dominated by the Roosevelt Field Shopping Center. The center was located right off an exit of the Meadowbrook Parkway. The shopping center sucked the life out of neighborhood retail, especially in nearby Hempstead. Diners like Al Gordon's Diner in Lynbrook, an O'Mahony Monarch model, soon became a thing of the past. A Brill diner was placed in Hempstead and just like any other village, Riverhead had a lunch wagon, this one run by Steves Neofotis. In 1946, Ed Gunning opened up the Old Country Diner, a Fodero, near the center to capture the business from the hungry shoppers.

Small roads that once connected villages became four or even six-lane parking lots at rush hour. The diners followed the movement east when it began in the late 1940s, popping up on these soon-to-be mega roadways. On the Sunrise Turnpike, located in the south side of Long Island, Virgil and Lee Tuttle placed a DeRaffele in Bellmore. John Chronis and M. Galanes placed a Mountain View in Hicksville.

In response to the population boom, diner manufacturers were called upon to build more and larger diners. The pace in these diners also picked up, they needed to serve more people faster. It is still true today. At the On Parade Diner in Woodbury, author Michael Engle ordered a BLT—it came in less than a minute! Long Island diners have a reputation for quick service.

The Apollo Diner in East Meadow is a remodeled 1962 Kullman.

The Paradise Island Diner is the former Sea Coral Diner, a Mediterranean that recently received a postmodern remodel, a popular trend on Long Island.

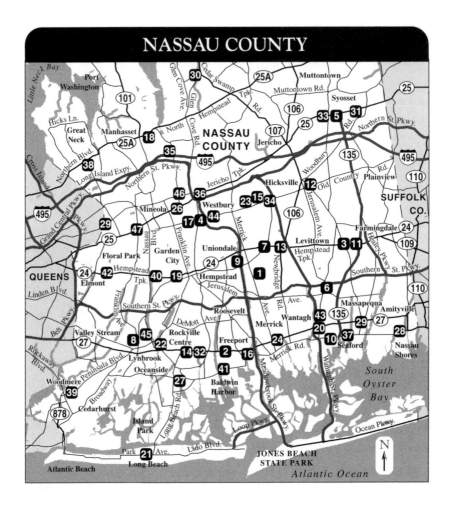

Some people wanted to escape the mad rush. Gerald Rhode left Cedarhurst in 1926, before the onslaught of suburbia, to run a diner in Oneonta in Central New York. Al and Helen Braunstein ran a chain of diners on Long Island with three friends. In 1955, they decided to take it easy and move upstate. They bought a diner in the sleepy village of Unadilla, which was on a truck route from Binghamton to Albany. Shortly afterward, they received a Master diner. Although Al said it got to be a real headache running a diner on the island, his experiences there made an impression on him. In a 1957 interview for the *Oneonta Daily Star*, Al said, "My years in the diner experience taught me that the kitchen is the heart of the diner." The next two owners of the Unadilla Diner, Lawrence Henchey and James Garvey, had also run diners on the south side of Long Island. Henchey learned

1 Apollo Diner: East Meadow (E)
2 Baldwin Coach Diner: Baldwin (E)
3 Bethpage Town House Diner: Bethpage (E)
4 Carle Place Diner: Carle Place (E)
5 Celebrity Diner: Syosset (P)
6 Circle M Diner: Wantagh (P)
7 Colony Diner: East Meadow (P)
8 Concord Diner: Valley Stream (E)
9 Dominican Restaurant #2: Uniondale (E)
10 East Bay Diner: Seaford (P)
11 Embassy Diner: Bethpage (E)
12 Empire Diner: Hicksville (P)
13 Empress Diner: East Meadow (P)
14 Golden Reef Diner: Rockville Centre (E)
15 Harvest Diner: Westbury (E)
16 Imperial Diner: Freeport (E)
17 Kiss the Chef Diner: Mineola (MS)
18 Landmark Diner: Roslyn (E)
19 Lantern Diner: West Hempstead (E)
20 Lighthouse Diner: Wantagh (PM)
21 Long Beach Diner: Long Beach (R)
22 Lynbrook Diner: Lynbrook (P)
23 Majestic Diner: Westbury (P)
24 Mary Bill Diner: Merrick (R)
25 Massapequa Diner: Massapequa (E)

26 Mineola Diner: Mineola (MS)
27 Mitchell's Restaurant: Oceanside (P)
28 Nautilus Diner: Massapequa (E)
29 New Hyde Park Diner: New Hyde Park (P)
30 Old Brookville Restaurant: Old Brookville (E)
31 On Parade Diner: Woodbury (P)
32 Pantry Diner: Rockville Centre (E)
33 Patsy's Pizzeria: Syosset (P)
34 Pollos El Paisa: Westbury (R)
35 Ravagh Persian Grill: Roslyn Heights (R)
36 Sea Crest Restaurant: Old Westbury (E)
37 Seaford Palace Diner: Seaford (P)
38 Seven Seas Restaurant: Great Neck (R)
39 Sherwood Diner: Lawrence (E)
40 Silver Star Diner: Franklin Square (P)
41 South Shore Auto Discount Center: Baldwin (R)
42 Stop 20 Diner: Elmont (E)
43 Sunrise Diner: Wantagh (E)
44 Thomas's Ham-n-Eggery: Carle Place (R)
45 Valbrook Diner: Valley Stream (E)
46 Williston Townhouse Diner: Williston Park (E)
47 Yesterday's Diner: New Hyde Park (E)

the trade while operating the Woodland Diners and Garvey ran the Rainbow Diner.

Occasionally, there was trouble in diners. In such a highly populated area, there was increased crime. Mrs. Irene Currier, who ran a diner in Westhampton with her husband, was murdered in her diner in 1959. It was the third murder by a gang of thieves who had previously hit the Diane Diner in Smithtown. Peter Vasilakos moved upstate after suffering a series of bad experiences at his diner on Long Island. In a 1989 *Times Union* interview, he said, "fifteen burglaries, three or maybe four holdups, and getting my head stitched up many, many times. Not a very nice place."

But this didn't stop many other people from trying to fulfill their dreams in the diner business. *Diner Magazine,* a periodical for diner owners, lists quite a few diners and annexes in the 1950s. Annexes were factory-built additions used to expand the seating capacity of existing diners. Nearly a third of the annexes announced by the magazine went to diners located on

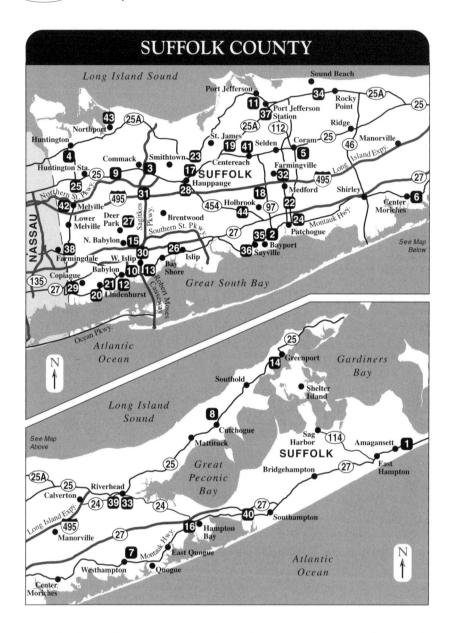

Long Island. Fordham Grizzard had a Fodero diner and annex built in the same year at Ford's Diner in East Farmingdale. The Commack Diner on the Jericho Turnpike received a Mountain View annex and Jason Trucks received a DeRaffele annex at his Dixie Diner in Mineola. Unfortunately, none of these diners exist today.

1 Art of Eating: Amagansett (MS)
2 Blue Point Diner: Blue Point (R)
3 Candlelight Diner: Commack (E)
4 Cooke's Inn: Huntington (E)
5 Coram Diner: Coram (P)
6 Country Cottage Diner: Center Moriches (E)
7 Crazy Dog Diner: Westhampton (R)
8 Cutchogue Diner: Cutchogue (MS)
9 Dix Hills Diner: Huntington (R)
10 Delphi Diner: West Islip (E)
11 El Nuevo Rincon del Tropico Inn: Port Jefferson (R)
12 Fortune Gardens Chinese Restaurant: Babylon (MS)
13 Forum Diner: Bay Shore (E)
14 Front Street Station: Greenport (R)
15 Garden Plaza Diner: North Babylon (P)
16 Hampton Bays Diner: Hampton Bays (E)
17 Hauppauge Palace Diner: Hauppauge (P)
18 Holbrook Diner: Holbrook (E)
19 Lake Grove Diner: Lake Grove (P)
20 Lindencrest Diner: Lindenhurst (E)
21 Lindenhurst Diner: Lindenhurst (P)
22 Metropolis Diner: Medford (P)
23 Millenium Diner: Smithtown (E)
24 Oasis Diner: Patchogue (R)
25 Oceancrest Diner: Huntington Station (E)
26 Oconee East Diner: Islip (E)
27 Olympic Diner: Deer Park (R)
28 Paradise Diner: Hauppauge (E)
29 Peter's Diner: Amityville (E)
30 Peter Pan Diner: Bay Shore (E)
31 Premier Diner: Commack (P)
32 Reina's (Gabino's) Diner: Farmingdale (R)
33 Riverhead Grill: Riverhead (R)
34 Rocky Point Townhouse Diner: Rocky Point (P)
35 Sayville Modern Diner: Sayville (E)
36 Seacrest Diner: Sayville (E)
37 Seaport Diner: Port Jefferson Station (E)
38 Spartan Diner: Farmingdale (R)
39 Spicy's BBQ: Riverhead (MS)
40 Southampton Princess Diner: Southampton (P)
41 Suffolk Diner: Centereach (P)
42 Sweet Hollow Diner: Melville (E)
43 Tim's Shipwreck Diner: Northport (R)
44 Towers Diner: Bohemia (E)

Besides annexes, some owners just bought incredibly large diners. These diners were shipped in many pieces, which were then assembled on site. The Peter Pan Diner in Bay Shore started out as one of these large diners before being either replaced or remodeled. Another, the Empire State Diner in West Hempstead, is now gone too.

As the 1960s rolled around, diner styles were changing. The growing population of suburban Long Island and New Jersey encouraged manufacturers to build larger and grander diners. With most diners on the island doing a booming business, many diner owners were either replacing or remodeling their diners. The styles shifted away from stainless steel to other materials, with more earth tones.

Although small diners were ideal for small lots in urban and village settings, these diners lacked the space and many owners lacked the money for expansion. This led to the demise of many of them. A few of these diners remained unchanged, perhaps surviving only because of a loyal customer base.

The extensively remodeled Sea Breeze Diner now sits closed in Garden City.

In the 1950s, there were probably as many as 400 diners on Long Island, with many located in the commercial districts. But as suburbia expanded, diners and commercial interests moved and the classic stainless steel diners disappeared. Only a few survive: The Mineola Diner, a Mountain View, sits on a corner on the Jericho Turnpike on a suburban strip at the edge of town. The Kiss the Chef Diner, a late 1940s Silk City, sits on a dead-end industrial street. The Cutchogue Diner, a 1941 Kullman, sits in the heart of that town.

## BRAMSON ENGINEERING COMPANY AND THE NEW AERO DINER

The only diner manufacturer on Long Island, Bramson, was located in Oyster Bay. They built only two diners. One, often referred to as The South Windham Diner, had been located in Willimantic, Connecticut, and was then known as the Boulevard Diner. In 1960 it was sold and moved to South Windham, Connecticut. Built in 1958, the diner, is a prime example of the modern stainless style of diner architecture most commonly built between 1935 and 1955.

In 2002, Michael Smith purchased the diner from the American Diner Museum, which had acquired it when the leased land on which the diner stood was sold. Smith had the diner moved to North Windham, Connecticut. Its new home is in River Plaza, a strip mall Smith owns. Now named the Aero Diner, it has been sensitively restored. A well-proportioned neon sign, glass block in the foundation, boomerang Formica on the tables, and retro waitress uniforms add to its nostalgic appeal.

Many diners in this period were owned by people of Greek origin. Many of these owners came up through the ranks, some starting out as dishwashers. A true American success story, these Greek owners had a lot to do with the movement of diners toward the Mediterranean style, and the emphasis on quality Greek cooking. The fact that Long Island consumes the most feta cheese of any region in the country belies this emphasis. The Greek-run diners typically feature favorites like moussaka, souvlaki, and pastitsio.

It makes sense that a Greek would be one of the major importers and producers of feta cheese. Nick Boboris, who runs Sirob Imports, was selling 5.5 million pounds a year in 1992. At that time, Nick, along with his brothers, was running the Royal Oak Diner in Bellport and the Expressway Diner in Hauppauge. The Expressway, located just off an exit of the Long Island Expressway but now demolished, was the former Lasalle Diner, which was moved from Queens Boulevard in 1971.

Harold Kullman, son of Kullman Diners founder Sam Kullman, introduced the colonial style diner in the early 1960s. Harold Kullman has stated that there was a resurgence in diners in the late 1970s and 1980s.

A *New York Times* article by Richard Scholem, "Not-So-Fast Food, to Stay," in January 1999 did a fantastic job describing the state of the diner on Long Island. Although it did not specifically touch upon the architectural changes happening in diners for the last fifteen years, it hinted about the reasons. For the previous fifteen years, diners on Long Island had gone almost exclusively to retro or postmodern styles. The semi-retro or transitional look mixed environmental styles with some postmodern elements. Some of the

The Garden Plaza Diner in North Babylon is a former pancake house remodeled in the postmodern style by DeRaffele in 1999.

materials used were dark-colored mirrored glass and polished granite. There was some stainless steel, but on these transitional diners, stainless was more of an accent like a border or trim. Many diners kept their mansard roofs, but instead of the shingle and terra cotta roofs of the 1970s, they tend to be either mirror-finished glass or porcelain enamel panels. This look is more prevalent in metropolitan New York City rather than in the five boroughs. Both of these styles exclusively focus on the exterior look of a diner.

The retro look has no environmental materials at all. These postmodern diners have mirror-finished stainless steel and glass block as their two primary materials. All of these diners have towering vestibules made of stainless steel and glass block. The On Parade Diner on the Jericho Turnpike in Woodbury and the Hauppauge Palace Diner in Hauppauge are two quintessential postmodern diners with towers that incorporate glass block. The Palace has modestly large windows with stainless steel above and below them, and horizontal lines of red in between the stainless. The roofline is curved, with a metallic look and a border of red just above the curve. The On Parade Diner is slightly different. The tower vestibule is multi-tiered and features glass block on the lower portion and designed pieces of stainless steel that pay homage to the stainless benders of classic diners. Above the windows is a row of mirror-finished stainless steel that is bent in a zigzag formation across the entire length, minus the large vestibule. The bathrooms are actually built onto the front of the diner to the left of the vestibule. The exterior features a mix of glass block, zigzag-patterned stainless, and the name of the diner in large letters. The roofline for this small room is done in curved stainless, also in a zigzag pattern.

The other type of roofline showcasing classic postmodern is DeRaffele's exaggerated reverse step. The Lighthouse Diner on the Sunrise Highway in Wantagh is just one of the diners on Long Island that exhibit this style. These diners that have the reverse step roofs also have large towers over their entrances or vestibules. This look is so popular that some non-authentic diners have copied the design. Everything on today's diners is custom designed rather than mass produced.

---

# DINER DRIVES

The orientation of Long Island, extending eastward from New York City, lends itself to diner drives that run west to east. Of the seven drives included here, six are west to east. Some of these drives start in New York City and continue east. A few run the entire length of the island over

100 miles. With a bit of planning, you may even be able to use the Long Island Railroad or the Long Island Bus System to visit some of the diners. More information can be found on their Web site at www.mta.nyc.ny.us/lirr/.

Unless specifically noted, all drives in Long Island will start in the west, closer to New York City. As you become familiar with Long Island, you will see that you could very easily head out on one diner drive, and come back on another by simply reversing the order.

## ROUTE 24

Route 24 extends across the center of Nassau County from Queens through Elmont, Hempstead, and Levittown to Farmingdale on the Suffolk County line. The first Route 24 diner east of Queens is the Stop 20 Diner on the north side of the road in Elmont. The diner, featuring dark marble and glass on its exterior, is known for its Elmont Burger, a patty with cheese, bacon, and an egg over easy. At Franklin Square, the Silver Star Diner specializes in American and Greek food with an emphasis on seafood. This retro-style DeRaffele sits on the south side of Route 24, closer to the road than a diner typically would be located because this is an older commercial district intended for a community of walking patrons.

Just before West Hempstead, the Lantern Diner sits on the north side of the road near the intersection with Nassau Boulevard. The diner sports a mix of environmental and postmodern styles, highlighted by a white stone facade with enormous windows. A half-mile south of Route 24, on Front Street in Uniondale, is the former Coliseum Diner, now called Dominican Restaurant #2. This diner boasts "Espesialidad en comidas Criolas y Americanas," meaning it serves Creole and American food. There is a giant mural

The Colony Diner on the Hempstead Turnpike is one of the few Swingles on Long Island. This one was built in 1985, one of the first in the postmodern style.

DeRaffele built the Bethpage Townhouse Diner on Hempstead Turnpike in the 1980s and renovated it in 1999.

of a Caribbean scene on its exterior wall, appropriate for a community that is largely Dominican.

Back on Route 24 in East Meadow, just to the east of Uniondale, there was a relatively rare Swingle Diner (#1286DKVDR), built in 1986 and remodeled by DeRaffele. The Colony is on the north side of the six-lane Route 25. Its tall entry tower is made of glass brick with blue trim all around. Now there is only one other Swingle on all of Long Island.

The Empress Diner is on the south side of the road, just before the Wantagh State Parkway. The retro-style diner has only an average size vestibule for that particular style. but would still make any classic diner's vestibule pale in comparison.

The last two Route 24 diners are in Bethpage, east of Levittown, just before the Seaford–Oyster Bay Expressway. The Bethpage Townhouse Diner and the Embassy Diner were both built or rebuilt by DeRaffele in the 1980s and renovated in 1999. The Embassy is located next to a movie theater, a popular location for diners in the past. Although there are varied makes and remodels of diners, DeRaffele has had the most significant presence on Long Island. In a recent survey of thirty-five named diners, DeRaffele models account for at least seventeen.

## ROUTE 27
Route 27 runs along the south shore from New York City all the way to Montauk Point at the eastern tip of Long Island. The Sunrise Highway is known as the route to the Hamptons. The highway splits off the Laurelton

Parkway in Queens, and much of it is six lanes. Farther east the road is four lanes, with limited access sections. The highway is never more than a few miles from the Atlantic coast. On your way east you'll first come upon the Concord Diner in Valley Stream, east of Rockaway Parkway. There has been a diner at this location since at least the 1930s. The current diner was built by Kullman in 1993 and remodeled by Musi a few years later. It has a distinctive square entryway in glass block. A mirror stainless-steel strip circles the diner above the windows and the front door. The diner is on a small piece of land on the north side of the road, just in front of an auto body shop and the Long Island Railroad.

It is easy to miss the Lynbrook Diner in Lynbrook. On the south side of the road, the diner sits nearly flush with the buildings to the left and right. With the other buildings so close to the road, typical in older commercial districts, you may not notice the diner until you're past it. The Lynbrook was built by DeRaffele in the 1960s and later remodeled. With blue glass roof trim and "bumped out" windows on the vestibule and left side, it typifies the postmodern styling. Just like many other Long Island diners, it is open twenty-four hours.

The Golden Reef Diner is down the road just a short hop in Rockville Centre. It is located next to the LIRR station and is known for its quick service. There has been a diner on this spot since 1922. The postmodern diner that stands there today named the Golden Reef was called the Oasis Diner in the mid 1950s. It was renovated by DeRaffele in 1992 and again in 2001, which removed its exaggerated modern facade. Although it has had its

Concord Diner-Restaurant is a Kullman/Musi from 1999.

Golden Reef Diner on Sunrise Highway in Rockville Centre is a 2001 DeRaffele renovation of the 1992 Oasis Diner.

share of renovations, it's not a flashy diner. It has a simple retro look to it, with a generally green tone to its exterior.

On the north side of the road, east of Wantagh Parkway, you'll find the Sunrise Diner in the village of Wantagh. All shiny mirror stainless-steel and blue glass trim, it was built in 1996 by DeRaffele. Among the specials sometimes found at the diner are mussels, something usually found only at Italian restaurants. The next diner is in view of the Sunrise Diner on the south side of the road across Wantagh Avenue. The Lighthouse, a 1956 Kullman, was originally the Wantagh Diner. Later, the Lighthouse was given an environmental remodel, with a stone facade, large metal mansard window awnings, and a lighthouse fixture on the roof. The diner was remodeled again by DeRaffele with a reverse step roofline and a large vestibule.

One of the two Massapequa diners are on Route 27. The Massapequa Diner is just west of the Massapequa Nature Preserve and sits on the south side of the road. Former owner George Tsaklianos, now president of the Nassau-Suffolk Diners Association, was asked by the *New York Times* in January 1999 why diner owners were Greek. He remarked, "Greeks are party people who like to sit, eat, have a glass of wine and talk." The other Massapequa diner, the Nautilus, is a Mediterranean-style Kullman just south on Merrick Road.

In December 2003, Friendly's, a northeast ice cream and food chain, proposed remodeling and operating a restaurant at the site of the All Star

Diner in Massapequa. Today, the diner that exhibited a classic postmodern style with a shiny mirror stainless roofline, large windows, and a pink marble exterior, is no more. Also gone is the South Bay Diner in Lindenhurst.

## ROUTES 27A AND 80
Just like Route 27, this road hugs the south shore of Long Island from Valley Stream in western Nassau County to Southampton on the South Fork where it joins Route 27 and continues on to Montauk Point. The road passes through some of the most densely populated areas of Nassau County and then through Suffolk County's sparsely populated areas of potato farms and vineyards. The most eastern reaches of Suffolk's South Fork have become well known as the Hamptons. This drive contains a wide variety of diners of varying sizes, shapes, and ages. Some have been converted into other businesses.

The route starts in Valley Stream as Merrick Road, which is very prominently marked, coming off the Sunrise Highway. Traveling eastward, you will come to the Valbrook Diner, on the border of Valley Stream and Lynbrook, a few blocks east of Rockaway Parkway. The diner sports a mirrored glass mansard roof-edge above the more traditional Mediterranean stone facade. This Musi diner, built in 1972, was updated by DeRaffele in 1988–89. Also of note is the Pantry Diner in Rockville Centre where three generations of the Mavroudis family have owned the diner since 1949. This is a colonial-style diner with a white fence at the roofline, a brick facade, and large windows. Located at the intersection of Merrick and Long Beach Roads there is ample off-street parking for patrons.

Freeport's Imperial Diner, east of Guy Lombardo Street, was more of a traditional colonial until it was remodeled recently. Apparently, the remodeling did the trick and brought back the customers, who keep coming for the good food. The latest remodeling was done by Progressive Designs, who gave the Imperial a retro postmodern appearance. Four miles east, in Seaford, is the highly visible East Bay Diner. Its latest remodel was done by Progressive Designs. The Seaford Palace Diner, just down the road in Seaford is your next stop. With its gleaming black glass and towering corner entryway topped by a sign proclaiming DINER, the Seaford stands out at the intersection of Merrick and Seaman's Neck Roads. Large portions and reasonable prices make this a worthy stop.

Farther on, in Massapequa and Massapequa Park are two diners, one right on the Sunrise Highway. The Nautilus Diner is near the western border of Amityville. This Kullman is a perfect example of a Mediterranean-style diner with a white stone facade, rounded windows, and red tile mansard roofline. The clean, well-kept interior maintains the classic, Mediterranean

Freeport's Imperial Diner was an early colonial-style environmental. Now the diner has been remodeled in postmodern style.

style. The Massapequa Diner is only a short jog north on Sunrise Highway before the Massapequa (Nature) Preserve. Patrons of these two diners go back and forth about why one diner is better than another. Both of these diners were remodeled by Kullman within the past ten years, though the Nautilus has not deviated from its Mediterranean looks.

In Suffolk County, Lindenhurst has two diners located close to each other. The first, just east of Broadway, is the Lindencrest Diner, built by De-Raffele in the 1990s. It is distinctive for its enormous entryway, blue glass roofline, large windows with black glass below, rough stone corners, and its park-like landscaping. By contrast, the Lindenhurst Diner is older, built in 1954, but recently modernized. After the remodeling, it would be hard to tell that this diner was built anytime before the 1990s. The Lindenhurst sports darkened windows trimmed in polished stainless steel and a red curved roofline.

In Babylon, the Fortune Garden Chinese Restaurant is a Kullman diner, built in 1959 as Jerry's Diner, and converted in the late 1990s. The original door is located at the corner of the diner and is still pristine in blue trim and stainless steel. The Fortune Garden's owners have added a canopy over the roofline. The Delphi Diner in West Islip is massive, with tan block corners, huge diner signage, lots of blue-tinted plate-glass windows, and tidy landscaping. The diner was built in the 1980s by DeRaffele. Bay Shore's Forum Diner recently remodeled by DeRaffele in 1996 and 2006 was originally built by Musi as a cross between exaggerated modern and environmental. As you pass through Islip and East Islip, Route 27A merges with

Route 27 in the Connetquot River State Park Preserve. A quick turn onto Route 80 will put you back on our diner drive.

One of the very few Paramount Diners located on Long Island is the Sayville Modern Diner on Main Street in Sayville. This is a village diner right in the middle of the shopping district. Built in the early 1960s and remodeled in 1993, it serves the local community as well as the occasional seasonal tourist. It is a combination of the exaggerated modern style of architecture with postmodern touches. The other diner in Sayville, the Seacrest, was built some time later by DeRaffele and reflects the latest in postmodern styling with a blue glass mansard roofline, large picture windows with a marble and glass finish.

The Blue Point Diner has been a mainstay in Blue Point since its erection by Mountain View in 1953 (#343). Its blue awnings have immense eye appeal and welcome the traveler. Unfortunately, for diner fans, the outside has been covered with vinyl siding, and the inside has been muddled into what people believe the 1950s should look like. In Patchogue, the Oasis Diner was formerly known as the Patchogue Townhouse Diner and Sante Fe Diner. Today, due to remodelings, the diner looks like a nondescript box.

Up the road in Moriches is the Moriches Bay Diner. This DeRaffele could be described as a "grown-up" environmental diner. The exterior mixes stone with polished granite while the interior is fresh and up to date.

There are quite a few miles before you reach the next diner. The Crazy Dog Diner began life as the Westhampton Beach Diner in 1952 when Mountain View #310 was set up on Montauk Highway. Adjustments were

Sayville Modern Diner on Montauk Highway in Sayville is a late modern village diner.

made in the late 1990s with the addition of a new kitchen area. This is, in fact, an upscale restaurant. *The New York Times* said ". . . the hot Crazy Dog is a new wave hybrid of cutting edge cuisine and old favorites." In 2001, the *Times* put it another way, "Here, diner is an architectural term, not a culinary one."

Your last stop on this long trip to the east end is at the Southampton Princess Diner. Originally built by DeRaffele in 1962, it has been serving its clientele for over forty years. Just like almost every restaurant in the region, the diner features fish on their menu.

## ROUTE 25 (JERICHO TURNPIKE)

This portion of Route 25 cuts across Nassau and Suffolk Counties. The route starts at the Cross Island Parkway on the edge of Queens and goes beyond Riverhead to Cutchogue. Route 25 is a well-traveled four-lane highway that passes in and out of old villages that have been swallowed up by the commercial and suburban development of the island.

Yesterday's Diner, east of Hillside Boulevard in New Hyde Park, the first village after you leave Queens, is the former Galaxy Diner. Built by DeRaffele in 1946 and remodeled in 1991, it features a wall mural depicting Marilyn Monroe, Humphrey Bogart, Elvis Presley, and James Dean, an homage to the 1950s. This 24/7 diner located on the north side of the road, is in exaggerated modern style with an under-window border of alternating black and white square tiles, colorful ceramic tiles, under-lighted overhang, and large rounded glass-block corner windows. The interior has pink marble counters,

Yesterday's Diner on Jericho Turnpike in New Hyde Park is the former Galaxy Diner, built by DeRaffele in 1948 and redone in 1997.

sunburst stainless steel behind the counter, pink and maroon terrazzo floors, and etched glass 1950s-themed touches.

From Yesterday's Diner, there is an alternate two-diner side trip to the north. For this option, take a left at the next major road, Lakeville Avenue. When you get to Hillside Avenue, which is also Route 25B, take another left and backtrack a few blocks to the New Hyde Park Diner, a DeRaffele re-styled postmodern eatery built in the 1970s and later remodeled. Continuing east on Hillside Avenue, just past Mineola Boulevard and Willis Avenue in Williston Park, the Williston Townhouse Diner is located on the north side of the road, an early example of the coming postmodern style. It is located in the quaint village of Williston Park beside the historic Long island Railroad (LIRR) station. A mural inside depicts a green and yellow 1930s O'Mahony that once stood at this location. Backtrack to Willis Avenue and go south until you return to the Jericho Turnpike. The Mineola Diner is on the northeast corner of the Jericho Turnpike and Willis Avenue. The Mineola Diner is a 1946 Mountain View diner, and one of the few classic diners still left on the island. The outside has vertical red flutes, very rare for a Mountain View, and classic cowcatcher corners. The inside is painted, but still maintains the charm of a smaller diner.

The next side trip is an absolute must! Continue south on Willis Avenue. (Or, if you never took the side trip to Hillside, take a right onto Willis and head south.) Just before the railroad tracks, take a left onto narrow East 2nd Street. The street becomes a light industrial area, not often visited by most residents of Mineola. But at the corner of Hudson Street is a classic Silk City Diner from the mid to late 1940s. Because of the area it serves, the diner is open from 5 A.M to 4 P.M, rather unusual for a diner, especially on Long Island. This diner knows how to accommodate its loyal customers. If they have the ingredients, they will make it, and sometimes, they'll even go out of their way to make it for you. Amazingly, the prices are more typical of what you might find in a small town, not on Long Island.

Second Avenue is basically a dead end, so turn around and head back to Willis Avenue and take a right. When you get back to the Jericho Turnpike, take another right and continue east. Demolished in 2008, the Jericho displayed massive "belly" windows, just like the Thru-Way Diner in New Rochelle that also met its demise in 2008.

In Old Westbury you will find the Seacrest Diner. The diner can be found just before the Jericho Turnpike merges with Hillside Avenue. This environmental diner with white rocks on the front, and a terra cotta roof has a full menu like any twenty-four-hour Long Island diner. The inside is still traditional, but it has been updated and is in good condition. The diner requires reservations on the weekends.

As you get into Syosset you'll find the Celebrity Diner, Swingle #262DV, which was built in 1962 and later remodeled to postmodern style, featuring black glass roof trim, mirror stainless, belly windows, and huge diner signage. The former Nostalgia Diner, now Patsy's Pizzeria, was remodeled in 1999 and has the reverse step stainless roofline that DeRaffele is known for. It is diagonally across the intersection with the Celebrity on the south side and Patsy's Pizzeria on the north. The On Parade Diner at the corner of Piquets Lane in Woodbury is the last diner on Route 25 in Nassau County. The diner is easily located on the south side of the road. It was remodeled by DeRaffele as a postmodern retro diner, all shiny with a mirror stainless exterior and a soaring glass-brick clocktower over the vestibule. It is a true eye-popper! Of special note is the terrazzo compass rose on the vestibule floor saved from the original diner. As you enter the diner, a small center room features the cashiers, dessert case, and a short wall of liquor. To each side is a dining room, one with a counter and more traditional diner setting, the other as a dining room with a mural on the far wall.

From here, the rest of the Route 25 diners are in Suffolk County. Passing through Huntington Station, the diners happened to locate on Route 110 and not on the Jericho Turnpike. In Commack, just off Route 25 on Veterans Memorial Highway, is the Candlelight Diner. This 1987 Kullman is open twenty-four hours a day. State and Main, a company formed by Randy Garbin and Chris Carvell, finished remodeling this diner in 2006.

Your next stop is Smithtown and the Millennium Diner. Located on the corner of Routes 25 and 111, the diner features a brick-clad facade with white trim. It was updated by DeRaffele in 2001. The Coram Diner at the

The Celebrity Diner on Jericho Turnpike is another Swingle diner on Long Island, built in 1962 and updated in the 1990s.

The On Parade Diner on Jericho Turnpike in Woodbury is a DeRaffele renovation of an original Kullman.

intersection of Route 112 in Coram used to be the typical environmental diner, but it too has joined the craze of retro postmodern diners felt on Long Island.

Twenty miles farther east in the town of Riverhead are two vintage diners from the 1940s. Spicy's BBQ was first built as two barrel-roof diners side-by-side. They were later joined by Kullman, which added a new front diner-wrap that bound them together. Two more circa 1940 Kullmans, the Riverhead Grill on Main Street and Cutchogue Diner on the Main Road round out your trip. The Riverhead Grill started out as a Paramount diner in 1932. Remodeled in 1937, it retained its character until its transformation by Kullman in the early 1940s. The center of attraction for shoppers in Riverhead, the Grill hosts a variety of patrons. Local politicians, courthouse personnel, tourists, and everyday people frequent the diner. Inside are brass chandeliers, comfortable booths, etched glass transom windows, and a long counter. The Cutchogue Diner, a 1941 Kullman, is a classic. After seeing a dizzying assortment of modern, environmental, and postmodern diners, the Cutchogue is a fantastic way to end this drive.

## OLD COUNTRY ROAD
This drive is entirely in Nassau County and is a heavily traveled commercial road dotted with shopping centers and malls. Because all of the diners are located on the north side of the road, the best way to attack this diner drive is to come from the Wantagh State Parkway in Westbury and head west.

DeRaffele renovated the Harvest Diner in Westbury in the early 1990s.

DeRaffele-built diners are predominant in Nassau County. The New Rochelle facility is close enough to ship diners to the island, and many of the earlier diners have been updated by the same company. DeRaffele indicates that three-quarters of his business today is remodeling.

The first diner on your drive is now known as Pollos el Paisa, which received a recent face-lift. The all-white facade was painted a glowing gold but it retains its exaggerated modern roofline with its under-eave lighting. The roof-edge is now a red tile mansard. From the outside, this 1962 DeRaffele could easily be mistaken for a Mountain View. The diner has received glowing reviews for its chicken.

The next three diners are within a mile of each other. Just up the road, two blocks west of Grand Boulevard, you come to the Harvest Diner, built by DeRaffele. It represents the Mediterranean style, with rounded windows, red terra cotta mansard roof, and stone facade painted light yellow. The Harvest offers a relaxed atmosphere and is open 24/7. The Majestic Diner is a DeRaffele as well, with a huge entryway and shiny stainless steel. Reverse step mirror stainless steel graces the roofline while the towering entryway is topped by a huge diner sign. The interior features gleaming stainless steel along the back wall of the counter.

Old County Road becomes the most commercial at Carle Place. There is every big box store you can think of, shopping plazas, and a mall. Across from East Gate Boulevard, Thomas's Ham-n-Eggery Diner, built in 1946, retains much of its original charm. Neon tubing circles the roof edge of this tan-colored diner. The menu ranges from French toast stuffed with lemon cream cheese and ricotta and topped with homemade blueberry sauce to

Greek specialties to liver and onions to a Cajun omelet with Louisiana andouille sausage. The last diner on this short trip is the Carle Place Diner, located on the corner of Old Country Road, Clinton and Glen Cove Roads, the first intersection west of the Meadowbrook State Parkway. This was a 1970s DeRaffele sensitively remodeled by DeRaffele in 1997 and recently updated by Progressive Designs. The brown marble exterior, the glass-block corners, and the huge entryway with its diner signage and grand appearance beckons shoppers from the Roosevelt Field Shopping Mall located across the street. The inside is done in brown wood tones, and still holds on to its cantilevered stools upholstered in red.

## ROUTE 25A

Starting in Queens County as Queens Boulevard, Route 25A is Long Island's northernmost east–west road. While not hugging the shore, the highway does travel through many northern villages. For your trip, the drive will end in Port Jefferson. At the start of the road, look for a four-lane busy highway. You'll also have to beware of double parking, a typical practice in urban areas for delivery trucks.

Your first stop is the Seven Seas Restaurant-Diner in Great Neck at the intersection of Lakeville Road. The diner sits on the north side of the road, also known as Northern Boulevard. The other three corners of the intersection are devoted to gas stations. This rare Swingle was built in 1958 remodeled around 1970, and drastically changed in the early 1990s. Displaying postmodern styling in warm, brown tones of glass and stone, the diner specializes in steaks and seafood. All baking is done on the premises.

Take a short ride south on Mineola Avenue (which turns into Willis Avenue) to the junction with the Long Island Expressway, and you will find the former Roslyn Diner. Today, the diner has been transformed into the Ravagh Persian Grill. Built by DeRaffele in 1958, it has been remodeled by new owners over recent years. In 1999 and 2000, the diner was transformed first into Hamid Kosher, then to the Roslyn Grill, and finally into its present incarnation.

Back up to Route 25A in Roslyn, you will find that the Landmark Diner lives up to its name. This village landmark sits on the north side of the route. A 1962 DeRaffele, it was updated in 1988, and is slated to be replaced by a two-story diner built by DeRaffele. The diner serves a full diner menu that features Greek food, and all their baking is done on the premises. Their location at the intersection of Route 101 serves Roslyn and the northern communities of Port Washington and Sands Point.

Continue east until you get to Glen Cove Road and make a turn north to visit the Greenvale Townhouse Restaurant. There will be a sign pointing

DeRaffele's Millennium Diner, renovated in the early 2000s, reflects a growing trend to find a new vernacular style for diners.

toward Glen Cove that will make finding this left turn much easier. This 1983 eatery is easily spotted with its brick and stone facade and shingled mansard roofline. The diner is located close to the road, in line with the other businesses in this older commercial strip. Go a little further north on Glen Cove Road and you will find the Old Brookville Family Restaurant at the corner of Glen Head Road. The diner faces the side road, making it a little harder to spot. This is the first environmental diner built by Kullman in 1972, done in red brick with white mullioned windows.

There are no more diners on Route 25A until you reach Suffolk County. In Suffolk, the road narrows to two lanes and passes the shore of Cold Spring Harbor. For a couple of miles, the road feels more like New England. After passing two non-vintage diners in the village of Huntington, you arrive in Northport, the location of Tim's Shipwreck Diner on Main Street. Tim's is a treasured town favorite where everyone eats, both locals and visitors. The walls proudly show off the community's history.

Don't miss the newly updated Millennium Diner in Smithtown. It was transformed in 2004 by DeRaffele from a colonial-style eatery into a classy village diner. Some miles east, Tropico Inn is a vintage Silk City (#5705), built in 1957 and now closed and gutted. This diner went through a number of changes over the years. First known as the Port Diner, then as the Happy Days Diner, it last served Port Jefferson's Latin-American community as a neighborhood meeting place.

While you are in Port Jefferson, head a short way south to Route 347 and the Seaport Diner, the last diner on this drive. The Seaport Diner is a unique mix of styles—its postmodern vestibule is topped with glass block, and its dark glass windows are outlined by stainless steel. The building is capped by six-foot wide columns covered with large stones and topped with glass blocks.

## ROUTE 110

Only a few major roads joining Long Island's north and south shores feature more than two diners. Route 110 runs just east of the Nassau–Suffolk county line. One of the few Swingle Diners extant on Long Island is Cooke's Inn in Huntington. Built in 1961 and well preserved by Juanita Cooke, the diner is filled with artifacts collected by Juanita during her years as a school teacher. The stone facade, curved cornice, and under-eave exterior lights add to the charm. Heading south, you cross Route 25 and into Huntington Station and reach the stately Oceancrest Diner. Built by DeRaffelle in the 1960s and later remodeled, the Oceancrest is a fine example of the then-popular Mediterranean-style of diner architecture, with its fieldstone facade, terra cotta tile mansard roofline, and large windows. In sharp contrast is the Sweet Hollow Diner in Melville. Located near the Walt Whitman Shopping Center, the diner has a striking presence with its pink and gray marble siding, and neon signage.

The Spartan Towers Diner, open 24/7, is easily recognized by its unique architecture. Two brick-red stucco towers and brown granite tiles bordered

Huntington's The Cooke's Inn on Route 110 is a Swingle built in 1961 and renovated in 2001.

with mirror stainless form a massive facade with silvered glass windows that make this a "can't miss" eatery. The interior echoes the exterior with lots of mirror stainless steel, sunburst stainless behind the counter, and granite tabletops. They offer a full menu with special diet offerings.

In Amityville, Peter's Diner recently moved in 2005–6 to its present site, taking over the long-closed Riviera Diner. The diner is exaggerated modern style, with a sawtooth roofline and under-eave lighting. The exterior is faced with beige and black granite. Light and dark shades of wood and Formica add to the natural, calm atmosphere inside the diner. An oval-framed, etched-glass rendering of the Parthenon is on one wall, with a hand-painted mural of a Greek island on another. Some diner-philes might wish to view the original Peter's Diner. Travel south a few miles to the LIRR overpass along Route 110. There you will find the old diner tucked away just south of the railroad. Its address is 236 Broadway.

# THE CUTCHOGUE DINER

### 1941 KULLMAN, RENOVATED 1987
Main Rd. (Rt. 25), Cutchogue • (631) 734-9056

The North Fork of Long Island has twenty of the more than fifty wineries that now grace the East End of Long Island. It is a tourist mecca, and what better place to eat than in the Cutchogue Diner.

In the August 1, 1941, issue of *North Fork Life*, the Cutchogue Diner is described as "A thirty-six foot creation . . . [Olin] Glover's new eatatorium seats 42 comfortably. . . . Maroon fluted porcelain decorates the outside with stainless-steel trim and an all-steel frame. Marble counters and uphol-stered booths give the diner a Pullman-car effect which is carried out by a Mexican mahogany trim." The center entrance door is flanked by glass block. There are lavish flower beds along the front of the diner, lending a welcoming look. The inside of the diner has the authentic classic feel, with tables and chairs set along the front wall. More booths were added in a later addition. There is an art deco motif in maroon and gold throughout as seen in the tiles below the counter, on the floor, and on the vinyl-upholstered chairs and stools. Art deco lighting glows between the wooden windows. A separate narrow section of horizontally fluted etched glass sits atop each window, evoking an old railroad dining car. A plaque mounted on the wall states, "Town of Southold, Suffolk County Landmark—1956." When the present owner, John Touhey, purchased the diner, he was quoted in *Newsday*, "I bought it as a preservationist. It's an art piece; it's like a painting. I was afraid someone would put those fake bricks up and get a long menu." The original green wooden barrel-roof diner was incorporated into the then newly built Kullman diner in 1941. It now serves as part of the expanded kitchen, restrooms, and storage areas.

The diner is locally famous for its large selection of homemade pies. Try their peanut butter luster and—in season—the strawberry-rhubarb pie. Be sure to ask for their old-fashioned mashed potatoes, lumps and all. Prices are reasonable, portions are generous, and the service is friendly. John Touhey says, "A diner is [about] who goes there, every bit as much as it is a restaurant with a counter and a grill." Birthdays are a tradition at the diner, and not just for staff members. Regular customers are feted, too. Cathy Dickson has been waitress and manager at the diner for more than fifteen years. Her mother, Lynn, also waitresses there. John pitches in when he is staying at his summer home in Cutchogue.

# TIM'S SHIPWRECK DINER

**1940s KULLMAN, RENOVATED 2003**

46 Main St., Northport • (631) 754-1797

According to the newspaper *Long Island Heritage,* the original Northport Diner, built by the Worcester Manufacturing Co., was rolled into place in 1924 on wheels using the trolley tracks already in place on Main Street and placed edgewise to the street. Former owner Otto Hess says that diner was about twenty-five-feet long. Its front was positioned in line with the other storefronts along Main Street. It replaced an older, trolley-car diner that had been there since the early 1900s. It remained in place until it was replaced by the present Kullman Diner in the early 1940s. Covered with photos dating back as far as the 1880s, the walls of the Shipwreck are a chronicle of Northport village history.

In the early days, the diner would open at 5 A.M. Regular customers were clammers and fishermen, Long Island Lighting Company workers putting up the smokestacks in nearby Asharoken, and employees from Davis Aircraft. Today, most customers are families with children who pack the place, and visitors to this historic village. The exterior remains virtually unchanged and the wooden booths and walls are original. The lighting was replaced in

The original Northport Diner in the 1920s.

the 1990s during the most recent renovation. It was during this renovation that the original wooden wheels were discovered. Parts of these wheels are on display. The diner was enlarged and brought up-to-date when an out-door patio eating area was also added. A part of the television show, *Full House*, was filmed there, as were parts of two movies, *The Hero Within* and, more recently, *In and Out*, starring Kevin Kline and Tom Selleck. In the film, the diner was temporarily renamed Darlene's Greenleaf Diner.

When asked if there is any favorite dish among patrons, owner Tim Hess quickly responds by saying, "My mom, Marion, makes the best home-made cheesecake and rice pudding!"

The Shipwreck is more than a local eatery. It is a treasured locale for the village of Northport and the surrounding communities. Local politicos meet there for lunch and visitors seek it out. People love it. Souvenirs including mugs, postcards, and refrigerator magnets are for sale.

# MARY BILL DINER
### 1948–49 SILK CITY #48210, RENOVATED
14 Merrick Ave., Merrick • (516) 378-9713

Situated close to the Long Island Railroad station in Merrick, this diner has been a fixture in the community for over fifty years. On a number of visits, we found that the satisfied customers seem to be the best advertisement for the diner. One said, "This place is like family." Another said, "The diner serves the best food in the area." As we talk with Mary Kokos, she frequently looks up to say "Hi!" or "So long," to a patron. She knows everyone by name. Their omelets are traditional neighborhood delights. In a *New York Times* article January 31, 1997, Richard Kessel, president of the Long Island Power Authority, and a frequent Mary Bill patron, said, "Diners sure have more than just food. When I'm in one, I feel like I'm home."

The menu is a satisfying blend of the usual diner food, with alternatives from "The Lighter Side" of the menu and salad platters for the health-conscious. They serve an impressive array of omelets, sandwiches, and grilled specialties.

The Mary Bill exhibits the classic Silk City architectural characteristics. Sloping barrel roof, stainless steel behind the cooking area, wooden sliding door on the end wall, a counter tiled in ivory, blue, and pink with comfortable stools, and wood-back booths, all add to the general ambiance of this old-time diner. A nice touch is the porcelain "Bell System" telephone sign on the wall. Some years ago, the exterior was covered over with brick in an effort to "modernize" the diner. On one visit, we discovered the original stainless steel and porcelain siding to the left of the front entrance where the brick had been removed.

Mary Bill Diner in Merrick the late 1940s.

# MINEOLA DINER
## 1946 MOUNTAIN VIEW #236
### 138 Jericho Tpk. (Rt. 25 at Willis Ave.), Mineola • (516) 877-1370

George Tzampanankis was born in Crete and came to the United States "for a better life." He started as a dishwasher and moved up to grillman before opening his own business, a deli in Queens. A second deli followed and then a coffee shop. His son, Chris, manages the takeout and delivery business today. George and his wife also own a deli in Suffolk County run by Rosalie and another son, Nick.

The diner's menu is varied, with traditional Greek dishes such as spinach pie, gyros, and souvlaki sharing a place with the usual diner fare, as well as turkey and veggie burgers. There are daily blue-plate specials, and a newer, lighter fare. Weekends are their busiest times.

Most cooking is done out front behind the counter. The grill, originally behind the counter, had been moved to a back kitchen by a previous owner. George moved it back to its proper location about four years ago. Above the grill is a unique clock. It has a stainless-steel background with a center crescent moon and swirling colored stars. Other diner paraphernalia graces the walls and back bar. The plates and coffee mugs are 1930s vintage and are always steamy clean.

The Mineola Diner has been featured in television documentaries and has been seen on the three major New York City networks. It has been written up in *The New York Times* and *Newsday* as well. When you enter through the heavy door, you may feel that you are stepping back in time. There is a feeling of gentle nostalgia. The neon sign outside is pure Americana and the diner is typical of Mountain View Diners—with round glass-block corners, interior square corners with recessed lights, and exterior cowcatcher corners.

# DINER DIRECTORY

## AMAGANSETT

**Art of Eating**
74 Montauk Hwy. (Rt. 27)
(631) 267-2411
*1946 Kullman and 1959 Silk City*
Formerly Honest Diner.

## AMITYVILLE

**Peter's Diner**
750 Broadway (Rt. 110)
(631) 789-4272
*Circa 1964 DeRaffele*
Remodeled 2005. Formerly
Riviera Diner.

## BABYLON

**Fortune Garden Chinese Restaurant**
101 W. Main St. (Rt. 27A)
(631) 422-6505
*1959 Kullman*
Formerly Jerry's Highway Diner.

## BALDWIN

**Baldwin Coach Diner**
790 Sunrise Hwy.
(516) 223-2161

**South Shore Auto Discount Center**
785 Merrick Rd.
(516) 546-2800
*1960s DeRaffele*
Formerly Baldwin Townhouse
Restaurant Diner.

## BAY SHORE

**New Forum Diner**
315 W. Main St. (Montauk Hwy./Rt. 27A)
(631) 666-4455
*Musi*
Renovated by DeRaffele 1996.

**Peter Pan Diner-Restaurant**
Bay Shore Rd. and Sunrise Hwy.
(631) 665-1788
Circa 1956.

## BETHPAGE

**Bethpage Town House Diner**
4011 Hempstead Tpk. (Rt. 24 at
Hicksville Rd./Rt. 107)
(516) 796-8842
*1980s DeRaffele*
Renovated 1999.

**Embassy Diner**
4280 Hempstead Tpk. (Rt. 24)
(516) 796-1132
*1980s DeRaffele*
Renovated 1999.

The Art of Eating on Montauk Highway in Amagansett is a combination of a 1940 Kullman and a 1959 Silk City that once operated as the Honest Diner.

## BLUE POINT

**Blue Point Diner**
145 Montauk Hwy.
(631) 363-9545
*1953 Mountain View #343*

## BOHEMIA

**Towers Diner**
4180 Veterans Memorial Hwy.
(631) 981-7155
Postmodern.

## CARLE PLACE

**Carle Place Diner**
151 Old Country Rd. (at Clinton and Glen Cove Rds.)
(516) 741-0336
*1970s DeRaffele*
Renovated 1997.

**Ham-n-Eggery**
325 Old Country Rd.
(516) 333-3090
1946.

## CENTER MORICHES

**Country Cottage Diner**
334 Main St.
(631) 878-6408
Duffy's Diner on this site, built in the 1920s, burned down in 1989.

## CENTEREACH

**Suffolk Diner Restaurant**
2101 Middle Country Rd. (Rt. 25)
(631) 981-9855
Built on-site in the postmodern style.

## COMMACK

**Candlelight Diner**
56 Veterans Memorial Hwy.
(631) 499-3918
*1987 Kullman*
Renovated by State and Main 2006.

## CORAM

**Coram Diner**
383 Middle Country Rd.
(631) 451-0489
Remodeled by DeRaffele 2008.

## CUTCHOGUE

**Cutchogue Diner**
Main Rd. (Rt. 25)
(631) 734-9056
*1941 Kullman*
Renovated 1987.

## DEER PARK

**Olympic Diner Restaurant**
1536 Deer Park Ave.
(631) 242-1902
*DeRaffele*
Renovated 2001.

## EAST MEADOW

**Apollo Diner**
630 Merrick Ave.
(516) 292-1620
*Circa 1962 and 1975 Kullman*

Patron Lucille Monti leaves Cutchogue Diner with a full stomach and a happy face.

**Colony Diner**
2019 Hempstead Tpk. (Rt. 24)
(516) 794-5159
*1985 Swingle #1285DKVDR*
Renovated 1998 by DeRaffele.

**Empress Diner**
2490 Hempstead Tpk. (Rt. 24
at Rt. 106)
(516) 796-0828
*DeRaffele*

## ELMONT

**Stop 20 Diner**
1336 Hempstead Tpk. (Rt. 24)
(516) 358-7142

## FARMINGDALE

**Spartan Towers Diner-Restaurant**
1580 Broadhollow Rd. (Rt. 110 at
989 Conklin St.)
(631) 293-8633
Renovated 1991–92.

## FARMINGVILLE

**Gabino's Diner**
777 Horseblock Rd.
(631) 698-1264
*1958–59 Kullman*
Renovated 2003. Formerly Chris's Diner.

## FRANKLIN SQUARE

**Silver Star Diner**
813 Hempstead Tpk. (Rt. 24)
(516) 326-9532
*DeRaffele*

## FREEPORT

**Imperial Diner**
63 W. Merrick Rd.
(516) 868-0303
Remodeled by Progressive Designs.

LARRY CULTRERA

The former Fabrizio's Diner in Greenport is the Front Street Station.

## GREAT NECK

**Seven Seas Restaurant**
607 Northern Blvd. (Rt. 25A at
Lakeville Rd.)
(516) 482-0980
*Circa 1958 Swingle*
Renovated.

## GREENPORT

**Front Street Diner**
212 Front St. (Rt. 25)
(631) 477-2484
*Silk City*
Renovated.

## GREENVALE

**Greenvale Townhouse Restaurant**
49 Glen Cove Rd.
(516) 625-5300
1983.

## HAMPTON BAYS

**Hampton Bays Diner and Restaurant**
157 Montauk Hwy. (Rt. 80 at Rt. 24)
(631) 728-0840
1980s.

## HAUPPAUGE

**Hauppauge Palace Diner**
525 Smithtown Bypass
(631) 979-4324
*DeRaffele*

**Paradise Diner**
579 Veterans Memorial Hwy.
(631) 724-1778
*DeRaffele*

## HICKSVILLE

**Empire Diner-Restaurant**
42 N. Jerusalem Ave. (at West John St.)
(516) 433-3352
*1952 DeRaffele*
Renovated 1966, remodeled by
DeRaffele 2001.

## HOLBROOK

**Holbrook Diner**
980 Patchogue–Holbrook Rd.
(980 Main St.)
(631) 471-7144
*1996 DeRaffele*

## HUNTINGTON

**Cooke's Inn**
767 New York Ave. (Rt. 110)
(631) 424-2181
*1961 Swingle*
Renovated 2001.

DeRaffele's 1996 Lindencrest Diner mixes environmental stone facing with late modern stainless steel and glass.

**Dix Hills Diner**
1800 Jericho Tpk.
(516) 499-5988
Remodeled.

## HUNTINGTON STATION

**Oceancrest Diner**
269 Rt. 110 (Walt Whitman Rd.)
(631) 421-4424
*1960s DeRaffele*
Renovated. Formerly Eagle Diner.

## ISLIP

**Oconee East Diner Restaurant**
749 Montauk Hwy. (Main St./
7 Islip Ave.)
(631) 581-2653

## LAKE GROVE

**Lake Grove Diner**
2211 Nesconsett Hwy.
(631) 471-5370
*DeRaffele*

## LAWRENCE

**Sherwood Diner**
311 Rockaway Tpk.
(516) 371-4616
*1987 and 1996 DeRaffele*

## LINDENHURST

**Lindencrest Diner**
338 W. Montauk Hwy. (at Broadway)
(631) 226-1010
*1996 DeRaffele*

**Lindenhurst Diner**
Wellwood Ave. (195 East Montauk
Hwy. at Delaware Ave.)
(631) 957-6650
1954, renovated postmodern style.

## LONG BEACH

**Long Beach Diner**
284 W. Park Ave.
(516) 670-9100
*2001 environmental.*

## LYNBROOK

**Lynbrook Diner**
401 Sunrise Hwy.
(516) 593-1661
*1962 DeRaffele*
Renovated by DeRaffele 1990s.

## MASSAPEQUA

**Massapequa Diner**
4420 Sunrise Hwy.
(516) 799-5234
*1970s DeRaffele*

**Nautilus Diner**
5523 Merrick Rd.
(516) 799-5880
*1970s Kullman*

## MEDFORD

**Metropolis Diner-Restaurant**
1711 Rt. 112
(631) 758-2427
*1992 DeRaffele*

## MELVILLE

**Sweet Hollow Diner**
100 Rt. 110
(631) 549-0768

## MERRICK

**Mary Bill Diner**
14 Merrick Ave.
(516) 378-9713
*1948–49 Silk City #48210*
Renovated.

## MINEOLA

**Kiss the Chef Diner**
106 E. 2nd St. and Hudson St.
(516) 739-5869
*Circa 1946 Silk City*

**Mineola Diner**
138 Jericho Tpk. (Rt. 25 at Willis Ave.)
(516) 877-1370
*1946 Mountain View #236*

## MORICHES

**Moriches Bay Diner**
62 Montauk Hwy.
(631) 878-6827
*DeRaffele*

## NEW HYDE PARK

**New Hyde Park Diner**
1601 Hillside Ave. (at 2nd St.)
(516) 354-2022
*1970s DeRaffele*
Renovated 2000s.

**Yesterday's Diner**
443 Jericho Tpk. (Rt. 25)
(516) 352-5290
*1946 DeRaffele*
Renovated 1997.

## NORTH BABYLON

**Garden Plaza Diner Restaurant**
1143 Deer Park Ave.
(631) 254-1425
*1999 DeRaffele*
Renovated.

## NORTHPORT

**Tim's Shipwreck Diner**
46 Main St.
(631) 754-1797
*1940s Kullman*

The Riverhead Grill on Route 25 in Riverhead is an early 1940s Kullman beneath an environmental remodel.

## OCEANSIDE

**Mitchell's Restaurant**
2756 Long Beach Rd.
(516) 255-9544
*DeRaffele*

## OLD BROOKVILLE

**Old Brookville Restaurant**
319 Glen Head Rd. (at Glen Cove Rd.)
(516) 671-1063
*1972 Kullman*

## OLD WESTBURY

**Sea Crest Restaurant**
4 Glen Cove Rd.
(516) 741-0580
1972.

## PATCHOGUE

**Oasis Diner**
275 E. Main St. (Montauk Hwy.
at Rt. 112)
(631) 748-5504
1940s. Formerly Patchogue
Townhouse Diner.

## PLAINVIEW

**Plainview Diner**
1094 Old Country Rd.
(516) 822-0766
Exaggerated modern.
Remodeled by Progressive Designs.

## PORT JEFFERSON

**Tropico Inn**
1527 Main St. (Rt. 25A)
(631) 478-0973
*1957 Silk City #5705*
Formerly Old Port Diner.

## PORT JEFFERSON STATION

**Seaport Diner**
5045 Nesconset Hwy.
(631) 928-7777
1980s.

## RIVERHEAD

**Riverhead Grill**
85 E. Main St. (Rt. 25)
(631) 727-9295
*1940s Kullman*
Renovated 1970s and 1990s

**Spicy's BBQ (Birdland)**
225 W. Main St. (Rt. 25)
(631) 727-2781
Joined side-by-side by Kullman 1940s.

## ROCKVILLE CENTRE

**Golden Reef Diner**
329 Sunrise Hwy.
(516) 764-9273
*1992 DeRaffele*
Renovated 2001. Formerly Oasis Diner.

**Pantry Diner**
525 Merrick Rd. (at Long Beach Rd.)
(516) 766-3615
1949, renovated.

**ROCKY POINT**

**Rocky Point Townhouse Diner**
400 Rt. 25A
(631) 821-1496
*DeRaffele*

**ROSLYN**

**Landmark Diner**
1023 Northern Blvd. (Rt. 25A at
Searingtown Rd.)
(516) 627-4830
*1962 DeRaffele*
Renovated 1999.

**ROSLYN HEIGHTS**

**Ravagh Persian Grill**
210 Mineola Ave. (at Long Island Expy.)
(516) 484-7100
1958, renovated 1999–2000. Formerly
the Roslyn Diner.

**SAYVILLE**

**Sayville Modern Diner**
136 Main St. (Montauk Hwy.)
(631) 589-9840
*Circa 1962 Paramount*
Renovated 1993.

**SEAFORD**

**East Bay Diner**
3360 Merrick Rd.
(516) 781-5300
Remodeled by Progressive Designs.

**Seacrest Diner**
229 West Main St.
(631) 567-5376
*DeRaffele*

**Seaford Palace Diner**
3689 Merrick Rd. (at Seaman's
Neck Rd.)
(516) 679-2488
1991.

**SMITHTOWN**

**The Millenium Diner**
156 E. Main St. (Rts. 25 and 25A
at Rt. 111)
(631) 724-5556
*DeRaffele*
Renovated 2000s.

**SOUTHAMPTON**

**Southampton Princess Diner**
32 Montauk Hwy. (and Rt. 27)
(631) 283-4255
*1962 DeRaffele*
Renovated by DeRaffele 1997 and 2000.
Formerly Holiday Grill Diner.

**SYOSSET**

**Celebrity Diner**
312 Jericho Tpk. (Rt. 25)
(516) 364-1970
*1962 Swingle #262DV*
Renovated 1990s. Formerly Town and
Country Diner.

**Patsy's Pizzeria**
407 Jericho Tpk. (Rt. 25)
(516) 802-3507
Renovated 1999.

## UNIONDALE

**Dominican Restaurant #2**
1019 Front St.
(516) 292-6336
Formerly Coliseum Diner.

## VALLEY STREAM

**Concord Diner**
99 4th St. (near Sunrise Hwy.)
(516) 872-9790
*1993 Kullman*
Renovated by Musi.

**Valbrook Diner**
160 E. Merrick Rd.
(516) 872-0465
*1972 Musi*
Renovated by DeRaffele 1988–89.

## WANTAGH

**Circle M Diner**
1132 Wantagh Ave.
(516) 221-8884
Remodeled by DeRaffele, 1976.

**Lighthouse Restaurant Diner**
3240 Sunrise Hwy.
(516) 828-8111
*1956 Kullman*
Remodeled by DeRaffele.

**Sunrise Diner**
3201 Sunrise Hwy.
(516) 221-5907
*1996 DeRaffele*

## WEST BABYLON

**Terrace Diner**
585 Sunrise Hwy.
(631) 587-8480
Postmodern.

## WEST HEMPSTEAD

**Lantern Diner**
564 Hempstead Pk.
(516) 292-1900

## WEST ISLIP

**Delphi Diner**
350 Montauk Hwy.
(631) 587-2003
*1980s DeRaffele*

## WESTBURY

**Harvest Diner**
841 Old Country Rd.
(516) 997-7838
*Circa 1980 DeRaffele*

**Majestic Diner**
498 Old Country Rd.
(516) 997-6010
*1997 DeRaffele*
Renovated by DeRaffele 1998.

**Pollos el Paisa**
989 Old Country Rd.
(516) 978-4363
*Circa 1962 DeRaffele*
Renovated 1999.

Originally built by DeRaffele around 1962, Pollos el Paisa was updated in 1999.

## WESTHAMPTON BEACH

**Crazy Dog Diner**
123 Montauk Hwy.
(631) 288-1444
*1952 Mountain View #310*
Renovated by Fodero with kitchen
addition. Formerly Westhampton
Beach Diner.

## WILLISTON PARK

**Williston Townhouse Diner**
1121 Hillside Ave.
(516) 746-2539

## WOODBURY

**On Parade Diner**
7980 Jericho Tpk. (Rt. 25)
(516) 364-1870
*Kullman*
Renovated by DeRaffele 2000s.

# HUDSON VALLEY

The Hudson River is named after Dutch explorer Hendrick Hudson. In 1609, Hudson explored the river, looking for a new, quicker route to the "Far East." Although he never did find this route, Hudson claimed this region for the Dutch. The Dutch settled in port towns like Peekskill, Newburgh, Poughkeepsie, Hudson, Albany, and New York state's first capital, Kingston.

As New York developed along with the newly founded United States, land routes became necessary. Many of the first roads were called "post roads," developed to get mail from one town to the next. U.S. Route 9W on the west side of the Hudson River and U.S. Route 9 on the east, follow the routes of two of the most important post roads.

Naturally, when cars facilitated road travel, diners began to pop up on these roads. Diners on U.S. Route 9W can be found in Catskill, Saugerties, Newburgh, and Highland. On the east side of the river on U.S. Route 9, Hyde Park, Poughkeepsie, Red Hook, Croton-on-Hudson, and Peekskill have diners.

Be it social, cultural, or economic, this region has always been partially dependent on New York City. With the Metro-North Railroad traveling south from Poughkeepsie, and I-87 heading into the Big Apple, people can easily commute into the city for work. The influence of the metropolitan region of New York City can also be found in many of the diners of the region. Just as fashion trends tend to emanate from New York City, the city is at the forefront of architectural changes. So it's easy to see why the Hudson Valley was up-to-date with the latest trends in the diner world.

Today, two-thirds of the diners in the Hudson Valley are either environmental style, or postmodern retro diners built within the last ten years. In the more populated areas closer to the Hudson, that number increases to over 80 percent.

There are a few exceptions, like the Center Diner in Peekskill, a rare 1940s National Dining Car, and Jessi's Diner, in Newburgh (formerly Callie & Bill's), a 1930s O'Mahony. But these two diners have not totally escaped the effects of modernization. Callie & Bill's has been bricked over, as Bill Korondores believed that his diner needed a new look to keep up with the other diners. The Center Diner once faced this fate before being restored by Daniel Zilka at the request of a former owner named Dimitios Georgatos.

Lunch wagons started popping up in New England in the 1870s and 1880s. They became commonplace in cities that were heavily dependent on various factories. Like New England, the Hudson Valley had its share of diner-supporting manufacturing jobs, but if you were to rely on city directories for their appearance in the valley, the lunch wagon did not appear in the Hudson Valley until the twentieth century. According to the city directories, Kingston got its first lunch wagon in 1904, followed by Newburgh in 1905, and Poughkeepsie in 1917. One would guess that the city directories did not hold the lowly lunch wagon in high esteem, at first. In 1905, the *Poughkeepsie*

A rare sight—a group of ladies going to the diner—at the original Colonial Diner in Kingston.

The Star Diner is set edgewise to the street in White Plains. Through an alleyway, you can see the outside of this early 1950s Silk City.

*News-Telegram* stated, "Business is sure to grow if it be profitable. See the hot frankfurter business. From one boy with a kettle, a few years ago, it has grown to two lunch wagons, two or more night lunch houses, and a man or two still using the kettle in the streets."

With fast cooked foods like the hamburger and hot dogs, lunch wagons were ready for business. Lunch wagon proprietor Simon King even introduced a new sandwich called a French Roast.

Lunch wagons at this time ranged from ones that barely had enough room for a cook and a counter, to some larger ones that had six to ten stools next to a counter. By the 1920s, lunch wagons became larger and longer, and less mobile. They also picked up the name "diner," for their resemblance to railroad dining cars. A few diners in the late 1920s used the name "dining car," even though there was no question that they were factory-built diners. Others, like the Queen City Lunch Car in Newburgh, combined the two terms. By this time, companies like O'Mahony and Tierney, who were practically at the Hudson Valley's back door, were building a diner a day.

With the coming of the diner, city directories become a dependable means to find out what cities had diners, and how many. In spite of the beginning of the Great Depression in 1929, diners began to pop up in more and more places. As one manufacturer said, everyone still had to eat. Villages like Millbrook, Monroe, Catskill, and Cornwall-on-Hudson became

The Cairo Diner in Cairo was saved from demolition, but its future is uncertain.

The Dobbs Ferry Diner replaced the Otero's Diner shown below. It is a classic example of a colonial-style diner.

home to diners. Larger places, like the cities of Newburgh, Poughkeepsie, and Kingston saw a multitude of diners move in.

A Tierney dining car advertisement of the time bragged that any village with a population of 5,000 could easily support a diner. Tierney also noted that White Plains, with a population of 27,000, had thirteen dining cars. Rye, with 5,300 residents, had three dining cars, and Stamford, Connecticut, with 40,000 people, had fifteen dining cars, all successfully operated. To note how important commuting into New York City was, Tierney's advertisement stated, "one car in White Plains derives practically all of its trade from commuters to New York and automobile traffic."

Lunch wagons started out with locations close to either railroad stations, factories, or city centers, so when the automobile started taking passengers from the railroads and trolleys, diner locations also started to shift. A few diners started popping up on the edge of town, along the major thoroughfares of the time. Robert Gardiner placed a Tierney diner in Wappingers Falls, which he ran for fifteen years. Another diner

This diner, built in 1950, was replaced by the current Dobb's Ferry Diner.

This Bixler diner sits on old Route 9 in Croton-on-Hudson. A rare pre—World War II survivor in Westchester County.

was Hank's By-Pass Diner in Kingston. When U.S. Route 9W was moved to bypass downtown Kingston, owner Henry Van Wezmaal had the idea to place a diner on the new alignment. Ironically, by the 1960s, U.S. Route 9W was once again realigned, and Hank's By-Pass lost much of its business.

By the 1940s almost every new diner in the Hudson Valley was made in downstate New York or New Jersey. The lunch wagon makers of New England, like Samuel Jones and Ephraim Hamel, were long gone. In the 1930s, the Bixler Company of Norwalk, Ohio, sent a few diners to Kingston, Poughkeepsie, Fishkill, and into Westchester County. The Bixler sent to Ossining in the early 1930s was said to be the largest diner in the Hudson Valley at the time. One was located right across from the now-closed Tierney plant, and another—still there today—went to Croton-on-Hudson. Otherwise, the diner manufacturers in vogue at the time were O'Mahony, Kullman, DeRaffele, and Silk City.

By the time World War II was over, many of the diners found in the Hudson Valley were ten to fifteen years old. Porcelain enamel, painted steel, and interior wood trim were out, and in their place was stainless steel. Diner owners that didn't have money to upgrade kept their aged diners, but others had their diners replaced. The Colonial Diner in Kingston started out as your typical barrel-roof diner. When the diner was first replaced by a new

Silk City diner, the two sat side by side. The old diner was used for the kitchen, while the new Silk City was used to seat the customers until the new diner could be completely equipped. The old Maybrook started out as a barrel-roof diner and was replaced with a 1950s Mountain View. In Monroe, two new diners came to the area. Thompson's Diner was a spacious 1948 Paramount. The New Monroe Diner was also built in 1948 by Master. The old Monroe Diner started out in the village's downtown, but was moved out on the highway, to the intersection of two major roads. Unfortunately, none of these diners exist today.

If you head up to Millbrook, on the other side of the Hudson River, you will find a diner that is thriving. The site of the current Millbrook Diner has seen three diners. The first barrel-roof diner, called the DeLuxe Diner, was removed in 1929 and replaced by a monitor roof diner. In 1952 the current stainless-steel diner was put in place by O'Mahony. The diner's best known waitress, Sarah Dean, who started working at the diner in 1955, remembers when the new diner sat on the village green, waiting for the switch. She says that the old diner was bought by a lady from the Catskills region, and is purported to be operating near Hunter Mountain.

The Millbrook Diner is still going strong. When U.S. Route 44 bypassed the village in 1953, they lost truckers; when Bennett College closed in 1977, they lost many of the girls at the all-female school; and they lost state troopers when the barracks on old Route 82 closed. Still, the people come, espe-

Now Rocco's Pizza, this diner in Patterson shows what seemed to be a great roadside setting for a diner.

cially on weekends, when there will most likely be a line out the door. Even Mary Tyler Moore has been there.

One way or another, most places of significant population saw new diners. Peekskill had the By-Pass Diner, and Brewster was home to Bob's Diner and Alton's Diner, which, with the inclusion of a dining room, had seating for 180. It was also located at the intersection of Routes 22, 202, and 6.

This early 1940s DeRaffele in Harrison has been converted into Trattoria Vivolvo, a fine Italian restaurant. Its owner intends to preserve the appearance of the diner.

This rare Mahony Diner sat just outside of Kingston on Route 28. Lee Konjas ran the diner with partner Angelo Papaleonardos before donating it to the American Diner Museum.

Highland received a 1946 Kullman, Dobbs Ferry got a diner, and Greenwood Lake had an early Mountain View first known as the Lake Diner. Highland was also home to another Kullman. Originally owned by Edward and Mary Costello, they sold the Bridge Circle Diner to Frank McCann, who came up from Brooklyn and changed its name to McCann's Diner.

A few diner manufacturers bucked the stainless-steel look, even if just for a few years. Mountain View held on to the vertical porcelain flute look, made so popular by Kullman, into the late 1940s. Mountain View, a New Jersey based postwar diner builder, made significant gains in the Hudson Valley.

The 1950s saw the creation of the Eisenhower Interstate System. Interstate highways allowed for non-stop travel from one location to another. There were no traffic lights or intersections, and speed limits were much higher. So entrepreneurs began to locate restaurants right off the exit ramps of the highways.

The College Diner, right outside of New Paltz in Ohioville, was one of the first diners to take advantage of a New York State Thruway exit location. With their convenient location, they could catch drivers getting off of the thruway for a break, as well as the people going to and from Poughkeepsie. With the popularity of the car fully ingrained into American culture and the growing popularity of the interstates, interchange diners did a great business. They did so much business that most of them expanded, and new ones were built to be much larger than owners of old diners would have dreamed of. The College Diner, built in 1976, became one of these new larger diners. Another environmental diner, the Plaza, was built on the west side of the thruway exit, closer to New Paltz.

Adam's Diner in Wingdale came from New Milford in Connecticut. This rural diner is open twenty-four hours.

In the 1970s, colonial-style diners like the North Castle Diner in White Plains became quite popular in the lower Hudson Valley.

In Newburgh, three diners can be found just off the interstates. The Neptune and Gateway diners operate off I-87 and the Alexis Diner is off I-84. The Alexis was originally the Lexus Diner, until the car company by the same name objected. All of these diners are large, and represent styles quite different from the last thirty years of the twentieth century.

Just before the environmental period came the short-lived Googie period, highlighted by exaggerated lines and large windows. If the lower Hudson Valley had any ultramodern Googie-style diners, they're gone now, but the two known diners that came the closest (with their large windows) were the New Poughkeepsie, then known as Cy's Seville Diner, and the Stadium Diner in Kingston.

During the 1960s, architectural styles were changing. People were tired of stainless steel and it was time for another style. This new look would became known as environmental, and the Neptune and College Diners are classic examples. These diners were built with stones or brick on their facades. The roofs, just like many of the stainless-steel diners, were not visible to the public, but many newer diners added a fake mansard roofline. Some of these mansard-roof diners were Mediterranean style, possibly influenced by the increasing number of Greek owners. Mansard roofs were mostly clad in wood shingles or terra cotta pantiles.

The customer base for these diners was and is dictated by the car culture. Every one of these diners has their own parking lot, even the New Poughkeepsie Diner in downtown Poughkeepsie, even though much of its business comes from government offices across the street from the diner. The Arlington Diner, just outside of Poughkeepsie, is located in an eastern suburb on a heavily trafficked road that has been home to diners since the 1930s. Another diner in this stretch of road is the Acropolis Diner.

The Hudson Diner in Middle Hope has been on U.S. Route 9W since the 1960s. It is a few miles north of Newburgh on a part of the road with moderate traffic. The New Windsor Coach Diner is in a southern suburb of Newburgh known as Vails Gate. Just about all of these diners fit the stereotype: Greek, family-run diners that have a menu nearing on novel sized, and serve good home-cooked food at reasonable prices.

The Dietz Stadium Diner in Kingston fits all three of our previous descriptions. The original diner served Kingston from 1960 to 1978, until it was replaced by the Georgiou family with another diner built by Paramount. They bought an environmental diner with a stone facade. Although the diner is at the edge of downtown, it has its own parking lot. Adam Snyder of the Kingston Museum of Contemporary Art says that growing up, the Stadium was known as "The Diner," where friends wanted to go out and meet. Besides their menu that contains Greek, American, and Mexican cuisine, the food is modestly priced, and they make their own potato chips. Both the owner, George Georgiou, and one of his waitresses, June Gardner, worked at the Royal Diner when it was first located on Albany Street. June has worked at most of the diners that have called Kingston home, including her first job at the State Diner, and later at the Empire and Colonial Diners.

The original Dietz Stadium Diner ran from 1960 to 1978. The building was replaced by a Paramount environmental diner in 1980, still in operation.

Environmental diners like the Dietz Stadium and Mt. Kisco Coach in Mt. Kisco were preferred by that town because planning regulations favored buildings with a colonial appearance. This is also the case in tiny Lake Carmel, where the New Carmel Diner looks like any other building in town.

In the 1990s, more and more people started to notice that the stainless-steel diners of their childhood were becoming scarce. In many parts of the country, people were saving old diners, and reopening them. Stainless-steel diners became hip again, stimulating a trend to build new diners in a style reinterpreted from the 1950s. Diners like the I-84 Diner in Fishkill and Johnny D's in New Windsor are perfect examples. The exteriors of these diners were made to be flashy—almost larger than life. The I-84 Diner demonstrates DeRaffele's interpretation. The exaggerated roofline along with the interior of this diner would make any environmental diner look small. And with Johnny D's, Kullman went back to their roots to a time when they were best known for their vertical porcelain flutes. On the inside, Johnny D's could be easily mistaken for a neighborhood bar, with mahogany-style wood. Not only did the size of these diners change, but so did the price tag. A 1950s diner would have cost an owner a five-digit price, but these retro diners easily topped a million dollars. Some diner owners knew that they couldn't afford these prices, so they renovated instead. In the Hudson Valley, DeRaffele and Paramount have captured most of the renovation business. Two of their recent jobs were the Hudson Diner in Middlehope done by DeRaffele, and the Gateway Diner in Highland, done by Paramount. Both of these diners were originally environmental style and are now using the nostalgic packaging of stainless steel to attract diners.

The Mount Kisco Diner is a typical environmental diner in a main street setting.

Paramount built the Mount Ivy Diner in Pomona in 1997. They went back to the classic vertical flutes that Kullman was so well known for.

This 1955 Kullman in Wappingers Falls has been converted to a furniture repair store, but shows a little bit of its original exterior.

Another retro diner is the Mount Ivy Diner. A blue porcelain enamel, vertical-fluted diner, built by Paramount, the diner's exterior is a tribute to the past, but that is where the vintage references end. "Archie" Ligares calls a diner the most expensive type of restaurant to build and run, since it requires extensive storage facilities for his wide-ranging menu. Just like some diners on Long Island, Archie has taken the Mount Ivy up a notch on the culinary

The Elizaville Diner came from Lebanon, Pennsylvania. Shown here a week after it arrived, it is now open.

scale. They have a fresh fish case for the day's seafood fare and Archie also uses a nutritionist in planning menus.

In 2008, the Thru-Way Diner in New Rochelle was demolished for a chain pharmacy, despite an online petition pleading for the diner's survival. Located off of an exit of I-95, the diner was originally built in the exaggerated modern style. The Thru-Way, being located in the same city as DeRaffele, could have been thought of as the demonstration model of the time for DeRaffele. In the 1990s DeRaffele was hired to remodel the diner. The post-remodel diner sported a blue mirror-glass roofline, stainless steel trim, and bumped-out tinted windows.

The Hudson Valley also has its share of vintage diners, like the Elizaville Diner, a Kullman diner recently moved from Lebanon, Pennsylvania, where it was known as the Eat Well Diner. Owners Brian Pitcher and Dale Strong have removed the non-original mansard roof and returned the diner to its former glory. Pitcher ran the West Taghkanic Diner before selling it to the Eisner family.

Classics continue to disappear, however. The former Bells Pond Diner was moved to Rumney, New Hampshire, where it is known as the Plain Jane's Diner. Mountain View diner #333 was moved from Kingston to New Paltz to be used as an ice cream parlor. Unfortunately, it never opened and the diner was moved again to Savannah, Georgia.

Just like any other city, the diners in Newburgh started out downtown, and primarily focused on the main thoroughfares, Broadway and South Robinson. In 1950, all of the diners could be found on these roads. Today, there are only two diners left downtown; many others were moved to the suburbs. One on Broadway is closed and the other, Jessi's, is located a block away on Lake Street. The former was in such bad shape in 2006 that there were no ceiling or wall panels. These diners suffer from two main problems: lack of parking and a rundown neighborhood. Both are unrecognizable as classic diners from the outside. The former Callie & Bills is faced with bricks, an attempt to modernize this 1930s O'Mahony.

In the 1940s there was a diner known as Harvey's Diner on Route 17K, west of Newburgh, but it's long gone. Where classic stainless-steel diners once stood, environmental diners flourish. The three diners that located in suburban Newburgh have a keen eye on the transportation habits of a car-driven culture. Two diners are located on Route 17K. The Neptune Diner, a 1960s Fodero, is situated to catch traffic coming off I-87. Come in at night, and you're likely to find a few police officers taking a break. Farther out Route 17K and at another I-84 exit is the Stewart Airport Diner. This diner is situated to catch the state highway, interstate, and airport traffic. The New Windsor Coach is on Route 32 south of downtown Newburgh. The diner is a typical 1960s environmental diner from DeRaffele. Formerly the Vails Gate Diner, the New Windsor Coach was remodeled by Paramount in 1997.

Recent remodels have caused environmental diners to become increasingly rare in this region. Johnny D's is a retro diner built by Kullman along Route 300, a major commercial strip. Although it retains classic diner features on the outside, the inside looks and feels more like a pub. Johnny D's

Johnny D's Diner in New Windsor is a fine example of a Kullman retro-style diner. Unfortunately, this diner looks more like a pub inside than a diner.

A glass ceiling makes this a uniquely designed diner.

is a chain of diners owned by Johnny Daskalis, called the "Hudson Valley Diner King" by the *Times Herald Record*. The diner even received a writeup for having the cleanest bathrooms in the county.

The Gateway Diner is also on Route 300, closer to the interstate, and was built in 2001 by Paramount. Frank Georgakopoulos, the owner's brother and manager of the diner, wanted something different than a retro diner. His "big fat Greek diner," as Frank calls it, has a facade of polished granite and three glass ceiling towers, one over the main entrance and two smaller ones at each end.

The Alexis Diner is at the intersection of U.S. Route 9W, the old north–south highway, and Interstate 84, the only way across the Hudson River from Newburgh. Another twenty-four-hour diner just like the Neptune and Gateway, this diner has received frequent makeovers, with Paramount coming in to remodel the diner in 1996. The Alexis has five dining rooms and needs all of them during the lunch rush hour. The marble in the main entranceway into the kitchen looks like it might have cost more than many classic diners. It seems that their success in business allows the owners to spare no expense when it comes to showing off their diner.

# DINER DRIVES

## U.S. ROUTE 9W

Driving for diners between Albany and New York City means following U.S. Route 9 on the east side of the Hudson River or U.S. Route 9W along the west bank. This route goes through Newburgh, where the George Washington House is located; Kingston, New York's first capital; and Catskill, Saugerties, and West Point.

In the 1930s, downtown Catskill had a diner, which was moved to the fringe of town on 9W as that road became an important transportation route. The 9W Diner, a Bixler run by the Fegraus family, also operated on the edge of town. Another diner operated in Catskill near the Rip Van Winkle Bridge in the 1960s, before being relocated off the Taconic Parkway at Rigor Hill Road. The Ambrosia is now the only diner in Catskill. This 1970s Kullman diner was brought up from Long Island in the 1980s and was first known as the Olympic Diner. In 1993 Dennis Pilarinos bought the diner from DeRaffele, which had been hired to do some remodeling work. Today, not only can you experience the classic diner breakfast or lunch, you can choose the Ambrosia to be the site of your private party, as DeRaffele added a seventy-seat banquet room in 2002.

This 1962 Paramount has had an additional dining room added, and has been renovated to make it look more environmental.

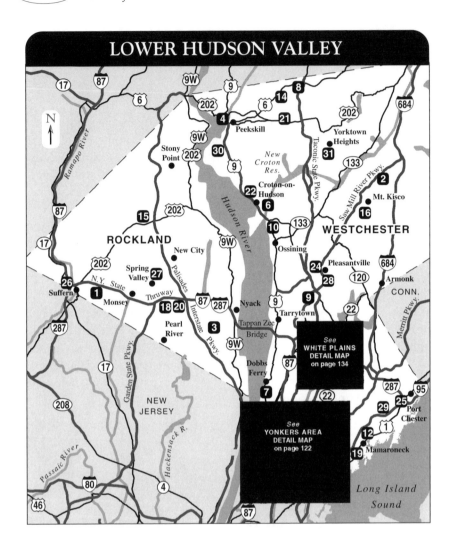

The next diner south of U.S. Route 9W is at the northern edge of downtown Saugerties. The Village Diner is a 1979 DeRaffele that replaced an older model that has been described as a trolley-style diner. The Village is a simple utilitarian diner with cantilevered stools and a stone and pebble facade.

After winding out of downtown Saugerties, you will see the Barclay Heights Diner on your left. It is a Kullman with a DeRaffele dining room added in 1979. The owner, Linda Lopez, is related to the owner of the Village Diner and also owns Selena's Diner in Tannersville. Barclay Heights is open

1 Airmont Diner: Suffern (P)
2 Bedford Diner: Bedford Hills (R)
3 Blauvelt Coach Diner: Blauvelt (E)
4 Center Diner: Peekskill (MS)
5 Columbus Diner: Mount Vernon (R)
6 Croton Colonial Diner: Croton-on-Hudson (E)
7 Dobbs Diner: Dobbs Ferry (E)
8 Doc James Cigars: Shrub Oak (R)
9 Executive Diner: Hawthorne (E)
10 Landmark Diner: Ossining (P)
11 Larchmont Diner: Larchmont (E)
12 Mamaroneck Diner & Pizza:
Mamaroneck (E)
13 Mirage Diner: New Rochelle (P)
14 Mohegan Diner: Mohegan Lake (P)
15 Mount Ivy Diner: Pomona (P)
16 Mount Kisco Coach Diner: Mount Kisco (E)

17 Mount Olympus Diner: Yonkers (E)
18 Nanuet Diner: Nanuet (E)
19 Nautilus Diner: Mamaroneck (E)
20 New City Diner: Nanuet (P)
21 New City Diner: Yorktown Heights (P)
22 Ocean House Oyster Bar and Grill:
Croton-on-Hudson (BR)
23 Odyssey Diner: Eastchester (E)
24 Pleasantville Colonial Diner: Pleasantville (E)
25 Port Chester Coach Diner: Port Chester (E)
26 Rockland Diner: Suffern (P)
27 Spring Valley Diner: Spring Valley (E)
28 Thornwood Coach Diner: Thornwood (E)
29 Trattoria Vivolo: Harrison (MS)
30 Westchester Diner: Peekskill (E)
31 Yorktown Coach Diner: Yorktown Heights (E)

twenty-four hours a day. If it wasn't for their good reputation, one would think a round-the-clock diner would never survive in such a small area.

Farther south in Kingston, the King's Valley Pancake House appears to be a generic brick restaurant on Route 32 (old U.S. Route 9W), but it is a 1997 Paramount. To get to this diner, you have to pass Kingston's version of the Miracle Mile, where the famous Rhinebeck Diner once sat.

The Sub Depot is on East Chester Street, the second-generation alignment of U.S. Route 9W through Kingston. This 1930s O'Mahony has had more than its share of renovations, but its barrel roof is still visible from the outside. The small diner has had many owners and has been opened and closed frequently in the last thirty years. Its first owners, Henry and Viola Van Wezmaal, ran it the longest.

From this point, you can take a slight detour to hit the Dietz Stadium Diner in Kingston, an environmental diner built by Paramount in 1980.

U.S. Route 9W becomes four lanes at Routes 299 (U.S. Route 44 and Route 55). This road is heavily traveled, as it is the main route from Poughkeepsie to the thruway. U.S. Route 9W cuts right through the tiny village of Highland, which has had a diner since the 1940s. Patrick's Diner arrived on January 3, 1946, sporting stainless and blue vertical flutes. The Kullman diner served meals until 1984, when it was replaced by a newer diner now known as the Gateway Diner. Current owner George Kapoulas says the old Kullman is now in Georgia. The diner has a longtime customer base. One patron, now

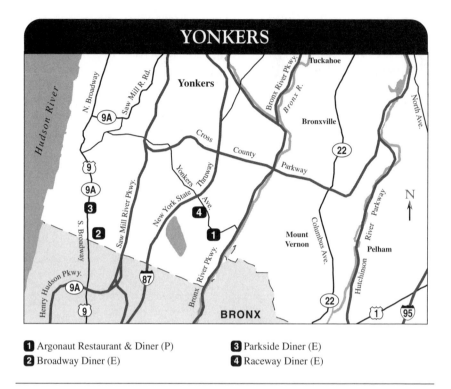

**1** Argonaut Restaurant & Diner (P)      **3** Parkside Diner (E)
**2** Broadway Diner (E)                    **4** Raceway Diner (E)

in her eighties, used to work at the diner for $1.50 a day. Employee Kathy Dolcemascolo would go to Patrick's when her father owned the Esso station next door. A couple from Australia likes the diner so much, they stop by three or four times a year.

South of Highland, U.S. Route 9W becomes more suburban. The Hudson Diner, formerly known as the D-B diner, can be found in the town of Middle Hope. About three years ago, DeRaffele remodeled this classic environmental diner by adding some neon and roofline trim. The current owners also run the Mohegan Diner in Westchester County. The whole family works together to run these diners. Myra oversees operations at the Hudson Diner. She was brought up in a diner, and she is raising her child in the Hudson. She says that her family members go back to Greece each year, paid for by the diner. "It is important to stick together," and working at the family diner definitely keeps the family close.

The last diner on this drive is the Alexis in Newburgh at the junction of I-84 and U.S. Route 9W. Always busy, this often-remodeled diner is open twenty-four hours. There are two dining rooms to each side of the main

The former D-B Diner in Middle Hope was a classic environmental diner. DeRaffele updated the diner to make it look slightly more flashy.

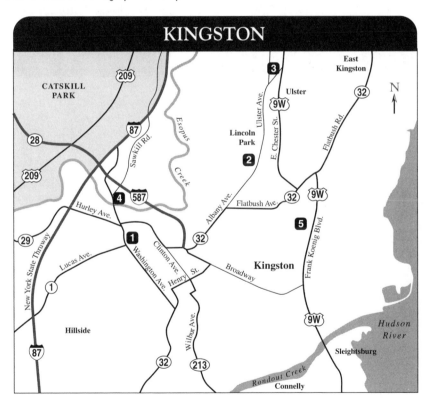

1 Dietz Stadium Diner (E)
2 King's Valley Diner (E)
3 Michael's Diner (E)
4 Olympic Diner (E)
5 Sub Depot (R)

diner. One side is trimmed in stainless steel while the other is trimmed in wood, with a mural on the wall.

## U.S. ROUTE 9

The two most common names for U.S. Route 9 are Broadway and the Albany Post Road. These names go a long way to describe the history behind this road that showcases thirteen diners. From the Revolutionary War, to the Industrial Age, to the era of Franklin Delano Roosevelt, this road is ripe with history. This drive will start in the south where U.S. Route 9 meets Interstate 84 and ends in Hudson.

On Broadway (U.S. Route 9) in Wappingers Falls you should notice Sunburst Furniture. Built in 1955 by Kullman, this diner is now being used to sell home furnishings. Some of the exterior and a little of the interior is still recognizable as a diner. The Dutchess Diner, a 1993 Paramount, is within sight of the Poughkeepsie Galleria and Southside Mall. Johnny's

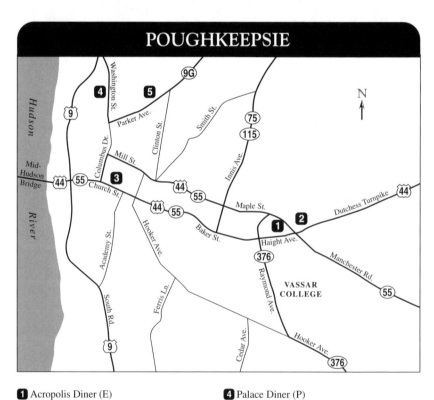

**1** Acropolis Diner (E)　　　　**4** Palace Diner (P)

**2** Arlington Diner (E)　　　　**5** Star Diner (E)

**3** New Poughkeepsie Diner (EM)

This 1950s Mountain View diner was once used on the campus of the Culinary Institute of America in Hyde Park. It now serves as the campus security office.

Diner once stood on the side of the northbound bypass around Poughkeepsie. In downtown Poughkeepsie, old U.S. Route 9 passes one block from the New Poughkeepsie Diner, a unique 1960s diner, dominated by windows. Two old U.S. Route 9 diners, the Tydol and Mid-Hudson, are gone. The Mid-Hudson was a barrel-roof diner, located just south of Marist College, and it was moved to Delafield Road when North Street was widened to allow U.S. Route 9 to bypass the downtown. It operated there a few more years before it disappeared.

The next diner on this quickly developing section of the road is in Hyde Park. A Mountain View diner, previously operated in New Jersey, sits on the campus of the Culinary Institute of America as the security office. Although the school's aim is to train the best chefs, at one time Barney Walitsky was in charge of a class called, "Coffee Shop Operations" that utilized the diner. He remarks, "You know a lot of students come here [to the diner] and say it doesn't mean anything, but I tell them that not everyone ends up in fancy restaurants." Also in Hyde Park, the Eveready Diner is one of the first retro diners built by Paramount.

Ron Dylewski remembers when there was a Silk City diner in Hyde Park called the Town 'n Country Diner. In the back (still standing today) was the mansard Mediterranean-style lighthouse room. "The Lighthouse room had a liquor license and clearly was aimed at making the place more family friendly during a time when diners were starting to seem dated," Dylewski adds.

A striking example of a forward looking postmodern diner built by Paramount in 1995.

Rhinebeck is home to the Beekman Arms, the oldest active tavern in America. The tavern opened in 1766 and was visited by George Washington in 1775. Two diners once called Rhinebeck home. The three-section Rhinebeck Diner was mammoth for its time. It was later moved to Kingston and is now in storage. The Halfway Diner is thriving as the "Historic" Village Diner in Red Hook, after spending about a year in Rhinebeck.

It's a good fifteen miles more to the final diner on this trip. The Diamond Street Diner on Warren Street in Hudson, a 1950s O'Mahony, has a name that pays homage to the brothels that once made the street famous throughout the country. Formerly the Columbia Diner, it is L-shaped and sports an exterior of stainless steel. The Bells Pond Diner, another 1950s O'Mahony, once sat a few miles south of Hudson, but it has been moved to Rumney, New Hampshire.

## I-84

The I-84 diner drive includes all the diners that are found off the exits of this limited-access highway. I-84 replaced U.S. Route 6 in the 1960s, allowing traffic between Pennsylvania and New England to bypass New York City. The interstate provides the diners with a good mix of local and long distance travelers. Of the five diners on the drive, the oldest two are at either end within older communities, while the newer three sit within the hustle and bustle of more recent suburbs.

Traveling east to west, the first diner on this drive is Bob's Diner in Brewster. I-84 hops right around downtown Brewster, and Bob's Diner is actually on U.S. Route 6, just about a mile from I-84. To the trained diner hunter, Bob's is an East Coast rarity. This 1955 O'Mahony is set up with booths at the other end of the diner in two rows instead of booths parallel to the counter. O'Mahony used this narrow setup for diners that were sent to the Midwest on railcars.

The Athenian I-84 Diner was set up near Fishkill by DeRaffele in 1971 and remodeled in 1997. This larger-than-life diner is DeRaffele's signature return to the classic diner look. With plenty of chrome and neon, this diner greets customers who are looking for a meal, any time of the day on the east side of the Hudson.

As you cross the Hudson River, I-84 joins the end of the U.S. Route 9W diner drive. The Alexis is the last diner on the U.S. Route 9W drive.

The Stewart Airport Diner is outside of Newburgh, where I-84 meets Route 17K. This 1973 Paramount is a typical mansard roof Mediterranean diner. The back wall (where the grill would be located in older diners), is

Originally built by DeRaffele in 1971, this view shows the Athenian I-84 Diner-Restaurant in Fishkill under renovation.

The current Athenian I-84 in Fishkill is a typical reverse-step postmodern DeRaffele.

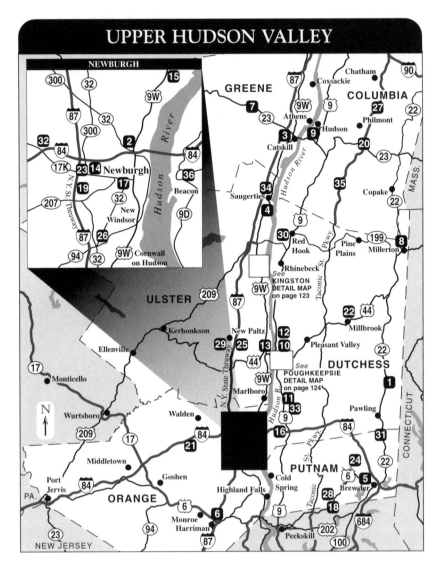

UPPER HUDSON VALLEY

covered with brown tiles and topped with roof-like shingles. By the time this diner was built, all the cooking was done in a separate kitchen to accommodate the larger dining room area. This diner has a yellow cupola more in keeping with a Chinese restaurant.

The last diner on I-84 before you reach the lower Catskills is the Maybrook Diner. Originally, there was a barrel-roof diner here known as the Modern Maybrook Diner that was popular with railroad employees. It was replaced by the current Mountain View diner, which retains much of its original charm, despite the wood-sided vestibule that was added later.

1. Adams (Star 22) Diner: Wingdale (MS)
2. Alexis Diner: Newburgh (P)
3. Ambrosia Diner: Catskill (P)
4. Barclay Heights Diner: Saugerties (E)
5. Bob's Diner: Brewster (R)
6. Bright Star Diner: Central Valley (E)
7. Cairo Diner: Cairo (BR)
8. Coach Ali's Millerton Diner: Millerton (MS)
9. Diamond Street Diner: Hudson (MS)
10. Diner: Hyde Park (R)
11. Dutchess Diner: Poughkeepsie (E)
12. Eveready Diner: Hyde Park (P)
13. Gateway Diner: Highland (P)
14. Gateway Diner: Newburgh (E)
15. Hudson Diner: Middle Hope (E)
16. I-84 Diner: Fishkill (P)
17. Jessi's Diner: Newburgh (R)
18. John's Kitchen: Mahopac (R)
19. Johnny D's Diner: New Windsor (P)
20. Martindale Chief Diner: Craryville (MS)
21. Maybrook Diner: Maybrook (MS)
22. Millbrook Diner: Millbrook (MS)
23. Neptune Diner: Newburgh (E)
24. New Carmel Diner: Carmel (E)
25. New College Diner: New Paltz (E)
26. New Windsor Coach Diner: New Windsor (E)
27. O's Eatery: Chatham (E)
28. Olympic Diner & Restaurant: Mahopac (E)
29. Plaza Diner: New Paltz (E)
30. Red Hook "Historic" Village Diner: Red Hook (MS)
31. Rocco's Pizza: Patterson (MS)
32. Stewart Airport Diner: Newburgh (E)
33. Sunburst Furniture: Wappingers Falls (R)
34. Village Diner: Saugerties (E)
35. West Taghkanic Diner: Ancram (MS)
36. Yankee Clipper Diner-Restaurant: Beacon (P)

## TACONIC STATE PARKWAY

In *Dutchess Magazine* Bill Fallon calls the Taconic State Parkway "the grand dame of roadways." The auto-only parkway goes north from the Kensico Dam in Westchester County to meet with I-90 near Chatham.

All four of the diners located at parkway exits were originally run by Bert Coons up to 1970. When he passed away in 1972, the Coons family sold off the diners one by one.

The diner drive starts at the junction of Route 82 and the Taconic State Parkway near Ancram. After spending a day at one of the many nearby state parks, the West Taghkanic Diner is a welcome sight. It is hard to imagine a more classic diner than the West Taghkanic. This 1953 Mountain View diner still shines with its chrome and red and blue highlights, and its restored neon sign is a classic. Current owners Rob and Anita Eisner have made sure that a trip to the West Taghkanic is just like taking a trip back to 1953.

The Martindale Chief Diner is located on Route 23 in Craryville. Sharing a Native American name and appropriate sign, this was the second diner on the parkway. This 1958 Silk City diner is as classic as you can get, especially when viewed from the right side, which highlights its large diner sign. Unfortunately, the classic neon sign has lost its neon, and the paint is chipping. But the inside is pristine. According to Dottie Coons-Drew, the daughter of Bert Coons, "The diner paid for itself in a year. People would drive the length of the parkway and have no where else to go but the diner."

The West Taghkanic in Ancram, one of four diners commissioned by Burt Coons along the Taconic Parkway. This one was built by Mountain View in 1953.

The third diner on the Taconic, now O's Eatery in Chatham, was built by Fodero in 1962.

Traveling north to Chatham, the next diner (now named O's Eatery) spent its first six years in Catskill. In 1969, it was moved to Rigor Hill in Chatham and named the Taconic Diner. This 1962 Fodero merges the colonial and environmental styles that were popular in the 1960s and 1970s. The western-style wagon wheel light fixtures and cantilevered stools are two examples. In the 1990s orange duct tape could be found on the stools and the booths, and the interior looked like a sterile cafeteria, in need of repair. By the turn of the twenty-first century, a big sign was hung above the door

# DERAFFELE MANUFACTURING COMPANY, INC.

The DeRaffele Company has been building diners since the early 1930s. Later they added banks, restaurants, and other modular buildings to their line. Angelo DeRaffele began working for "Pop" Tierney at the Tierney Dining Car Company in New Rochelle in the late 1920s, along with his friend Joseph Fodero. Each learned the business thoroughly and they went their separate ways. Fodero went to New Jersey and opened his own diner-building enterprise. DeRaffele remained on River Avenue in New Rochelle, later moving to larger quarters on Palmer Avenue. Phil DeRaffele began working for his father, Angelo, during high school and after a year at a Manhattan

Phil DeRaffele and Mario Monti at the DeRaffele facility.

design school was soon designing his own diners. In fact, he designed his first diner at age seventeen. He joined the firm full time in 1948, just before the company moved to its present location. He took over the business when Angelo died in 1957. At the present time his three sons, Phil Jr., Stephen, and Joseph work for the company. Two grandsons, Phil III and Keith, have also worked in the family business. Phil, now in his mid-seventies, still works full time designing diners. At this writing, his latest will be a two-story diner in Roslyn to be named The New Landmark Diner. It will replace the present Landmark Diner on Northern Boulevard. In a recent interview, Phil commented about the state of the DeRaffele Company, ". . . at this point, for every new diner being built, our company is doing three renovation jobs on older diners." The DeRaffele Company does business based on these principles: build a quality diner; respect your customers, they are individuals; and prepare to be flexible.

Phil modestly states. "The success of diners today is not based on the glamour [of the architecture]. It's the operation, the food, and the service that are important." Throughout New York State, DeRaffele diners comprise 30 to 40 percent of diners still in operation, with the greatest concentration being downstate.

Phil DeRaffele III, the grandson of the present CEO, has started his own diner business. It is called American Diner Corporation and it is also located in New Rochelle. The company is currently focused primarily on renovations. At present they have completed two projects and have three more in the works.

proclaiming that the original management was back—Dottie Coons-Drew, daughter of Bert Coons, who had sold the diner in 1987 but still held the mortgage. She had come back to restore the diner and its reputation. In 2005, Coons-Drew sold the diner to Otto Maier, who operates it as O's Eatery.

The last Bert Coons diner was located near the end of the Taconic Parkway on Route 295 in New Lebanon. The 1964 Fodero was sold to Barney LaPlante in 1977 and quickly moved to New Lebanon where it was known as the Indian Head Diner. In 1992, the diner was sold to Jimmy Dilis, who greatly altered the exterior and reopened it as Jimmy D's Pizza Royale. The remodeling moved editor Randy Garbin of *Roadside Magazine* to give the diner a Lou-Roc Award. The award, named for the Lou-Roc Diner in Worcester, Massachusetts, is given to diner owners who destroy the look of their classic diners through intensive renovations.

### U.S. ROUTES 1 AND 22

This diner drive follows U.S. Route 1 from the Connecticut border south to New York City. U.S. Route 1 goes from Presque Isle, Maine to Key West, Florida. It is only in New York for a short distance but it passes no less than five Westchester County diners. U.S. Route 1 is a four lane commercial road that goes in and out of centuries-old cities and leafy suburbs. It could be called the DeRaffele Highway, as they have had some part in every diner listed.

Mere minutes from the DeRaffele factory, the Thruway Diner exhibited belly windows, popular in the 1990s.

The first diner on this drive is the Port Chester Coach Diner located where U.S. Route 1 crosses over to run south of interstate I-95. A DeRaffele update from 1999, the exterior is in the postmodern style with blue glass roof trim, blue glass mansard coverings, a white stone facade, grand landscaping, and statuary at the entry. This is a typical semi-postmodern remodel done by DeRaffele. Continue south on U.S. Route 1 and turn right on Osborn Road. Then turn left on Halstead Avenue in Harrison to Trattoria Vivolo, a 1940s DeRaffele, updated into an elegant Italian restaurant. The exterior has the classic dark red vertical porcelain enamel strips under the windows, a silvered, round-edged roof line and a doorway situated at the narrow end of the building. This gem has been maintained in almost pristine original condition by its owner.

Take a left after passing the Trattoria onto Route 127, which will bring you back to U.S. Route 1. The Mamaroneck Diner and Pizza is at 405 East Boston Post Road. It features bumped-out windows, polished granite in between, stucco below this treatment, and plantings in front of the diner. The Nautilus Diner at 1240 Boston Post Road is one of the largest diners in Westchester County. This DeRaffele is an update of an old Mediterranean-style diner. It has a blue mansard roof, large arched-top windows, and a white stone exterior. The owners have also opened up two diners in Maryland, both built by DeRaffele.

A little farther south on U.S. Route 1 in Larchmont is another DeRaffele, this one built in 1993, and known as the Larchmont Diner. This contemporary diner has a gray and dusky rose exterior.

In downtown New Rochelle, home of DeRaffele, take a right onto North Avenue. About a mile up the road is the Mirage Diner, located across the street from Iona College. This 1970s DeRaffele was updated in the 1990s with a curved reverse-step stainless-steel roofline, large curved windows, and glass-block foyer walls. Like most newer diners, there is minimal counter space compared with older versions where the counter dominated the floor plan.

Continue down U.S. Route 1 and take a right onto Pelham Parkway, right after the Hutchinson River Parkway. The Columbus Diner in Mount Vernon stands at the intersection with Columbus Avenue (Route 22). Originally a classic Mountain View with a built-in dining room at one end, this diner currently sports an environmental remodel. The interior features wood tones, brass chandeliers, large booths at each end, and counter seating for about twelve patrons. The terrazzo floor is original, but the original Formica ceiling is obscured by acoustic panels.

The Odyssey Diner is located in Eastchester. This DeRaffele exhibits a metal mansard roof and a stone facade with a mostly glass back addition.

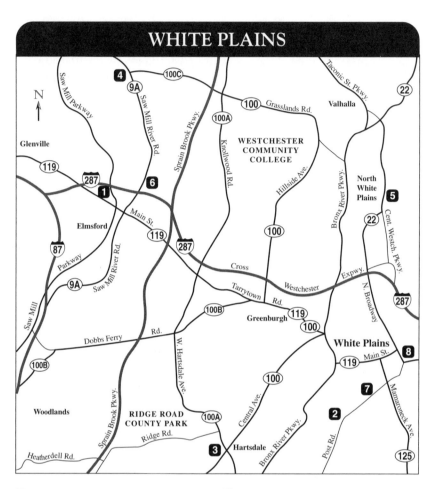

# WHITE PLAINS

1 El Dorado Diner: Elmsford (E)
2 El Miski: White Plains (MS)
3 Fountain Diner: Hartsdale (E)
4 Golden Star Diner & Restaurant:
  Elmsford (E)

5 North Castle Diner: White Plains (E)
6 Red Fox Diner: Elmsford (E)
7 Star Diner: White Plains (MS)
8 White Plains Coach Diner: White Plains (E)

---

There are two classic and two newer diners in White Plains. The first diner, a Mountain View formerly known as the Oasis Diner, now does business at 16 West Post Road as El Miski. Specializing in Peruvian cuisine, the diner has been slightly altered on the inside, but the outside is original. The Star Diner is a late 1940s Silk City that is set edgewise to the street at 66½ East Post Road, and has a remodeled facade. The diner's pristine front side can be seen from the alley. The Star offers great homemade soups and is packed throughout the day.

The White Plains Coach Diner is located at 50 Westchester Avenue. To get there from the Star Diner, head north on East Post Road (Route 22). The splendid-looking postmodern DeRaffele sits across the street from the Galleria, a local shopping mall. The blue glass roof trimmed diner has its own parking attendant during busier times of the day.

Continue west on Westchester Avenue and turn onto Route 22 north, which is now marked. The North Castle Diner at 720 North Broadway (Route 22) is a DeRaffele colonial-style diner, with a gray stone and brick facade, white mullioned windows, and a white cross-hatch fence around the roof.

From the North Castle Diner, turn around and follow the signs to I-287 West. Take exit 4 (Elmsford) then turn left off the ramp and right onto the access road for Route 119. Drive past U.S. Route 9A and you will quickly see the Eldorado Diner on the right, just up a small hill. This DeRaffele diner has a stone facade and a mirror finished mansard roof. The old neon sign still is on top of the diner. Across the street is a closed diner last known as the Starlight Coach Diner. Turn around and go past this diner and then take a left onto U.S. Route 9A north. The Red Fox Diner will be on your right a short way up at the highway. There was once a classic 1950s diner on this location, but it has since either been replaced or remodeled into a DeRaffele with polished granite, flat windows, and some mirror finish accents. On the

On a drive dominated by newer diners, there are a few gems left to see. El Miski in White Plains serves Peruvian food.

left, about less than a mile up is the shell of a former diner. This 1961 Swingle is now gutted and has been closed for a long time.

Continue north to the Executive Diner just outside of Hawthorne. There is some stainless above the door, surrounded by a stone facade. The diner has pieces of many styles. Perhaps this was once a brick clad diner, later remodeled by DeRaffele.

Follow Route 141 just north of the Executive. You will quickly come to a T in the road where 141 is not signed. Take a left here and about a mile or so up the road you will take a right onto Kensico Road. The Thornwood Coach Diner in Thornwood is visible on the right. Another diner built by DeRaffele, it has an all-glass back side with a combination of mirror finish glass and glass blocks on the corner.

Out of the parking lot, follow Marble Avenue through the intersection with Route 141 and head to downtown Pleasantville. This will bring you to the Pleasantville Colonial Diner. Rather unique compared with the other diners on this trip, it is the third diner to grace this location (the first was a Bixler). The diner has a slate mansard roof and stainless bands surrounding the windows, which sit above polished granite. Medium gray stones are used between the windows. Inside are terrazzo floor tiles and a ceiling bordered with a band of stainless steel. From there, head onto the Saw Mill Parkway and head north to I-684. This interstate will drop you off onto Route 22 north.

The next diner is just north of Patterson. The last three diners on the trip are all classic stainless-steel diners. Two of them are late-model Silk

DeRaffele built the Pleasantville Colonial Diner to fit in with its village setting.

Citys. The oft-changed Rocco's Family Restaurant and Pizza is Silk City #5804. While the exterior is as nice as the day it rolled out of the factory, the interior has received its share of drastic remodelings. The diner went through more than five name changes before emerging as a pizza place.

The Adams Diner is about ten more miles up the road at Routes 22 and 55 in Wingdale. A well-known truck stop, it is also a family place. Try their homemade soups. This stainless steel diner of unknown origin is open twenty-four hours. In the quaint village of Millerton, you will find Coach Ali's All-American Diner, Silk City #5871. It has been minimally remodeled by the present owner, who is a partner in the Adams Diner in Wingdale. The diner is slightly newer in age than Rocco's Pizza, and has larger windows and quilted stainless-steel panels on the exterior.

# AMBROSIA DINER
## 1970s KULLMAN
### RENOVATED BY DERAFFELE 2001 AND 2002
321 West Bridge St. (at U.S. Rte. 9W), Catskill • (518) 943-1047

The diners of the Hudson Valley are mostly run by Greek owners, and there's almost a guarantee of good food. The Ambrosia started out as a typical 1970s diner, somewhere on Long Island. The diner was moved to Catskill in 1984. (Catskill had been without a diner for nearly twenty years. Bert Coons had moved the last diner in town to the Taconic Parkway and reopened it as the Parkway Diner.) In 1988, the diner was doing business as the Olympic Diner. The same owner also ran the Olympic Diner II in nearby Ravena. Both of these diners were located on U.S. Route 9W. The Ambrosia Diner was given its name by the current owner, Dennis Pilarinos. Mr. Pilarinos bought the diner from Phil DeRaffele in 1993. DeRaffele was hired to do a remodeling on this diner in 1992. When the opportunity arose, DeRaffele decided to purchase it. The remodeled exterior facade is a combination blue enamel and mirror stainless. A ribbon of black and white ceramic tiles underlines the windows.

The interior layout is a familiar one, with the counter and booths area and restrooms taking up about half of the square footage. This half has a terrazzo floor and is decorated with mirror stainless, especially the counter area. The countertop is black granite, as is the one at the cashier's station that stands in the center of the diner. The other half of the diner consists of a carpeted dining room with tables and chairs and booths around the perimeter. There are mirrors on one wall that are placed at a height so that when customers are seated they don't see reflections of other people in the dining room. A seventy-seat private party room was added by DeRaffele in 2002.

Pilarinos is very much involved in the community. He sponsors a Little League baseball team. The diner sponsors a Professional Bowlers Association event every April. Kiwanis meets here regularly as does the fire company's ladies auxiliary. The local Red Hat Society meets here monthly. With today's larger size, diners become the perfect place for groups like these to come together.

# BOB'S DINER
## 1955 O'MAHONY, RENOVATED 1996
27 Main St. (U.S. Rts. 6 and 202), Brewster • (845) 278-2478

Bob's Diner has been in the Sprague family for over fifty years. Thomas, the current man behind the counter, became the owner-operator at age nineteen. Bob's is a village diner, nestled in the heart of Brewster. The diner is close to the Metro-North Railroad station, the town hall, the village hall, and the post office.

Some patrons came to the diner even before it became Bob's Diner. One of the old-timers tells of dating the pretty ticket-taker at the Cameo Theater, Brewster's lone movie house. When the movie house closed for the night, they would walk to the diner (then called Martin's) for a late-night treat. Another customer comes in every day and must sit in "her" seat at the counter. What would happen if she can't get her seat? Hopefully, we'll never find out.

As for food, you can have the usual burgers, or you can choose a bison burger or a veggie burger. There are creative wraps, such as veggie-mozzarella with a tasty dressing. And perhaps the best thing for anyone who likes diners, the prices are very affordable.

The exterior was clad in board siding during one of its renovations, covering over its original stainless steel. It has a ten-stool counter. A sixteen-seat booth dining area, an office, and a new kitchen were added, but the majority of meals are prepared out front behind the counter. The grill and soup-cooking equipment remain in view. Over the counter area is the original art-deco style stainless-steel work with a centerpiece clock.

Bob's Diner is the hub of activity after local town and village meetings. Officials come after meetings and some, like the village's mayor, can often be found in the diner. The placemats announce offerings at the Brewster High School adult education classes. The diner also offers discounts for Metro-North employees and motorcyclists.

# CENTER DINER
## 1939 NATIONAL
### 13 Bank St. (near U.S. Rt. 6), Peekskill • (914) 737-7409

Peekskill is a city that is trying to redefine itself as an arts enclave. Fortunately they have an art deco gem built by the National Diner Company, Fodero's predecessor. The Center Diner is the kind of place that true fans of diners dream of. Today, there are only two National Diners still in existence and, while both are well preserved, only the Center Diner is open for business. (The other, Charlie's Diner in Pittsburgh, Pennsylvania, was recently for sale, and will very likely be moved in the near future.)

The Center Diner has a monitor roof and original speckled porcelain enamel panels exhibiting its name. These panels had been covered during a past renovation, but in the 1990s, Daniel Zilka of the American Diner Museum was asked to restore the diner to its original beauty. The covering was removed and revealed the original porcelain in beautiful condition. The interior still has the original wood-covered walls, four-inch ceramic square tiles, and a black marble counter. About ten years ago, the counter was shortened to allow for the installation of two additional larger booths.

This is a village diner, set in the middle of the block amid storefronts. It has many loyal patrons who are regulars at the diner. The mainstay of the waitstaff, Ann, recently announced her retirement. She had been there for more than eighteen years and served under three owners. The cook has been there for more than ten years, and homemade soups are a specialty of the diner.

Because the city of Peekskill is undergoing an urban-renewal program to make it one of Hudson Valley's key artists' colonies, grant money has been secured for the development of much-needed housing and studios for painters and sculptors. Peekskill now has a score of artists-in-residence whose studios and galleries offer convenient viewing and shopping hours.

The Paramount Center for the Arts, at nearby 1008 Brown Street, is the former Paramount Theater, built and owned by Paramount Pictures in the 1930s to showcase the studio's newest releases. It is undergoing restoration. Prominent theater architects Rapp & Rapp designed the theater, dubbed a "movie palace" at the time. The theater has a seventy-foot ceiling, 1000 plush seats, and a Wurlitzer organ. A grass-roots non-profit committee saved the building from demolition in the 1980s. There is an upstairs gallery featuring New York-based artists, and an artists-in-residence program featuring multi-cultural presentations. Live performances run the gamut from stage shows to motion pictures. It is rapidly becoming an important regional arts center.

# NEW COLLEGE DINER

## 1976 DERAFFELE

500 Main St., New Paltz • (845) 255-5040

Usually, when someone replaced a 1963 Kullman with a colonial-style 1976 DeRaffele, diner purists would be disappointed. Although the silver diners get the national spotlight, two-thirds of the diners in the Hudson Valley are environmental or newly built. But fear not, diner fans, some of these environmental-style diners of the 1970s and 1980s still provide the quintessential diner food, even if the cooking is done behind swinging doors in a large kitchen, instead of at a grill behind the counter.

As Daniel Zilka, director of the American Diner Museum, notes one of these days, environmental diners will be rare and there will be a group of diner enthusiasts working to save them.

With the popularity of postmodern remodeling, it very well might happen sooner than later. After almost thirty years, it's quite an accomplishment that the diner looks just like it did when it was first placed there. Owner Dimitios Vlanis explains why the diner looks like it does, "It's OK to make the diner silver if it was originally silver, but this diner was made for the spirit of '76." And in 1976, the environmental colonial-style diner was in. When you sit down and get your menu, the first thing that pops out is that the prices are affordable. Vlanis notes, ". . . it's better to be with people than alone." And with prices like these, it's easy to see why he's rarely alone. The owners and employees even had spirited discussions when it came time to raise coffee prices from 75 cents to a dollar.

While the New College Diner doesn't get a lot of the State University of New York–New Paltz crowd, it does get many people who are traveling to and from Poughkeepsie. The diner sits only a quarter of a mile off exit 18 of I-87 (the New York State Thruway). Ironically, about six miles closer to Poughkeepsie you will find the Gateway Diner, which was remodeled by Paramount to look retro with shiny stainless steel in the autumn of 2003.

Even though the College Diner attracts travelers, the regulars are what makes the business. Vlanis comments, "We've been blessed to have a great clientele, some people come in 4 to 5 times a day." The diner has very few specials, but what they do have is well-made and affordable.

# PALACE DINER

## DERAFFELE, 1981, RENOVATED IN 2004

194 Washington St. (near U.S. Rt. 9), Poughkeepsie • (845) 473-1576

The Palace Diner celebrated its twenty-fifty anniversary in 2005. The diner's new exterior is dramatic and eye-catching, reflecting the latest in architectural design. Stepped stainless steel graces the cantilevered canopy of the roofline. Colorful black, green, and cream tiles form a horizontal zigzag line below the windows.

The new interior features elegant dark wood panels, bordered by blonde wood frames in the two large dining room. The smaller, less formal counter area uses the same dark and light woods as the two dining rooms, reversing the shades of borders and panels. Granite is used on the countertop and the floor. The floor pattern consists of large squares of black and speckled beige with small rust-colored diamond insets.

The Palace philosophy is: "Our goal is to provide our customers with an enjoyable dining experience. To that end we try to accommodate all special dietary preferences—tell us what you want and we will do our best to deliver it to you." Most diners just have a philosophy, or a catchy phrase that attempts to embody the owners feelings, the Palace has a mission statement: "We understand that food is the energy of life and good food brings joy and pleasure."

The full menu includes breakfast, lunch, and dinner with daily specials. Holiday meals, including family-style Thanksgiving dinners, are a local tradition. There is an extensive wine list, beer selection, and cocktail bar, as well as an espresso bar. There is also an on-premise bakery that offers cakes, cookies, pies, danishes, muffins, and bread as takeout items.

The Palace Diner has been a popular local dining spot for many years. It has a wide cross section of patrons, from college students to local politicos to theater people. The artists and patrons of the nearby Bardovan Theater and the Civic Center come in for late night dining after the shows. Robin Williams and Sinbad are just two of the many visitors. Local groups such as the Sweet Adelines come in on a regular basis after their weekly rehearsal.

The Vanikiotis family is firmly rooted in the community. They also own and operate The Daily Planet, an American Diner on Route 55 in nearby LaGrangeville, the Brass Anchor Restaurant on Point Road in Poughkeepsie, and Barnaby's on Route 32 in New Paltz.

# THE "HISTORIC" VILLAGE DINER

## 1951 SILK CITY #5113

7550 North Broadway (U.S. Rt. 9), Red Hook • (845) 756-6232

On January 7, 1988, the "Historic" Village Diner became the first New York diner listed on the National Register of Historic Places, even though this 1951 Silk City is incorrectly listed as being built in 1927.

First located in Rhinebeck, the diner was named the Halfway Diner because Rhinebeck is halfway between New York City and Albany. The diner only lasted a year in Rhinebeck before it was bought by Bert Coons and moved to Red Hook. The Village Diner lost much of its Taconic Parkway business when the parkway was extended north to Route 82. The menu now states, "After years of catering to travelers on Dutchess County's major highways, the 'Historic' Village Diner now enjoys continued popularity as a community-oriented restaurant."

The diner has a wide-ranging menu with homemade Belgian waffles and Silk City French Toast as breakfast specialties. Lunch and dinner items include a variety of homemade soups; Vintage Burgers made with grilled chicken breast, tomato, bacon, lettuce, onion, and mayonnaise on a hard roll; the Silk City Special, made with grilled turkey, bacon, tomato, lettuce, onion, and mayonnaise on a hard roll; and other tasty specials. A salad bar

The interior of the Red Hook Historic Village Diner.

adds a healthy touch. Tea is served in insulated thermoses, a rare convenience, and beer and wine are also available. Desserts are made on premises. A separate dining room was added in the 1980s.

Bard College is nearby, and film students from the college like to use the diner as a setting. A Japanese music video was made at the diner and was shown on Japanese MTV. Gift items, including mugs, sweatshirts and T-shirts, classic menus, postcard packs, diner coffee, and a matted lithograph of the 1951 Village Diner are for sale.

A kitchen fire in late 2004 caused the diner to close for several months. The subsequent renovation brought the diner back to life, with some new siding, painting, and a general clean-up. They also added a full basement, with office and storage space. At the same time the kitchen was updated to include a charbroiler.

Melissa (Wambach) Griffin worked in the diner for fifteen years before she and her husband Ryan Griffin became owners. Melissa's dad, Richard Wambach, designed the diner's menu and logo.

# DINER DIRECTORY

## ANCRAM

**West Taghkanic Diner**
1016 Rte. 82 (at Taconic State Pkwy.)
(518) 789-3925
*1953 Mountain View #399*

## BEACON

**Yankee Clipper Diner Restaurant**
397 Main St.
(845) 440-0021
*1946 O'Mahony*
Renovated by Paramount 1998.

## BEDFORD HILLS

**Bedford Diner**
710 Bedford Rd. (Rt. 117 at Green Lane)
(914) 241-4808
*1950s Mountain View (?) DeRaffele*
Renovated 2005.

## BLAUVELT

**Blauvelt Coach Diner**
601 Rt. 303
(845) 359-5159
c1979.

## BREWSTER

**Bob's Diner**
27 Main St. (U.S. Rt. 6)
(845) 278-2478
*1955 O'Mahony*
Renovated in 1996.

## CAIRO

**Cairo Diner**
*1926 Tierney*
In storage.

## CARMEL

**New Carmel Diner and Restaurant**
63 Gleneida Ave. (at Rt. 52)
(845) 225-5000
*DeRaffele*
Renovated 2000s.

## CATSKILL

**Ambrosia Diner**
321 West Bridge St. (at U.S. Rt. 9W)
(518) 943-1047
*1970s Kullman*
Renovated by DeRaffele 2001 and 2002.

## CENTRAL VALLEY

**Bright Star Diner**
220 Rt. 32
(845) 928-2877
*1972 DeRaffele*
Renovated 1992.

## CHATHAM

**O's Eatery**
309 Rigor Hill Rd. (at Taconic
State Pkwy.)
(518) 392-1001
*1962 Fodero*
Originally the Taconic Diner.

The Martindale Chief Diner near Craryville is a 1958 Silk City that retains its beauty inside and out. The neon has been removed from their roadside sign.

## CRARYVILLE

**Martindale Chief Diner**
Rt. 23 (at Taconic State Pkwy.)
(518) 857-2525
*1958 Silk City #5807*

## CROTON-ON-HUDSON

**Croton Colonial Restaurant and Diner**
221 South Riverside Ave. (U.S. Rt. 9A and Rt. 129)
(914) 271-8868
*1971 DeRaffele*

**Ocean House Oyster Bar and Grill**
10 U.S. Rt. 9A (45 North Riverside Ave. at Farrington Rd.)
(914) 271-0702
*Circa 1933 Bixler*

## DOBBS FERRY

**Dobbs Diner**
434 Broadway (U.S. Rt. 9 at Wargrove and Rochambeau Aves.)
(914) 674-0850
*1950s Kullman,* remodeled environmental.

## EASTCHESTER

**Odyssey Diner**
465 White Plains Rd. (at Crest Ave.)
(914) 961-8855
*DeRaffele*

## ELMSFORD

**Eldorado Diner**
55 W. Main St. (Rt. 119E)
(814) 592-6197
*1960s Kullman*
Renovated by DeRaffele 1990s.

**Golden Star Diner & Restaurant**
267 Saw Mill River Rd. (U.S. Rt. 9A)
*1961 Swingle #1161DV*
Closed.

**Red Fox Diner**
138 Saw Mill River Rd. (U.S. Rt. 9, North Central Avenue)
(914) 592-4641
*1950s Mountain View or O'Mahony*
Renovated by DeRaffele 1990.

## FISHKILL

**Athenian I-84 Diner-Restaurant**
853 Rt. 52 (at I-84)
(845) 896-6537
*DeRaffele*
Renovated by DeRaffele 1997.

## HARRISON

**Trattoria Vivolo**
301 Halstead Ave.
(914) 835-6199
*1940s DeRaffele*

## HARTSDALE

**Fountain Diner**
31 South Central Ave.
(914) 428-5457
*Circa 1980 DeRaffele*

## HAWTHORNE

**Executive Diner**
26 Saw Mill River Rd. (U.S. Rt. 9A)
(914) 592-5415
*1965 DeRaffele*
Renovated by DeRaffele 1996.

## HIGHLAND

**Gateway Diner**
U.S. Rt. 9W (52 Vineyard Ave.)
(845) 691-6326
*1992 Paramount*
Renovated 2005.

## HUDSON

**Diamond Street Diner**
717 Warren St. (Rt. 23)
(518) 828-1310
*1950s O'Mahony*

## HYDE PARK

**Culinary Institute of America**
433 Albany Post Rd. (Rt. 9)
*1950s Mountain View*
Used as security offices.

**Eveready Diner**
540 Albany Post Rd. (Rt. 9)
(845) 229-8100
*1995 Paramount*

## IRVINGTON

**River City Grille**
6 South Broadway
(914) 591-2033
1943.

## KATONAH

**Blue Dolphin Diner**
175 Katonah Ave. (near Rt. 35)
(914) 232-4791
*1930s Kullman*
Renovated.

## KINGSTON

**Colonial Diner**
*Silk City.*
In Storage.

**Dietz Stadium Diner**
127 N. Front St.
(845) 331-5321
*1980 Paramount*

**King's Valley Diner**
617 Ulster Ave.
(845) 331-3254
*1997 Paramount*

**Michael's Diner**
1071 Ulster Ave.
(845) 336-6514
1970s.

**Olympic Diner**
620 Washington Ave.
(845) 331-2280

**Sub Depot**
336 E. Chester St.
(845) 339-7399
*1930s O'Mahony*
Remodeled.

## LARCHMONT

**Larchmont Diner**
239 Boston Post Rd. (U.S. Rt. 1)
(914) 833-2062
*1993 DeRaffele*

## MAHOPAC

**John's Kitchen**
149 Sheer Hill Rd. (U.S. Rt. 6)
(845) 621-1698
*Homemade 1910s*
Renovated.

**Olympic Diner-Restaurant**
Box 930 U.S. Rt. 6 (at Miller Pl.)
(845) 628-0876
*DeRaffele*
Renovated 2002.

## MAMARONECK

**Mamaroneck Diner & Pizza**
405 East Boston Post Rd. (U.S. Rt. 1)
(914) 698-3564
Renovated by DeRaffele 1995.

**Nautilus Diner**
1240 West Boston Post Rd. (U.S. Rt. 1)
(914) 833-1320
*1970s Kullman*
Renovated by DeRaffele 1990s.

## MAYBROOK

**Maybrook Diner**
940 Homestead Ave. (Rt. 208 and I-84)
(845) 427-5067
*1954 Mountain View #440*

## MIDDLE HOPE

**Hudson Diner**
5500 U.S. Rt. 9W
(845) 562-4625
Circa 1960, renovated 1991, renovated
by DeRaffele 2002.

## MILLBROOK

**Millbrook Diner**
3266 Franklin Ave. (Millbrook Ave./
U.S. Rt. 44)
(845) 677-8736
*1948 O'Mahony*

## MILLERTON

**Coach Ali's Millerton Diner**
Main St. (U.S. Rt. 44E)
(518) 789-3480
*Silk City #5871*

## MOHEGAN LAKE

**New Mohegan Diner**
1992 E. Main St. (U.S. Rt. 6)
(914) 528-2585
*1976 DeRaffele*
Remodeled 1990 and 2005.

## MOUNT KISCO

**Mount Kisco Coach Diner**
252 Main St.
(914) 660-5676
*1950s DeRaffele*

## MOUNT VERNON

**Columbus Diner**
749 Columbus Ave.
(914) 668-7969
*Mountain View*
Remodeled.

## NANUET

**Nanuet Diner**
120 W. Rt. 59
(845) 632-2200
*1990s DeRaffele*

**New City Diner**
127 Rt. 304
(845) 624-1400
*1990s DeRaffele*

## NEWBURGH

**Alexis Diner**
5023 U.S. Rt. 9W (at I-84 and North Plank Rd.)
(845) 565-1400
*Homemade 1990, and Kullman 1996*

**Gateway Diner**
1292 Rt. 300
(845) 567-1200
*2000 Paramount*

**Jessi's Diner**
34½ Lake St. (Rt. 32)
(845) 561-2009
*1930s O'Mahony*

**Neptune Diner**
82 Rt. 17K
(845) 564-2112
*Circa 1965 Fodero*

**Stewart Airport Diner**
240 Rt. 17K
(845) 564-1650
*1973 Paramount*

**Viscinti Limousine**
145–7 S. Robinson Ave. (U.S. Rt. 9W at Dickson St.)
*Paramount*
Converted to other use.

## NEW PALTZ

**New College Diner**
500 Main St.
(845) 255-5040
*1976 DeRaffele*

**Plaza Diner**
27 New Paltz Plaza
(845) 255-1030
1970s.

## NEW ROCHELLE

**Mirage Diner**
690 North Ave.
(914) 235-2568
*DeRaffele*

## NEW WINDSOR

**Johnny D's Diner**
909 Union Ave. (Rt. 300 at Line Rd.)
(845) 567-1600
*1995 Kullman #90216*
Kullman, renovation 1996.

**New Windsor Coach Diner**
351 Rt. 32
(845) 562-9050
*1997 Paramount*

## OSSINING

**Landmark Diner**
265 S. Highland Ave. (U.S. Rt. 9)
(914) 762-7700
*DeRaffele*
Renovated 2000.

## PATTERSON

**Rocco's Pizza**
2908 Rt. 22
(845) 878-7900
*1958 Silk City #5804*
Interior renovated 2003.

DeRaffele remodeled the Landmark Diner-Restaurant in Ossining in 2002 to bring it up to date in the postmodern style.

## PEEKSKILL

**Center Diner**
13 Bank St.
(914) 737-7409
*1939 National*

**Westchester Diner**
300 Old Albany Post Rd. (U.S. Rt. 9A)
(914) 734-4949
*1950 Mountain View*
Renovated.

## PINE BUSH

**Cup & Saucer Diner**
82 Boniface Dr. (at Ted Rd.)
(845) 744-4969
*2001 Paramount.*

## PLEASANTVILLE

**Pleasantville Colonial Diner**
10 Memorial Plaza
(914) 769-8555
*1982 DeRaffele*
Renovated 2002–3.

## POMONA

**Mount Ivy Diner**
1669 U.S. Rt. 202
(845) 354-0100
*1996 Paramount*

## PORT CHESTER

**Port Chester Coach Diner**
317 Boston Post Rd.
(914) 937-0008
*DeRaffele*

## POUGHKEEPSIE

**Acropolis Diner**
829 Main St.
(845) 452-6255
*1962 Paramount*
Renovated by Paramount 1993.

**Arlington Diner**
251 Dutchess Tpk. (U.S. Rt. 44E)
(845) 452-1554
*1972 DeRaffele*
Renovated 1980s, renovated by Paramount 1992.

**Dutchess Diner**
799 South Rd. (U.S. Rt. 9)
(845) 297-8100
*1993 Paramount*

**New Poughkeepsie Diner**
59 Market St. (near U.S. Rt. 44 and Rt. 55)
(845) 452-7397
*1964 Kullman*
Renovated 1997.

**Palace Diner**
194 Washington St.
(845) 473-1576
*DeRaffele 1981*
Renovated by DeRaffele 2004.

**Star Diner**
121 Parker Ave. (U.S. Rt. 9G)
(845) 473-7272
*1960s DeRaffele*
Renovated 2004.

## RED HOOK

**The "Historic" Village Diner**
7550 N. Broadway (U.S. Rt. 9)
(845) 756-6232
*1951 Silk City #5113*
Renovated 2004–5.

## SAUGERTIES

**Barclay Heights Diner**
140 Main St. (U.S. Rt. 9W)
(845) 246-4610
*Circa 1964 Paramount*

**Village Diner**
130 Main St. (at U.S. Rt. 9W)
(845) 246-9596
*1979 DeRaffele*

## SHRUB OAK

**Doc James Cigars**
Rt. 132 (near Taconic State Pkwy.)
(914) 962-9388
*Possibly by O'Mahony*

## SPRING VALLEY

**Spring Valley Diner**
25 E. Central Ave. (Rt. 59W)
(845) 425-3900
Closed.

## STONY POINT

**Hogan's Family Diner**
56 South Liberty Dr.
(845) 429-9603
Homemade.

## SUFFERN

**Airmont Diner**
210 Rt. 59W (at Airmont Rd.)
(845) 368-0020
*DeRaffele, 2000*

**Rockland Diner**
41 Lafayette Ave.
(845) 357-2139
*DeRaffele 1960*
Remodeled.

## THORNWOOD

**Thornwood Coach Diner**
525 Kensico Rd.
(914) 769-8844
*DeRaffele*

## WAPPINGERS FALLS

**Sunburst Furniture**
7154 Broadway (U.S. Rt. 9)
*1955 Kullman*
Other use.

The 1981 Palace Diner in Poughkeepsie was renovated by DeRaffele in 2004.

## WHITE PLAINS

**El Miski**
16 W. Post Rd.
(814) 684-8640
*1950 Mountain View #288*
Formerly the Oasis Diner.

**North Castle Diner**
720 N. Broadway (Rt. 22)
(914) 684-8540
*DeRaffele*

**Star Diner**
66 1/2 East Post Rd.
(914) 664-8702
*Circa 1950 Silk City*

**White Plains Coach Diner**
50 Westchester Ave.
(914) 428-5700
*1990s DeRaffele*

## WINGDALE

**Star 22 Diner**
Rts. 22 and 55
(845) 832-9647

## YONKERS

**Argonaut Restaurant & Diner**
1080 Yonkers Ave.
(914) 237-5055

**Broadway Diner**
590 South Broadway (U.S. Rt. 9)
(914) 969-9998
*DeRaffele*

**Mount Olympos Diner**
1 Fort Hill Rd. (at Rt. 100)
(914) 961-4617
*DeRaffele*
Renovated 1990s.

**Parkside Diner**
390 South Broadway
(914) 965-3438
*1930s DeRaffele, remodeled.*

**Raceway Diner**
833 Yonkers Ave.
(914) 965-3438
*1960 DeRaffele*

## YORKTOWN HEIGHTS

**New City Diner**
3825 Crompond Rd. (Rt. 35 and
U.S. Rt. 202)
(914) 788-9877
1999 DeRaffele; 1920s Kullman and
1950s DeRaffele were formerly on site.

**Yorktown Coach Diner**
340 Downing Dr. (at Front St.)
(914) 245-2191
*DeRaffele*
Renovated circa 2000.

# THE CAPITAL DISTRICT

The Capital District is sited on the river named for Hendrick Hudson. Hudson was the first European to sail up the river. He reached the confluence with the Mohawk River in 1609; although he failed to find the passage to the Far East, he did encourage settlement of the Albany and Troy area.

Troy has always vied with Albany as the center of commerce, but when it came to the number of lunch wagons, both of these cities lost out to Schenectady, because Albany and Troy both had ordinances restricting lunch wagons from a very early date. Albany's ordinance prohibited lunch wagons from parking at the same spot for more than five minutes.

Schenectady didn't pass such an ordinance until 1912. General Electric and the American Locomotive Company operated in this twenty-four-hour factory town, which employed many shift workers who were also regular lunch wagon patrons. The city directories listed at least nine wagons in the first decade of the twentieth century. By the time the ordinance was passed, many of these wagons had become stationary.

In 1922, an O'Mahony lunch car known as the Palace Lunch was bought by Todd and Lee and placed on Jay Street. There was another Palace Lunch in Gloversville. By the 1940s, there were ten diners in Schenectady.

The lunch wagon had a niche in Glens Falls. A 1904 article in *The Glens Falls Times* illustrates the attitudes of established institutions toward the increasingly popular lunch wagon service: "The night lunch wagon has just made its appearance in London and is regarded with great novelty. The night lunch wagon has been an established dyspepsia breeder in Glens Falls for many years, and it is strange that it has not been introduced in London before."

The large number of wagons on the streets were due to Albert Closson, who built lunch wagons. Closson patented a design for lunch wagons in 1903, after running his Crystal Palace at Monument Square in Glens Falls every night for eight years. In his advertisement for the wagon, Closson noted, "The owner is a genial fellow and parts his hair in the middle."

Glens Falls had at least four Closson wagons on the streets, and nearby Whitehall, a canal town of about 2,000 people, had four wagons, of which

Note the Closson Lunch Wagon on the street in Whitehall. The wagon could be brought to wherever the customers were.

Samuel Rivette owned two Closson wagons in Glens Falls, the home of Albert Closson.

at least three were made by Closson. Saratoga Springs, by then known for gambling, horse racing, and extravagant Victorian hotels, had at least two Clossons. In Portsmouth, New Hampshire, home of one of the last lunch wagons, the first wagon—that ran from 1912 to 1940—was a larger model, built by Albert Closson.

Today, Glens Falls seems to have totally forgotten about Albert Closson and his wagons. The most popular diner that did business in Glens Falls was the Palace Lunch, a 1921 O'Mahony. Anthony DeJulia and Edward Lee were the first owners. The diner was demolished, along with a few city blocks, to make way for the civic center. Ironically, Glens Falls has no more authentic diners, but the former Miss Glens Falls Diner, which did business in the city from 1938 to 1958, still lives on as the Northampton Diner in Northville.

The next small influx of diners into Saratoga and Glens Falls came thanks in part to Ward & Dickinson. The Commercial Dining Car, built by the company called Saratoga's Railroad Avenue home. Peter McNeil was its last owner in the 1940s. He also owned the 20th Century Diner in Albany.

Three Ward & Dickinson diners were sent to Glens Falls. The Central Lunch replaced a Closson lunch wagon in front of a Park Street taxi stand. Wayne and Wesley Brownell took over the diner from their father Louis for a short time before finding new jobs. By World War II, when Glens Falls was picked as the ideal American city by *Look* magazine, the diner was closed and in poor shape. One of the other diners was used just like a mobile lunch wagon and was towed to local factories before being shipped off to Port Henry on Lake Champlain. One diner of unknown origin made it to the village of Granville. In this village on the Vermont border, the diner was called the Chanawaka Dining Car, run by Chester and Clarence Petty. Raymond Petty also had a lunch wagon in Granville at the same time.

The Adirondacks may lack diners today, but that doesn't mean this mountainous region in upstate New York is void of diner history. In the first

The Silver Diner was built by expanding two Pullman Cars lengthwise. It was a long-time favorite in Schenectady since it opened in the 1930s.

part of the twentieth century, a lunch wagon could almost always be found in the villages serving the lumber trade. As industry, particularly lumber and mining businesses, left the Adirondacks, so did most of the wagons. Very few were replaced by diners, and even fewer of those are around today.

One lunch wagon entrepreneur, T. H. Buckley, summered in Ogdensburg. He set up his wagons throughout the northern Adirondacks, finding local businessmen to operate them on leases, usually for three years. R. H. Hanna of Plattsburgh was one of his lessees. Buckley thought so much of him that he offered Hanna the job of going to Buffalo during the Pan-American Exposition to run his kiosks.

With all the lunch wagons that dotted the Adirondacks, it would not be surprising if one were still around in someone's barn. Morrisonville, Antwerp, Pyrites, Tupper Lake Junction, Alburg, Westport, and Mineville all had lunch wagons. A unique wagon moved into South Colton on the northwest side of the Adirondacks in 1946. The Black and White Lunch Wagon was moved to South Colton from Watertown by Vincent Murphy. A few months later, before Murphy opened the lunch wagon, he enlisted in the Army and put the wagon up for sale.

Canton had a lunch wagon that made national news. Two St. Lawrence University students, Eddie Maier and Eugene Contois, bought an old lunch

Some lunch wagons found their way onto the open road. William Todd and his wife are shown in front of this one located between Glens Falls and Lake George.

LARRY CUILTRERA

The Bill Gates Diner from Bolton Landing was a Jones trolley car built in Troy. It is in the collection of the Champlain Valley Transportation Museum in Plattsburgh.

wagon they named The Palais Royale. They worked their class schedule so that while one was taking a class, the other was working at the wagon. These enterprising young men paid their way through college this way. After new owners took over in 1924, the wagon caught on fire and was destroyed.

Fire in lunch wagons seemed to be a constant fear in the north country, especially in the winter months. In 1902, John Pogue of Watertown purchased a Buckley lunch wagon. The blurb in the newspaper stated, "the gas tanks are on the roof so that there is no danger of fire." Perhaps the worst accident was at the McManus Diner in Potsdam in 1934. This Ward & Dickinson diner had its front wall bowed out by a gas stove explosion. Two customers, Robert Tambling and a man named Gibson, were hurled to the floor from their stools. The temperature at the time of the accident was minus twenty degrees. In 1928, the Clinton Diner, a Tierney, was located next to a theater that was gutted by fire. The diner survived and their employees helped with the cleanup of the theater. Phillips Diner in Ogdensburg was destroyed in 1972 by a burning theater wall that collapsed on the diner. Fortunately, the proprietor and employees had time to get out.

Besides several lunch wagons, Lake Placid had two diners. Isador Urfirer brought one diner to town in 1937 and named it the Little Diner. Harold McLaughlin bought a Ward & Dickinson that had previously been located in Anderson, Indiana. His favorite customer was Muffins, a mongrel. The dog received three meals a day, and the waitresses and countermen set up a collection each year for Muffins's license fee. In 1940, Muffins was entered in the Lake Placid Kennel Club spring show and won a pink ribbon for having the most breeds.

Saranac Lake had a 1929 O'Mahony. Tom McVeedy bought the $10,500 diner and received a $400 rebate for returning the wheels. In 1970, the grill was moved to the back kitchen.

In the diner era, Ward & Dickinson made a decent dent in the Adirondacks. Besides the Wardies in Lake Placid and Potsdam, they also placed diners in Tupper Lake, Malone, and two in Ogdensburg. Short-lived General Diners enterprise placed cars in Malone and Canton. Guy's Diner and the Flying Saucer Diner operated in Massena. There is a diner in Massena that— although greatly remodeled—is rumored to have been built by Kullman. Spanky's Diner is famous for something other than food. In her book *Haunted Northern New York,* Cheri Revai says that as many as seven ghosts haunt the basement of this diner. The diner's owner, Alex Krywanczyk, said that he saw a tray picked up and flung across a counter.

Although the Worcester Lunch Car Company seemed to have a monopoly on the New England diner market at one time, few were placed outside the New England states. It's almost as if there was an invisible barrier at the eastern New York State line. While Ohio has two Worcesters today, so far only one can be verified that was originally located in New York. That particular one went to Mechanicville, a main railroad junction for trains coming from New England through the Hoosac Tunnel. In 1927, the Hunter Brothers bought a Worcester to replace an older lunch wagon and named their new diner the West Virginia Diner, since it was located on the property of the West Virginia Pulp and Paper Mill. John Lavigne worked at this diner in 1941 during his summer college break. He says that the diner was mostly used by mill management and officials at the start, but it later became a gathering place for the employees to hold lively "bull sessions."

Albany has five diners, more than any other city in the state except the Big Apple. Albany was once home to the Miss Albany Diners chain. Neefman and Stillman Pitts, the owners of the chain, had seven diners, mostly built by Brill, though at least one was a Ward & Dickinson. One diner was moved to Menands, near a popular amusement park and ballfield, while another was moved across the river to Rensselaer. The chain did not make it to World War II, and different people bought most of the diners, leaving one on lower Central Avenue run by Stillman Pitts. Three of the diners were replaced by newer diners, one being an O'Mahony and another a Comac. Troy and Schenectady also had a couple of "Miss" diners that were built by Brill.

The Miss Troy Diner, the last diner in Troy, was demolished in 2006 to provide more space at a neighboring garage. The last renters, Chris and Theresa Martin, had a great business going, and showed reverence for this rare Brill. The diner once operated 24/7, catering to the late-night crowd coming back to Troy after a night at the Lebanon Valley Racetrack.

The Capital District does have one "Miss" diner left, and many "don't miss" diners as well. The Miss Albany Diner was the name given to a Silk City operating on Broadway after its appearance in the movie *Ironweed*. This diner, which was a replacement for an older Ward & Dickinson, is known for its unique brunch menu. Perhaps the most well-known vintage diner in Albany is Jack's Diner on Central Avenue. Jack's Diner was originally part of the Miss Albany chain. The Brill diner was replaced by a now-rare 1949 Comac. Even more unusual is that the diner has only had three owners. Although the current owner, Jack Murtagh, has passed the spatula off to his son, he can still be found at the diner much of the time.

Fire destroyed another diner in 2006. The Speedway Family Diner in West Lebanon had been in business since 1932. The diner always benefited from being located on U.S. Route 20 and close to the Lebanon Valley Speedway. During racing season the diner would stay packed until 2 A.M., two hours after closing. The Speedway Diner may have been the last remaining diner of an unknown manufacturer that also built Al Ruth's Diner in South Bend, Indiana.

Just before World War II, another diner chain started up. Hubert Monette started with two Morris Lunches in conventional buildings, then bought two Sterling diners and placed them on Broadway and Central Avenue, two major thoroughfares. In 1948, he bought a Fodero, and placed it near the Albany Medical Center. In 1952, he sold out to the Nedicks

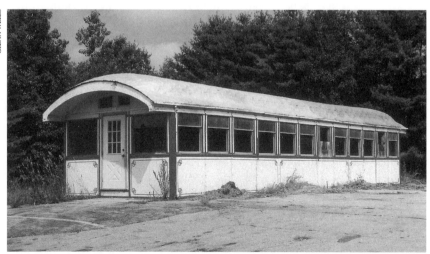

GLENN WELLS

The Jonesville Diner was originally one of the Morris Diners in Albany. This diner was donated to the American Diner Museum and has since sold to a private owner in the Chicago area.

The last of the Morris Diners. This Fodero, the Quintessence, sits in a residential neighborhood in Albany with only on-street parking—a rare location for a new diner in 1948.

Company of New York City, who were managing the Metro and Little Nick diners. Nedicks ran the two Sterlings until they were moved to Jonesville, New York and Pittsfield, Massachusetts. The Fodero stayed in the same location but went through many name changes, ending with Quintessence. Now closed, Quintessence was known for its Chicken Pataki, named for the governor of the state who served from 1995 to 2006. They proclaimed that if you buy it, "we'll pay the tax." At the time of this writing, the Quintessence was undergoing renovations.

Many people associate diners with truckers, though this is only partially true. If a diner sat on the highway with a big enough parking lot, then truckers were likely to be found there. The Duanesburg Diner, at the intersection of Routes 7 and U.S. Route 20, has room for truck parking, and both roads are major routes for truck drivers. In Colonie, Charlie's Northway Diner was known as a trucker's diner when it was featured in *Classic Diners of the Northeast* by Donald Kaplan and Alan Bellink. Shortly after the book was released, the diner became a Chinese restaurant. Now, most truck drivers stay out on the interstates, so there are no truck-stop diners in the region anymore.

Mickey Koutouzis managed both the DeRaffele Little Nick and the Nedick's (a Fodero-built diner) with an iron fist. His son John recalls that he had tricks to keep everyone in line. "He would park his car in the lot across the street from Little Nick and watch the night shift with binoculars, to make sure everything was ship shape." One time, he caught his night cook sharing a steak with a waitress. In the morning he went through the night's receipts and asked the cook where the fifth steak was in the cooler. Other owners knew that Mickey did a fantastic job running diners, and he was asked to become partners in new ventures in Menands and Colonie. But Mickey didn't believe in partners, he wanted to run a diner his way.

John says that his father hired many drunks as dishwashers, and if they didn't show, he had to fill in as dishwasher after school. John started doing this at age eleven. But Gus "Chico" Flores wasn't one of the drunks, he was a dependable dishwasher who quickly worked his way up and became an

Originally Little Nicks Diner on Central Avenue, this diner was moved to Stillwater before being moved to Wellborn, Texas, by current owner Eric Shulte.

CONRAD HOFFMAN

The most original Bixler diner extant languishes in Coeymans.

excellent short-order cook. Even though he initially didn't speak any English, he learned quickly, and soon became Mickey's number one cook. Chico even followed Mickey over to the Miss Glenmont Diner when he bought it in 1968. Before orders were written down, they were simply called out, and Chico could handle this with the best of them! He could keep track of four orders even with variations like extra cheese or no tomatoes. He could even catch a waitress trying to take part of another waitress's order, having forgotten to call in her own.

## URBAN DINERS

Former Schenectady historian Don Huelett remembers meeting his wife at the Van Curler Diner, named for the hotel across the street. Diner operators in the city of Schenectady were not as likely to replace their 1920s and 1930s–era diners as owners in other places. The most popular diner was by far the Silver Diner, a converted Pullman car. Today, the diner sits in limbo, awaiting a possible new life and a new owner. James Cecilian, the grandson of the original owner, wrote to the local newspaper, imploring the city to find a new owner in order to preserve the history of the once-popular diner. Other diners in the city were the Victory, Ladd's, CrossTown, Modern, and the Oven and Griddle.

In Troy, the 5th Avenue Diner and 2nd Avenue Diner were in Lansingburgh and the Congress Street Diner and Troy Diner were downtown. One resident of Lansingburgh remembers that the 5th Avenue Diner was where families and students of Lansingburgh High School went after games and other school events. Each group had their own time to be at the diner. The 2nd Avenue Diner was a place where people went after the bars closed for the night. He remembers one night when the cook was so drunk that he told a customer that if they wanted their eggs cooked, they would have to do it themselves.

All of these diners have been gone since at least the 1970s. Albany has lost quite a few too, these include the Bassett, Charlie's, Roger's, Metro, Market, and the 20th Century Diner. Four diners are left in Albany, including Dan's Place II. This diner holds unique hours, opening up at 3 A.M. to catch the early workers and the very late night bar crowd. The diner is in the middle of a mixed residential-commercial block of Washington Avenue. You wouldn't know it was an actual old barrel roof diner, unless you went inside. This is one of the rare places where you really get the feeling of what it was like in the 1930s, with a typical lunch crowd consisting of locals, businessmen, and police officers, all shoulder to shoulder.

Around 1939, a diner was moved from Albany to Cohoes, possibly the Central Lunch Car run by Stephen Brayman. In a newspaper picture and caption announcing the diner's arrival, the caption read, "Belle of the Gutter." Fire Chief John Kelley was the first owner of the diner while it was located in Cohoes. The town, known as the Spindle City (for all the textile work done there), amazingly only had two lunch wagons.

## SUBURBAN DINERS

Suburban diners tend to be located on high-traffic commercial strips. A majority of these are environmental diners built in the 1960s or later, quite spacious and featuring big kitchens. Johnny B's, the former Miss Glenmont Diner, sits on a major road used to get in and out of town. The diner was moved to the current location from the other side of U.S. Route 9W. There was a fire in the original diner and it was replaced by the current 1961 Silk City. This part of U.S. Route 9W is not commercial; it is a gateway to the southern suburbs of Albany.

Heading west out of Albany on highly commercial Central Avenue, you will find the Gateway Diner, and its large neon sign, right next door to the Westgate Plaza which opened in 1957. This plaza was one of the first attempts at a shopping area located outside of the traditional downtown locations. In 1957, the Albany *Times Union* called this area of Central Avenue the "city's western hinterlands." Later, this section of Central Avenue starting at Everett Road would be known as Albany's Miracle Mile, with neon as far as the eye could see. The Gateway attempted to take advantage of hungry shoppers who wanted a quick meal before going home or continuing to shop. This diner had more of a Space Age feel to it, until two sunrooms were

This Paramount, the Tops Diner in Rotterdam, is dwarfed by the replacement on-site restaurant. The Tops was demolished in 2006.

added on each side of the door; a 2008 remodel further changed the appearance. The Gateway serves as one of the Capital District's only twenty-four-hour diners.

Central Avenue originally had a trolley line that connected the cities of Schenectady and Albany. In the 1930s a phone book lists the Colonie Diner at trolley stop 26, a reference to the location of that diner that would be lost on practically everyone today.

You will find the Farmer Boy Diner closer to Schenectady. The current 1992 Paramount replaced an older environmental Swingle diner. Based on pictures on the wall in the current diner, the Swingle is the third diner to call this location home. The original looks to be a late 1930s O'Mahony, very similar to Eddie's Paramount Diner in Rome. The Farmer Boy is located on a section of Central Avenue that has experienced a commercial boom. Surrounding it are several commercial establishments and some run-down mid-century motels. Just down the road is the Colonie Diner. The diner sits in front of a plaza, where it has been since it opened in 1962. At that time, the diner's style was classic exaggerated modern, with a zigzag roofline and large windows. Today, its appearance has been toned down a bit.

The Wolf Road Diner is on Wolf Road, another commercial artery that intersects with Central Avenue. Dennis Spathis has run this diner since 1991. The Swingle diner came from Menands and was called the Tiffany Diner for a brief time after arriving in Colonie. During this period, the past owners filed for bankruptcy and reorganized. Back in Menands, Teddy Vasilakos saw an empty foundation, ready for a diner, and bought a new one for the location. This newer diner is also a Swingle. The interior almost feels like the din-

This Paramount diner, the Farmer Boy, is the fourth diner to grace this location in suburban Colonie.

The Menands Diner in Menands is a typical Swingle diner from 1983.

ing room in someone's home. Behind the cash register are framed copies of three excellent reviews the diner has received from local newspapers.

A possible Manno diner sits on Troy Schenectady Road in Latham. The former Acropole and Village Diner sits on a busy four-lane road and now goes by the name Route 7 Diner and is under new ownership. The diner has always done a respectable business on a section of road that is slowly but surely being taken over by one commercial establishment after another. Although this road has been a four-lane road for a long time, until recently it was largely residential. The former Village Diner added a dining room sometime after opening, which made the place look more like any other restaurant.

The Country View Diner is in the town of Brunswick on the road to Vermont from Troy. Built by Swingle in 1988, it was known as the Stagecoach Diner. Within the past five years, DeRaffele remodeled the diner with stainless steel and glass block. At one time, the diner was known as the Collar City Diner (a reference to Troy's past).

Retro diners are inspired by classic fifties diner styles, but on a much grander scale. The three located in the Capital District are located in suburban areas, two in commercial strips. The third, the Alexis Diner in Troy, a 150-seat DeRaffele built in 1999, is slightly more isolated, but is still on a major road near the community college and the Rensselaer Business Park on Route 4. Alexi Lekkas, the owner of the Alexis Diner started out as a dishwasher in the 76 Diner. Its style is not as extreme as the Metro 20 Diner, which operates at the back entrance to Crossgates, the largest mall in the region. The Alexis Diner is done in blue and silver, with some mosaic tiles below the windows, and a simple foyer. On the other hand, the Metro 20 has a four-tier reverse-step roofline, and a large foyer of glass block. The diner is mostly stainless steel on the outside and is highlighted in grayish blue and checkerboard tiles. The Circle Diner, a Kullman has the grandest foyer. There is more glass block and stainless steel on this red and silver diner, which harkens back to Kullman's past glory.

# DINER DRIVES

Before the advent of the interstates, travelers driving through Albany between Boston and Buffalo followed U.S. Route 20 to Albany and then either continued west on that highway or switched to Route 5. Travelers passing through Albany between New York City and Montreal followed U.S. Route 9 or U.S. Route 9W up the Hudson Valley to Albany and continued north on U.S. Route 9 or U.S. Route 9N. Because of the traffic, many Capital District diners were attracted to these same routes, creating what are now the region's two diner drives.

### U.S. ROUTE 20/ROUTE 5
U.S. Route 20 enters New York State about ten miles west of Pittsfield, Massachusetts, home of one of the former Morris Diners from Albany. The first diner you come to in New York State is Jimmy D's Pizza Royale in New Lebanon, formerly the third Taconic Parkway diner. Neither the name nor appearance of this restaurant is diner-like, but a diner it is.

The 9 & 20 Diner, formerly the Countryside, sits at the junction of the two major roads in Castleton.

Dewey's Diner in Albany was originally Cy's Diner from Kingston. The owners have flirted with the idea of removing the vinyl siding.

The road continues through rural New York until it merges with U.S. Route 9. Here the 9 & 20 Diner, a 1941 Silk City, sits. Currently closed, the diner was a popular stop on the way in and out of Albany. Like any good diner, people remember it for their blue plate specials. Heading into Albany today, the area becomes more suburban, but it was not always that way. When the East Greenbush Diner came to town in 1979, this Swingle was almost secluded. The real congestion starts where Route 4 begins. This is the approximate site of the former Travelers Diner.

Nearing Rensselaer, you would have passed Pat & Bob's Diner at one time. It is now located in Wakefield, New Hampshire. Our next diner is the Riverside Diner in Rensselaer, which replaced a Carrol's Restaurant, which in turn replaced the Dixie Diner. The diner was known as Vivian's Diner for over twenty-five years, until recently when the new ownership changed its name. This Swingle is a plain looking stucco building with a metal mansard roof.

After crossing the Hudson River into Albany, head west on State Street, which becomes Central Avenue. Fork left on Washington Avenue until you spy Dan's Place II at 494, between North Lake Avenue and Quail Street. The diner did business somewhere else in Albany before it was moved to this location in 1953. The diner is a popular stop after a late night at the bars for college students from The College of St. Rose or the State University of New York Albany. But at lunchtime, you can find just about anyone at Dan's Place, including cops, locals, and business people.

Turning right on Quail Street, go back to Central Avenue to our next one-of-a-kind diner. There are only three known Comac diners and Jack's Diner at 547 Central Avenue is the best preserved. Jack Murtagh has been running the diner for forty years. Everything about this diner is worth a trip, and Jack prides himself on roasting turkey right in his kitchen.

Heading out of Albany on Central Avenue, we hit the aptly named Gateway Diner at 899 Central Avenue. Like many twenty-four-hour diners, you'll find a typical Greek menu. This diner gets all types of crowds, including shoppers, state employees, and suburbanites coming back from the bars in downtown Albany. Driving west, under the railroad trestles, we pass the former site of the DeRaffele diner known as Little Nick's Diner. Like some other diners in Albany, it was managed by Nedick's of New York City. The diner was moved to Stillwater around 1973 where it was known as Carol's Diner, run by the late Carol Lasher. The diner is still in business as Hullabaloo's Dessert Depot in Wellborn, Texas, after being saved at the last minute by the American Diner Museum.

Continuing on Central Avenue, take a right on Wolf Road to 219, and the Wolf Road Diner in Colonie, a 1970s Swingle. Dewey's Diner on Fuller

## MAD PRIORITIES

What is the difference between an engineering mind and a restaurateur's mind? Well Cliff Brown might just be the perfect person to answer this question. Retiring from a job as an engineer, he and his wife, Jane, bought the Miss Albany Diner (MAD) in 1988. Through many years of trial and error, Cliff has come up with rules and concepts that help keep the diner in order to this former engineer.

Perhaps his most unique accomplishment is the MAD priorities:

1) Deliver hot food
2) Take payment
3) Bus tables
4) Take orders
5) Make coffee
6) Empty bus boxes
7) Process orders
8) Refill coffee cups

Obviously, there's some logic behind this order, and the first two are the most important ones for good reason. Cold food tastes bad, and no one seems to complain about being ignored if a waitress is bringing food to other tables. The second is a pet peeve of Cliff's, and something that many people take for granted until it happens to them. How many times have you been out in a restaurant, and you're ready to leave, but for the life of you, you can't get the waitress to give you the check? Cliff understands that the time before you get your food and

Road in Albany is a Kullman with light blue flutes peeking out on half the diner. Dewey's originally came from Kingston where it was known as Cy's Diner. The diner was moved to this spot in 1965 by Lillian Dewey to replace an on-site diner that burned down in 1964. Dewey's is open 7 A.M. to 2 P.M. Monday through Friday. It is a family run place with very loyal customers. The employees make customers, even first timers, feel welcome. They have that special personality you find in some diners, an ability to be caring and joking at the same time, though it can come off as gruff or even rude to people out of the diner loop.

Fuller Road meets U.S. Route 20 again about a mile down the road. Take a right and pass Crossgates Mall. The Metro 20 Diner in Guilderland sits at the back entrance to the mall. It is a classic DeRaffele diner with reverse-step stainless steel on the roofline. DeRaffele likes the look of this diner so much, they have a framed photograph of the diner at night in their offices in New Rochelle. Owner Demetrios Michael is a long-time Capital District diner owner.

---

while you are eating is the restaurant's time. But once the customer is done and ready to leave, that's the customer's time. A very important part of the experience of dining is to be able to get out quickly when you want to leave.

Cliff took care of this problem the only way he thought it would make sense—give the bill to the customer as soon as the waitress puts in the order. More than a few customers are confused by this, thinking you have to pay right there and then, so Cliff added these lines to the bottom of the bill:

"To serve you better, receiving your bill now assures:
1) The kitchen has your order
2) Shows what U ordered
3) When finished, no waiting"

Other things that Cliff has instituted in his diner include no substitutions. He says you can't order a car without a trunk, and at MAD there are certain items you can't remove from your order. If people ask for food prepared in different ways, then the food will not be the same each time. So no substitutions helps to maintain the consistency of the food they are known for. Cliff writes in his menu, "If you want less of anything, it is still the same price. The food cost savings is minuscule; the overall cost of preparing, seating, and serving remains the same."

His latest words were conceived when he was dining at a restaurant with his family while on vacation. "When a child's behavior draws the attention of other dining patrons, maybe an acting school would provide a better destination than public dining."

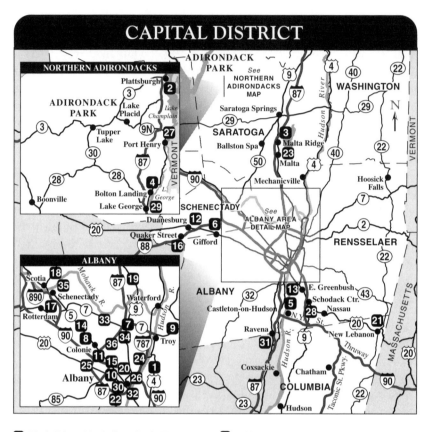

**CAPITAL DISTRICT**

1 Alexis Diner: North Greenbush (P)
2 Bill Gates Diner: Plattsburgh (BR)
3 Bloomers: Malta Ridge (MS)
4 Bolton Beans: Bolton Landing (BR)
5 Bridge Diner: Coeymans (BR)
6 Chuck Wagon Diner: Princetown (MS)
7 Circle Diner: Latham (P)
8 Colonie Diner: Colonie (E)
9 Country View Diner: Brunswick (E)
10 Dan's Place II: Albany (R)
11 Dewey's Diner: Albany (MS)
12 Duanesburg Diner: Duanesburg (R)
13 East Greenbush Diner: East Greenbush (E)
14 Farmer Boy Diner: Colonie (E)
15 Gateway Diner: Albany (R)
16 Gibby's Diner: Quaker Street (MS)
17 Gilly's Diner: Schenectady (E)
18 Glenville Queen Diner: Glenville (E)

19 Halfmoon Diner: Halfmoon (E)
20 Jack's Diner: Albany (MS)
21 Jimmy D's Pizza Royale: New Lebanon (R)
22 Johnny B's Diner: Glenmont (MS)
23 Malta Diner: Malta (E)
24 Menands Diner: Menands (E)
25 Metro 20 Diner: Guilderland (P)
26 Miss Albany Diner: Albany (MS)
27 Miss Port Henry Diner: Port Henry (BR)
28 9 & 20 Diner: Castleton (MS)
29 Prospect Mountain Diner: Lake George (P)
30 Quintessence: Albany (MS)
31 Ravena Diner: Ravena (E)
32 Riverside Diner: Rensselaer (E)
33 Route 7 Diner: Latham (E)
34 '76 Diner: Latham (E)
35 Silver Diner: Schenectady (R)
36 Wolf Road Diner: Colonie (E)

The Metro 20 Diner in Guilderland is a postmodern DeRaffele with a reverse step roofline.

The last diner on our trip is fifteen miles down the road in Duanesburg. U.S. Route 20 starts out as four lanes, with lots of commercial establishments, but quickly turns rural as Route 146 heads off to Schenectady. The rest of the trip is a two-lane highway, reminiscent of what the route heading west from Albany would have looked like about half a century ago. The Duanesburg Diner is a rare 1930s Bixler Diner. It is possible that there was also another Bixler on U.S. Route 20, where Route 155 goes to Altamont. The Duanesburg Diner has been remodeled quite a bit on the outside and has an additional dining room, but the diner section still has the original booths and stools, and the barrel-roof ceiling. Open from breakfast to dinner, the diner has daily specials each night. It's a difficult choice between the Duanesburg and Gibby's Diner, just a few miles down Route 7 in Quaker Street. Gibby's is a small Mountain View that is pristine inside. The diner was bought by Gibby Wolfe in 1952, when Route 7 was the only road from Binghamton to Albany. I-88 opened in the 1980s, but business has not been hurt in the least. When asked by *Roadside Magazine* in 1999 if he thought the interstate was hurting his business, Gibby mused to a customer, "I wonder when they'll open the highway?" Gibby has now retired from the business, handing it over to his daughter Colleen Glindmyer. To the customers, however, the quality of food has not changed.

## U.S. ROUTE 9, U.S. ROUTE 9W, U.S. ROUTE 9N

This route can be described as "Diners on the 9s." Your trip starts on U.S. Route 9W in Ravena. This part of the highway is mostly rural, with occasional businesses located at intersections in and around Ravena. Ravena once had what may have been a Paramount diner that became part of an auto dealership's offices before finally being demolished. The environmental-style Ravena Diner, however, still operates on U.S. 9W. The next diner north does not appear until the outskirts of Albany. Johnny B's in Glenmont is a typical late-model Silk City Diner that once operated as Uncle Milty's and Miss Glenmont Diner.

In Albany, take a left onto Madison Avenue and then another left onto New Scotland Avenue to get to the Quintessence Diner, a closed Fodero. Diners this size were typically located in the suburbs, not in urban neighborhoods such as this one. Follow U.S. Route 9 north toward Latham. The road becomes more residential as it leaves Albany. In the vicinity of Siena College and Hoffman's Playland, U.S. Route 9 becomes more commercial again and widens into a four-lane highway filled with auto dealerships, plazas, and stores.

Down the road, on the left is the Latham '76 Diner, an environmental diner with a spirit of '76 theme that is open twenty-four hours a day. Former owner Alex Loupessis operated the diner from about 1973 until he passed away in 2007. The '76 Diner, like the Miss Albany, took the initiative to ban cigarette smoking before the state of New York passed its law. The diner may also be home to the largest diner menu in upstate, if not all of New York.

The former Miss Glenmont Diner, now Johnny B's, has turned from a popular truck stop on Route 9W to a nice place to bring the family.

They offer three types of Philly cheesesteaks, and six kinds of pasta sauces, just to name a few examples of their menu's vastness.

Just up the road is the Circle Diner. To get there, make sure you stay in the right lane and don't go under the Latham Circle. The Circle Diner sits on the northeast side of the rotary. This 1998 Kullman was done in retro style, costing over $2 million. The owners of the Circle Diner brought in executive chef Bill Hohenstein, who created a fine-dining menu. But you can still get the classic diner meatloaf or choose from one of the specials more typical of diner fare.

A 1960s traveler continuing up U.S. Route 9 bound for the Adirondacks would have passed rural motels, gas stations, and two diners, the Linwood and Crescent. Today, those diners are gone and the road is now lined with businesses, including the Halfmoon Diner on the corner of Grooms Road and U.S. Route 9. The diner is an environmental-style DeRaffele that owner Peter Vasilakos had built in 1988. After fifteen burglaries and three holdups at his restaurant on Long Island, he decided that a change of scenery was in order. The Halfmoon Diner is also the only diner near Clifton Park. U.S. Route 9 north of the town retains the charm of an older road. Old motels and a cottage camp can be found closer to Malta. The next diner is at the corner of U.S. Route 9 and Route 67 in Malta. The brick-faced, colonial-style Malta Diner was built in 1993 by DeRaffele for Steve and Debbie Gouvis. They wanted a stainless-steel retro diner, but the town of Malta ruled against that design, and forced them to go with the style they have today. Just a few miles up the road in Malta Ridge is a classic Fodero now known as Bloomers. Previously, this diner had been an Italian restaurant and before that was called the Malta Ridge Diner. Sophie and Joseph Parker, along with their son Paul, took over the diner in 1995 and renamed it Chez Sophie Bistro. It was famous for Sophie Parker's fine French cuisine. In 2006, the Parkers moved their restaurant to the Saratoga Hotel and put the diner up for sale. The diner has been grandfathered into Malta, which maintains ordinances that encourage buildings to have a colonial appearance. Many people who vacationed in the Adirondacks remember Malta as more of a haven of roadside motels and restaurants than the colonial-themed bedroom community it is becoming.

The road becomes increasingly rural, and there are no diners until you reach Lake George. At one time, however, there were diners in South Glens Falls and Queensbury. Queensbury was once home to the environmental style Aviation Diner, a named shared with a local mall. Approaching Lake George, the road becomes more commercial and tourist oriented, especially after passing the Great Escape Amusement Park. The roadside is crowded with stands selling T-shirts and ice cream, miniature golf courses, and classic motels. There is also a diner, the Prospect Mountain, a Diner-mite model, the first in New York State, just delivered in December 2007. It replaced the previous diner on site, a rare doublewide Silk City from 1950 that was destroyed by fire earlier that year. Lake George is a resort town, and the Prospect stays open all night on the weekends during the peak season. The diner still serves classic diner food, along with a broader array of menu items. They are known for their bacon cheeseburgers.

In Lake George, U.S. Route 9N hugs the lake. North from here the road is only two lanes and it's easy to get behind a slow-moving vehicle. In Bolton Landing, the former Service Diner, Worcester #791, built in 1946, is now Bolton Beans, a coffee shop that just recently started serving breakfast and lunch, Fortunately the owner, who rents out the diner, is very sensitive to its preservation and does not allow many alterations. Bolton Landing was once home to the Bill Gates Diner (no relation to the famous billionaire). The diner was originally a trolley car built by the Jones Car Company of Troy. After retirement, the trolley was bought by the Liapus brothers from Glens Falls and taken to Bolton Landing, where they set up on a lot leased from Nettie Gates. The brothers sold the diner in 1949 to Nettie's son, Bill. The diner closed in 1981 and it was given to the Adirondack Museum in 1989, which restored the diner and put it on display at their Blue Mountain Lake Museum. Since then, Bill's son, author William Preston Gates, has written many articles about his parents' diner. The diner has since been loaned to the Champlain Valley Transportation Museum, which operates on the former Plattsburgh Military Base.

This Fodero diner in Malta Ridge has been used as an Italian restaurant and a French bistro.

The only Worcester diner in the state. The diner now serves as the Bolton Beans coffee house, and sits where the Bill Gates Diner once did business in Bolton Landing.

The last diner on our trip, in Port Henry, is probably the most worthwhile of any, architecturally speaking. The Miss Port Henry Diner is high on the list of many diner fans, even though it is off of the beaten path. This Ward & Dickinson standard model diner was originally used in Glens Falls as a lunch wagon, brought each night to its factory-based clientele pulled by a horse. In 1933, it was brought to Port Henry and attached to a restaurant already on location. The diner was covered over, but in the 1990s a new owner realized what he had, and worked to restore the place to its original condition.

# MISS ALBANY DINER
## 1941 SILK CITY #4195
893 Broadway, Albany • (518) 465-9148

Running a diner and working as an engineer usually do not go together but Cliff Brown, the owner of the Miss Albany Diner, is not your typical diner owner. Besides having his own diner-management philosophy, he also has a diner that is on the National Register of Historic Places. In the 1920s, a Ward & Dickinson diner was delivered to this Broadway site. In 1941, owner Lillian McAuliff replaced it with a yellow and burgundy Silk City diner for $14,000, saving $4,000 by trading her old Ward & Dickinson. But Silk City never took the diner, and it was left on the back of the lot to rot away.

Lillian's son, Cliff Brown, remembers that she was very sensitive to criticism. Anyone who complained about her soup was readily thrown out. No matter, she still had a tremendous customer base because of the diner's location on one of the main north–south roads between Montreal and New York City.

The diner appeared in the 1987 film *Ironweed*, starring Jack Nicholson and Meryl Streep. For the movie, the diner's name was changed from Street Car Diner to Miss Albany, which it has remained ever since. Cliff and Jane Brown bought the diner shortly after the movie.

If you look up when you first get into the diner, you'll see three large french fries, each with a number and a description on how they are cooked, so that you can order your fries just the way you like them. The unique menu includes, for example, a turkey Waldorf—turkey, Granny Smith apples, bacon, crumbled blue cheese, and honey mustard on rosemary ciabatta. The brunch menu is just as fancy, including such items as the MAD Irish Toast—french toast with pecan cream cheese drowned in butterscotch Irish whiskey sauce. They also take care of the little things. For example, their fruit juices have no high-fructose corn syrup.

Today, Jane has mostly retired from the diner and Cliff can be found either conversing with customers, or in his office working on the books. They have left much of the kitchen work to their son Bill.

# MISS PORT HENRY DINER
## 1927 WARD & DICKINSON
### 3 Church St., Port Henry • (518) 546-3400

Every so often you hear a good news story about a historic building being restored. The Miss Port Henry is one of these stories. The Ward & Dickinson dining car came to town in 1933, and was remodeled many times over the years. In 1992, the business was bankrupt and closed. The diner was bought by Mike Darius, who noticed the wheels for the diner in the base-

The interior of the Miss Port Henry Diner in Port Henry.

ment. Darius had enough vision to attempt to restore the diner to its original luster, but was unable to come up with the needed money. Fortunately, Linda Mullen and Hank D'Arcy bought the diner and started the restoration process. They hired Edward LeClair to do the carpentry work, and the rest is history.

D'Arcy and Mullen ran the diner for a few years. They even invited the first owner of the diner, then ninety-seven-year-old Grace Tario, to the grand opening in 1996. Unfortunately, they sold the diner to different owners, and the diner underwent gradual changes to its appearance. One owner painted the diner black, instead of the original green, and added carpeting to the booths. Fortunately, the current owners, Greg and Jennifer Moore, seem willing to give the diner some stability.

They have provided a breakfast and lunch menu, along with homemade soups, and have begun adding unique specials here and there. Just like any good family-run business, they roast their own turkeys and take pride in the simple, yet important, facets of operating a diner. Their waitress, April, enjoys the cozy feeling and friendly customers at the Miss Port Henry. The diner gets more than its share of visitors from out of town. Many of them take a picture or two of this one of a kind Ward & Dickinson dining car.

# JACK'S DINER
## 1948 COMAC
547 Central Ave., Albany • (518) 482-9807

Albany has two diners on the National Register of Historic Places, the Miss Albany Diner and Jack's. Jack's is one of only two Comac diners still in pristine condition; it was never remodeled. Built in 1948, Jack's has a stainless-steel exterior with alternating yellow and green porcelain enamel strips. Inside, the diner is red and off-white. When it opened, an advertisement in the *Altamont Enterprise* stated, "From its gleaming, all-metal exterior to the harmonious counter and table setting, Jack's Diner presents the most modern decor for dining pleasure."

The first diner at 547 Central Avenue was a Brill, and one of the original seven Miss Albany Diners. Jack Saunders bought the diner from the Miss Albany chain around 1940, ultimately replacing it with the current Comac, which he bought with $13,000 he won in a craps game.

Jack Murtagh was the diner's accountant and also worked at a Mechanicville paper factory. He was about to be transferred to New York City when he heard the diner was going up for sale. As Paul Grondahl stated in the *Albany Times Union*, Murtagh "had a defining life moment: the big meatloaf or the Big Apple."

The meatloaf won out, and Murtagh bought Jack's in 1964. The diner is actually better known for its turkey. Jack's Diner serves real roasted turkey all the time, no substitutions. If you order a simple turkey sandwich, get ready for thick-cut pieces of turkey, just like Thanksgiving leftovers. The rest of the menu is tried and true, just as you would expect at a neighborhood diner.

Recently, Jack officially retired and sold the diner to his son Thomas, who has been working there for many years. Jack still does the books, acts as an unofficial greeter, and does any other job that is needed. He still has the diner business in his blood, and it seems that his family does too. Jack's wife works the register and other family members help out as well.

When the Comac was brought in, a full-page ad was placed in the *Altamont Enterprise*. The ad pointed out the convenience of the diner for shoppers coming into Albany from the west. When Jack Murtagh bought the diner in 1964, he said the diner was jam-packed Thursday, Friday, and Saturday nights. Today, with Central Avenue struggling for its identity in a suburban world, very few shoppers stop in for a bite. Jack says that it's almost all locals who patronize the diner, besides the few diner fans that come in to catch the magic of the vintage diner and the daily routine. The diner has been featured in commercials, including one for the state of New York. Jack Murtagh is a recipient of the Walter Scott Award, given by the American Diner Museum for his service preserving the positive image of diners.

**FEATURED DINERS**

# GIBBY'S DINER
**1953 MOUNTAIN VIEW #307**
Rt. 7, Quaker Street • (518) 895-2063

# DUANESBURG DINER
**BIXLER**
Intersection of Rts. 7 and U.S. Rt. 20, Duanesburg • (518) 895-8843

In 1952, Gilbert "Gibby" Wolfe bought a diner from the Mountain View Company and placed it on Route 7 in Quaker Street. At the time, Route 7 was the main road from Schenectady to Binghamton. Gibby's Diner soon gained an excellent reputation for large portions and fresh homemade food. This popularity allowed Wolfe to have three additions built on the diner, the most recent in 1984.

Gibby has since passed the diner on to his daughter and son-in-law Colleen and Glen Glindmyer. The diner is open from Wednesday to Sunday, and closed the entire month of January.

By the time I-88 was finished in 1983, the diner was already fully ingrained in the dining public's heart. The diner has become more like a country restaurant, with large portions of home-cooked food. The meatloaf

Gibby's Diner.

Duanesburg Diner.

is made from the original recipe used when the diner opened. Gibby's serves up three pork chops when most places only give you two and they bake their own fresh bread each day.

The nearby Duanesburg Diner has graced the intersection of Route 7 and U.S. Route 20 since 1937. The diner started out as the Duane Diner, but it was covered with a stone facade at an early date. The bathrooms are in the basement and a dining room was added later.

In the diner section, there is a painting of what the diner looked like in the 1950s. It shows the stone siding and the dining room, but a different roofline. In the picture, the diner has more of a billboard roof, which announces "Full Course Dinners" and "Ham and Eggs" and includes a clock on the end facing the road. Over the years, the diner has had many different names, and even survived a serious fire.

Luis Patino and his family have owned the diner since 1996. They changed the name to the Duanesburg Diner to pay homage to the community. The diner still has the original stools, wood booths, and a linoleum floor, but the counter is not original.

Monday's special is always chicken cacciatore, and on Thursday it's Salisbury steak. The other daily specials rotate. When you're done with the meal, there is always a good assortment of traditional desserts like puddings and pies.

# DINER DIRECTORY

## ALBANY

**Dan's Place II**
494 Washington Ave.
(518) 463-9102
*1920s O'Mahony*
Formerly known as Thruway Diner.

**Dewey's Diner**
45 Fuller Rd.
(518) 482-9406
*1940 Kullman*
Formerly Cy's Diner from Kingston.

**Gateway Diner**
899 Central Ave.
(518) 428-7557
*1971 DeRaffele*
Remodeled 1997, 2008.

**Jack's Diner**
547 Central Ave. (Rt. 5)
(518) 482-9807
*1948 Comac*

**Miss Albany Diner**
893 Broadway
(518) 465-9148
*1941 Silk City #4195*

**Quintessence**
11 New Scotland Ave.
*1948 Fodero*
Closed.

## BOLTON LANDING

**Bolton Beans**
Lakeshore Dr.
(518) 644-3313
*1946 Worcester Diner #791*
Known as Service Diner.

## BRUNSWICK

**Country View Diner**
855 Hoosick Rd.
(518) 279-1566
*1988 Swingle*
Remodeled by DeRaffele.

## CASTLETON

**9 & 20 Diner**
1842 U.S. Rt. 9
*1941 Silk City*
Closed.

## COEYMANS

**Bridge Diner**
Rt. 144
*1930s Bixler*
Closed.

## COLONIE

**Colonie Diner**
1890 Central Ave.
(518) 456-1550
*1962 Fodero*
Remodeled.

**Farmer Boy Diner**
1975 Central Ave.
(518) 456-2243
*1992 Paramount*

**Wolf Road Diner**
219 Wolf Rd.
(518) 459-5214
*1973 Swingle*

## DUANESBURG

**Duanesburg Diner**
Jct. Rt. 7 and U.S. Rt. 20
(518) 895-8843
*1930s Bixler*
Remodeled.

## EAST GREENBUSH

**East Greenbush Diner**
751 Columbia Tpk.
(518) 477-8483
*Paramount*

## GLENMONT

**Johnny B's Diner**
21 Frontage Rd.
(518) 434-3761
*1956 Silk City #5661*
Originally the Miss Glenmont Diner.

## GLENVILLE

**Glenville Queen Diner**
210 Saratoga Rd.
(518) 399-3244
Environmental.

The Circle Diner is Kullman's postmodern diner in Latham.

## GUILDERLAND

**Metro 20 Diner**
1709 Western Ave.
(518) 456-3876
*1997 DeRaffele*

## HALFMOON

**Halfmoon Diner**
231 Grooms Rd. (Rt. 91)
(518) 371-1177
*1988 DeRaffele*

## LAKE GEORGE

**Prospect Mountain Diner**
Canada St. (U.S. Rt. 9)
(518) 668-9721
*Diner-Mite 2007*

## LATHAM

**Circle Diner**
813 New Loudon Rd.
(518) 785-3324
*1998 Kullman*

**Route 7 Diner**
1090 Troy Schenectady Rd.
(518) 783-5129
*Possibly a 1973 Manno*

**'76 Diner**
722 New Loudon Rd.
(518) 785-3793
*1972 DeRaffele*

## MALTA

**Malta Diner**
2476 U.S. Rt. 9
(518) 899-5099
*1993 DeRaffele*

## MALTA RIDGE

**Bloomers**
2853 U.S. Rt. 9
*1954 Fodero*
(518) 584-4484
Originally the Malta
Ridge Diner.

## MENANDS

**Menands Diner**
563 Broadway
(518) 465-1869
*1986 Swingle*

## NEW LEBANON

**Jimmy D's Pizza Royale**
U.S. Rt. 20 and Rt. 22
(518) 794-8161
*1964 Fodero*
Remodeled.

## NORTH GREENBUSH

**Alexis Diner**
294 N. Greenbush Rd.
(518) 286-2603
*1999 DeRaffele*

## PLATTSBURG

**Bill Gates Diner**
Champlain Valley Transportation
Museum
12 Museum Way
(518) 566-7575
*Jones Trolley Car*

## PORT HENRY

**Miss Port Henry Diner**
5 St. Patrick Pl.
(518) 546-3400
*1927 Ward & Dickinson*

## QUAKER STREET

**Gibby's Diner**
Rt. 7
(518) 895-2063
*1953 Mountain View #307*

## RAVENA

**Ravena Diner**
11 Madison Ave.
(518) 756-9898
*DeRaffele*

## RENSSELAER

**Riverside Diner**
314 Columbia Tpk.
(518) 434-3268
*1979 Swingle*

## SCHENECTADY

**Gilly's Diner**
920 Crane St.
(518) 374-7840
*1979 Swingle*

**Silver Diner**
Erie Blvd.
Two railcars spliced together.
Closed.

# THE CATSKILLS

In its heyday the Catskill region was a world-class summer destination, a nearby escape from the heat of New York City, and a place to see the funniest comedians. The railroads, which reached the heart of the Catskills in the 1870s, opened up the area, especially to the citizens of New York City. The Catskills became a summer playground, especially for the Jewish community from the city, who discovered that it was a wonderful place to get away from the heat in pre-air conditioning days. This influx helped the region gain the nickname of the "Borscht Belt." Phil Brown writes in *Catskill Culture*, "in the Catskills they [the Jewish] could have a proper vacation like regular Americans, but they could do it in a very Jewish milieu." And that vacation included the all-American diner.

The halcyon days of the Catskills are gone and most of the grand hotels are either decaying or have vanished completely. A few are left, to serve the minority of families that still go to the Catskills each year. A modest tourist industry remains, largely focused on outdoor activities and weekend getaways. Amazingly, the Catskills still features a number of diners, though a quarter are closed, at least as of this writing.

In addition to the Catskills, the region also includes part of the Shawangunks on the east side of the Delaware and Hudson Canal corridor now used by U.S. Route 209. Diners in the Catskills include all those from Ker-

1. Americana (Crossroads) Diner: Grand Gorge (MS)
2. Ashley's Pizzeria & Café: Greenwood Lake (MS)
3. Circle E Diner: Hancock (E)
4. Cup & Saucer Diner: Pine Bush (P)
5. Diner: Loch Sheldrake (R)
6. Diner: Phoenicia (MS)
7. Diner: Platt Clove (MS)
8. Diner: Westbrookville (R)
9. Diner: Wurtsboro (MS)
10. Downsville Diner: Downsville (R)
11. Goshen Plaza Diner: Goshen (E)
12. Liberty Diner: Liberty (E)
13. Monroe Diner: Monroe (E)
14. Munson Diner: Liberty (MS)
15. Papa's Family Diner: Walton (P)
16. Phoenicia Diner: Phoenicia (E)
17. Port Jervis Diner: Port Jervis (R)
18. Quickway Diner: Bloomingburg (R)
19. Rainbow Diner: Kerhonkson (R)
20. Robin Hood Diner: Livingston Manor (R)
21. Roscoe Diner: Roscoe (E)
22. Route 209 Diner: Ellenville (R)
23. Selena's Diner: Haines Falls (MS)
24. Sullivan Diner: Parksville (R)

honkson on U.S. 209 south to Goshen, west to Port Jervis, up the Delaware River to Deposit and Stamford, and east to Grand Gorge.

Lunch wagons were not as numerous in this largely rural area, but many of the villages, and the biggest city, Middletown, had lunch wagons. Many of these villages were stops on the Ontario and Western Railroad, which also brought passengers into the wilderness of the Catskills. The

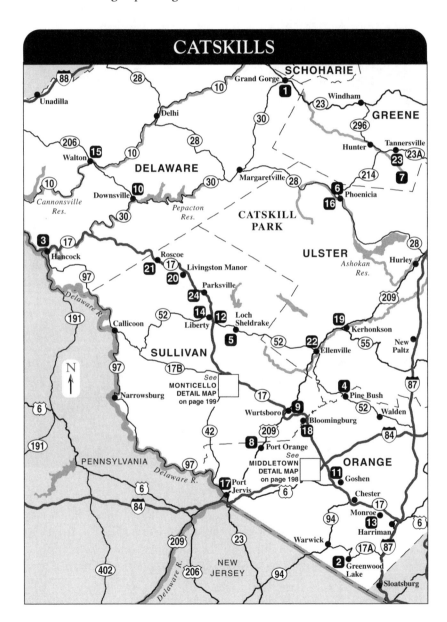

WILLIAM RHODES

Although Gager's Diner in Monticello has been remodeled, it once had the classic diner look of a Manno.

Diners next to gas stations were a popular combination.

Gaynor family ran at least three wagons in Middletown. Jack Gaynor bought an early Kullman diner, but moved it to Connecticut in the 1930s. Gaynor ordered a lunch wagon from Tierney in 1912 that he planned to locate in Goshen, but the wagon was badly damaged on the train ride up, so he refused to accept it. Harold Gager started with a wagon in Ellenville, and later moved it to Monticello. In between, he became the third person to fail at running a lunch wagon in Walden. While in Monticello, he upgraded to a barrel-roof O'Mahony. The diner was a popular Monticello institution, which allowed his son to replace it with a Manno. With the decline of the region, the diner failed. It became a Chinese restaurant around 2000, and it now sits closed.

Gager's Diner opened up in 1934. Around this time, his menu included roast beef, roast pork, or creamed chicken on a biscuit for 45 cents. You could also get meatballs and spaghetti for 40 cents. All of these menu items included soup.

Just like every other region, diners began to flourish in the late 1920s with the increasing popularity of the automobile (and the decline of the railroads). Route 17 is the main road through the region, serving Goshen, Middletown, Monticello, Liberty, Hancock, and Deposit on its way west to Binghamton. Every town along the way had a diner, and eventually diners started to find their way to the edge of town. Two such diners were the White Bridge, which was located just outside of Liberty on Route 17, and Felberg's Diner in Fosterdale, which was located with a gas station.

The current Miss Monticello Diner sits on the original alignment of Route 17. Carl Saloman and his father opened the Model Diner in 1928, bringing it in from Paterson, New Jersey. At the time, there were two other diners/lunch wagons in Monticello. Philip Schuren owned one of them. In a 1947 interview for *Diner Magazine* Carl said, "When we opened up on Bank Street, everyone was shaking his heads, telling us this was a one-season town." The Salomans survived, but they nearly called it quits twice in the first two years. Carl's mother pulled the diner through with her fantastic

WILLIAM RHODES

Eugene Bates attempted to open this diner in Stamford. A tragic car accident cut the dream short.

cream pies. Carl remembered that, during this time, most of the checks were for pie and coffee.

In 1936, they bought a new diner for $20,000, again from Paterson, and renamed it the Miss Monticello Diner. They were so busy in the summer that they had to add a dining room to the back of the diner for overflow. When World War II arrived, Carl went to serve in the Navy. When he came back, things had changed drastically. On the positive side, he picked up a partner in Art Hindley. Fortunately George Wagner, his cook since 1930, kept the diner going at home. Back at the diner, Carl found that it was tough to get any help, let alone good help. The government was controlling the prices for which meals could be sold and there was a thriving black market for supplies. Art said, "Business really boomed the day Carl walked back in here." But that only solved one problem. They both knew that despite the tight labor market, they had to find reliable workers. To keep good help, they were willing to offer shorter hours and higher wages—eighty dollars a week. They applied to the Veterans Administration for a newly formed on-the-job training program that would partially pay to train veterans coming back from the war who wanted to work in a restaurant.

As the Depression lifted, prosperity returned to the Catskills. Sections of Route 17 were rebuilt as a four-lane highway. Livingston Manor's Robin Hood Diner was built at the end of one of these sections. Although the diner is now encased in stone and brick, this Silk City's interior still exhibits

This shows a diner built when stainless steel was becoming unpopular, and just before the environmental phase kicked in.

An early Mountain View diner is now Ashley's Pizzeria in Greenwood Lake.

much of its original charm. It has a rounded ceiling, typical of Silk Citys of this vintage. Renovations made to the Port Jervis Diner, a Silk City in Port Jervis, make it barely recognizable as a diner at all. An even worse fate hit another Port Jervis diner. In February 1971, heavy snow that had accumulated on an adjacent building caused it to collapse and crush the diner, killing four people.

A 1940 Silk City known as the Lawrence City Diner once operated along Route 17 in Chester. The diner was connected to twenty-four deluxe cabins and a bar and grill—everything tourists would need as they headed toward the Catskills.

Talk to anyone in Liberty about diners, and more than likely they will bring up the old Triangle Diner. The Triangle Diner burned in a devastating fire in 1995. Much more than the diner was lost—the community lost a local meeting place and hangout popular after games and events. In 1938, Abe and Evelyn Novick bought the Cy's 9W Diner in Newburgh and had it moved to what was then Route 17, across from Grossinger's Resort. Hymie Heller and William Sunderland bought the diner later that same year. When the four lane was completed through Liberty, the diner was in a good location, just off the exit ramp.

On May 27, 1939, the *Middletown Times Herald* announced the opening of the Royal Clipper Diner. The Jerry O'Mahony diner had many innovations for its time. Glasses and silverware were treated with a Violet Ray Sanitizer

This Mountain View was a popular diner in Middletown run by Walter Burton.

that promised to make it the "most sanitary diner in this part of the country." Walt's Diner was a 1950 Mountain View Diner #332, and was located on Route 211. Walter Burton ran the diner from 1950 to 1970. After him,

OOMPA'S LINDA SCHIELE

Many diners came to the Catskills as used diners from other locations. This Kullman, Selena's Diner in Haines Falls, formerly did business in New Jersey.

Murray and Rhoda Farber took over the diner. They were also running a 1964 Manno called the Colonial Diner. For a small company, Manno had a hand in at least three diners in Sullivan County (including Gager's and one later demolished in Pine Bush).

As the environmental diner became more popular in the metropolitan regions during the 1960s, older diners were relocated to more rural areas. In Hancock, George Evanitsky, new owner of an on-site diner bought the former Syosset Diner, which operated on Long Island. He opened on Mother's Day in 1965, it was destroyed in a fire twenty years later. George's daughter, Liz, had the diner replaced by a ready-made unit built by DeRaffele. Down Route 17, along what will be the last limited-access section of the road completed sits the former Restop Diner. This Paramount diner that once had their trademark silver balls on the corners, came from Wayne, New Jersey in 1969. With the bypass planned at its Parksville location, this diner will probably have to be moved.

These aren't the only diners in the area that once operated in New Jersey. Belmont Bates was a New Jersey businessman who was spending his weekends in the Catskills. He soon decided that many of these Catskill villages needed a diner. In 1969, he had the opportunity to acquire Oompa's Diner, which had been operating near Lakewood, New Jersey, for ten years. The diner was scheduled to be replaced by a movie theater. It took most of a week just to move the first piece of the diner. The diner didn't open in Haines Falls until 1973, when everything was in place, and an operator was found who hailed from Albany. Today it is called Selena's Diner.

While this diner was being readied, another diner found its way into the Catskills. On a country road in Platt Clove, sits the former Silverton Diner of Silverton, New Jersey. Linda Schiele, Belmont's daughter, ran this diner from June 1971 to March 1972, when the diner was forced to close due to damage from frozen pipes. Linda fondly remembers groups of horseback riders coming to the diner from Woodstock. Since then, the diner has been used for storage.

Belmont Bates's brother, Eugene attempted to open a diner in Stamford. He bought a diner from Warwick, New York and had it moved to his farm. Unfortunately, Eugene died in an automobile accident, and the dream of a diner opening in Stamford went along with him.

Lin's Wood Shop in Platt Cove has not been open for more than thirty years. It is used for storage today.

The Americana Diner sat in a field north of Grand Gorge rotting away. The Miecznikowskis took on the daunting task of restoring and moving the diner to Grand Gorge.

The Munson Diner was moved to Liberty from Manhattan by a group of local investors. The intention was to find an operator and use the diner as a tourist attraction, but it took a long time.

The former Americana Diner serves the very small village of Grand Gorge, at the headwaters of the East Branch of the Delaware River. It had been moved to Gilboa when the Gilboa Dam was being built. Four men from Oneonta, including Nick and Joe Rizzo, called the complex that included the diner, the Mine Kill Lodge and Diner and opened in September of 1969. The diner was rotting away in nearby Gilboa until it was saved by Willy and Grace Miecznikowski.

The diner is not in perfect condition and the original stools have been replaced by four-legged stools. The diner reopened in 2005, but by the summer of 2006, it was already listed for sale. New owners renamed the diner the Crossroads Diner.

Two diners sit near the Esopus Creek in Phoenicia. The Esopus is popular with people interested in whitewater tubing. Four times a year, the city of New York releases extra water into the creek, making for a more adventurous ride. The Phoenicia Diner is a rarity for its location. This 1960s style diner has large windows and would look more at home in the suburbs. There is also an abandoned Silk City diner on the old road to Kingston. According to a neighbor, it seems like the current owner has no intention of selling the diner, and it probably hasn't served a meal in at least thirty years.

# DINER DRIVES

The two diner drives for the Catskills contain 70 percent of the diners in the region. The first drive follows U.S. Route 209, extending from Port Jervis to Kingston. U.S. Route 209 stays in a valley the whole way, alongside a former canal bed. The second diner drive follows Route 17 through the southwest Catskills. Route 17 is the shortcut west from New York City and the route taken by college students heading for universities in Binghamton, Ithaca, and Elmira.

### U.S. ROUTE 209

Near the border of New Jersey and Pennsylvania, Port Jervis is left with only one diner, although one can hardly tell that Port Jervis Diner is a Silk City. Ten miles north in Westbrookville, a Master diner is covered in wood siding, but retains much of its original features on the inside. In 1976, the diner went by the name Riviera Diner. The diner has been closed for at least a decade. In the fall of 2005, a car drove through the front of this diner, coming to a rest at the edge of the counter.

LARRY CULTRERA

Harold Gager started in his lunch wagon/diner career in Ellenville in the 1930s. Former mayor Henry Schipp also had Schipp's Diner there. In 1931, fire broke out at Schipp's, but the damage was repaired by

The former Charlotte's Diner in Ellenville, now the 209 Diner, was recently covered with plywood. This picture reveals a two-piece Silk City diner.

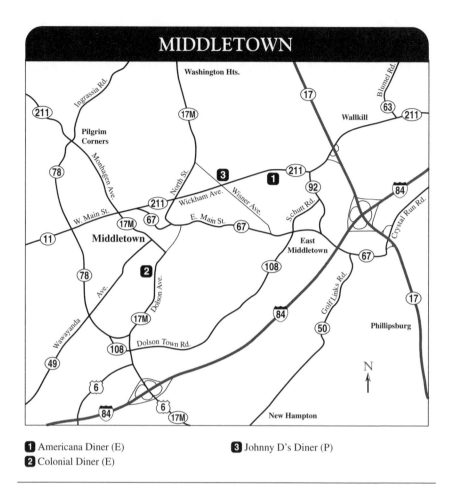

# MIDDLETOWN

1 Americana Diner (E)
2 Colonial Diner (E)
3 Johnny D's Diner (P)

---

"lunch car experts from New Rochelle," according to a Middletown newspaper. Just north of Ellenville's downtown is the 209 Diner. This Silk City's exterior has been covered in plywood, but the interior is well preserved, including the factory-built bathroom. The Rainbow Diner in Kerhonkson is another remodeled diner. This environmental diner covered in pebble panels dates to the 1950s and originally operated in New Jersey.

## ROUTE 17

Route 17 enters the Catskills region around Goshen. The Goshen Plaza Diner sits just off the Goshen exit. This environmental-style diner was built in 1985 by Paramount and serves many of the officials and lawyers working in the Orange County seat of Goshen. The quality and quantity of the food keeps them coming back.

# MONTICELLO

1 Blue Horizon Diner (E)     3 Miss Monticello Diner (R)
2 Gager's Diner (R)          4 Tilly's Diner (MS)

The Colonial Diner operates on old Route 17 at the eastern edge of Middletown. Manno originally built the Colonial Diner around 1969. In the 1990s a New Jersey-based company was hired to remodel the diner using polished stone and other postmodern materials. The company, Pappas & Kavrakis, left a tag, just as most of the diner manufacturers do. The diner is well known for being a late night hangout, with unique clientele and waitstaff. The former Johnny D's Diner sits on the other side of downtown. It is on the location of Walt's Diner, a Mountain View-built diner. It's not known if the current diner is new or a remodel, but the polished dark glass and stainless steel trim looks nothing like a Mountain View.

The Americana Diner also operates in Middletown on Route 211, on the way to Route 17 from downtown. The Americana is a mansard Mediter-

The Riviera Diner in Westbrookville was run into by a car recently. The front of the car reached the counter.

The classic interior of an O'Mahony diner is shown at the Quickway Diner in Bloomingburg.

ranean diner built in 1976 for John Gordon and Harry Sakolis. They serve cocktails and specialize in fresh seafood.

West on Route 17 from Middletown, the Quickway Diner can be found just off the Route 17K exit in Bloomingburg. This O'Mahony is covered with vinyl on the outside, and has a larger addition where it seems most people

The Royal Diner in Wurtsboro is a Silk City that was remodeled by Erfed.

sit. Teek and Vee, the owners, also run a car dealership right behind the diner. The diner has a Greek-inspired menu.

Travelers following old Route 17 west over Shawangunk Mountain came to the next diner on the edge of Wurtsboro. Now closed, the former Royal Diner is a Silk City best known for being remodeled in 1963 by Edward Fedkenheuer Sr. and Edward Fedkenheuer Jr., better known as Erfed. While the outside reflects Erfed's Googie stylings, the inside is pure Silk City.

Two diners once operated on Broadway in Monticello. Gager's Diner is now closed, but the Miss Monticello Diner continues to serve hungry patrons with delicious, dependable fare. The diner has undergone an environmental remodeling, though you can still tell on the inside that it was once a classic stainless-steel diner. Tilly's Diner is on the western edge of town near the racetrack. It's a popular place for breakfast and lunch. The Blue Horizon Diner is located north of Monticello on Route 42. It is an environmental diner built by DeRaffele, located in a commercial strip just off Route 17. Eight miles up the road in Liberty, the Liberty Diner sits very close to the former site of the Triangle Diner. The Liberty is a nondescript newer diner, which probably filled a gastronomical void when the Triangle burned, but can't fill the shoes of an institution.

Liberty is also the location of the Munson Diner from Manhattan, known as the "Seinfeld Diner," referring to its appearance in the Bizarro episode of *Seinfeld*, in which Elaine meets three guys who are the opposites of Jerry, George, and Kramer. The diner was moved to avoid demolition, and reopened for business in December 2007. Much of the original interior has been remodeled.

The former Hollywood Diner is in Loch Sheldrake, five miles east of Liberty on Route 52. This shell of a Kullman Challenger diner from the 1930s sits near the lake. The diner thrived in the days when there was a summer bungalow colony in Loch Sheldrake. The diner spent time as a laundromat and has been stripped of its fixtures.

Back on Route 17 and continuing west, you come to Parksville and the last traffic light on Route 17. This will change soon, when this stretch of

Tilly's Diner has long been a mainstay near the Monticello Racetrack.

The Hollywood Diner in Loch Sheldrake is a Kullman Challenger model that last did business as a laundromat.

The Roscoe Diner in Roscoe started in 1962 as a classic diner but was later remodeled and enlarged.

This DeRaffele, the Circle E Diner in Hancock, replaced a diner that was destroyed by fire in 1985.

road will become limited access. The Sullivan Diner (now closed) might need to be moved if it is to be opened once again. This diner is a 1948 Paramount, and once had the famous Paramount wedding-cake corners topped by metal balls. In the 1990s, the diner was covered with green siding, which was recently painted yellowish-brown.

Before the expressway opened, people heading west into Livingston Manor would pass by the Robin Hood Diner. This Silk City diner has a semi-barrel roof on the inside. Silk City abandoned that ceiling type in the late 1950s. The Robin Hood is covered in bricks and has had some changes on

Paramount built Papa's Family Diner in Walton in 1992. It is one of the simpler postmodern diners, but is still a work of beauty and a tribute to classic diners.

the inside, but the food is still true to its diner roots. A longtime employee at the grill is the son of the owners of the former Hollywood Diner in Loch Sheldrake. He has been working in diners for twenty-five years, first at the Hollywood before coming to the Robin Hood.

Leave Route 17 at Roscoe to find the famous Roscoe Diner. Many college students from schools in Binghamton and Ithaca will tell you that they always stop at the Roscoe Diner. Inside the Roscoe there are no less than a hundred pennants from different colleges adorning the walls. When the Roscoe opened in 1967, it was a regular stainless-steel diner. Today, the environmental diner features several additions and renovations.

Downsville is fifteen miles north of Roscoe on Route 206, near the Pepacton Reservoir. This is the largest of the seven reservoirs built by the city of New York to supply water for the city. As you enter Downsville, there is a barrel-roof building on the left that used to be a diner. Just a few hundred feet beyond is a plain Kullman diner with light blue vinyl siding, the Downsville Diner.

On the other side of Bear Spring Mountain, the village of Walton is host to Papa's Family Diner. This 1992 Paramount is a postmodern retro diner inspired by the stainless-steel diners of the 1950s. Papa's served 99-cent breakfast specials until 2004 and most items on the menu are still a real bargain.

# GOSHEN PLAZA DINER
## 1985 PMC
Rt. 207, Goshen • (845) 294-7800

In a *Times Herald-Record* reader poll covering Orange County, the Goshen Plaza Diner was voted the region's favorite diner. The Goshen Plaza is a simple environmental diner built by PMC in 1985. The interior is very utilitarian—no flashy design or colors. The coffee cups and dishes, however, provide a splash of color. But the decor is clearly secondary to the food.

Current owner Lisa Tsikolas took over the diner when her father "Kory" Antoniadis passed away a few years ago. Like other diners, her main competitors are the fast-food chains. She firmly believes that people need to be aware of what they are eating. Are they eating food made from fresh ingredients, or food made with preservatives to keep it fresh on a thousand-mile trip. With this in mind, the diner uses all fresh ingredients, right down to the herbs and vegetables. And to make sure these ingredients are used properly, she has brought in a chef, a trend in diners today.

Diners are known for quantity and quality, and at the Goshen Plaza this is very true. When they say soup comes with the daily specials, they don't mean a cup, they mean a bowl. And like any respectable diner, the soups are homemade. Prepackaged soups don't meet the standards that Lisa has set. Specials also come with dessert, and not just pudding or jello, but anything in the dessert case, displayed right in the center of the diner.

Lisa has been in the diner business much of her life. She started working at the Starlite Diner in downtown Middletown. Around 1980, her family bought an old diner in downtown Goshen. They ran the diner for five years before selling it and buying the Goshen Plaza. Manager Shirley Radulski has also worked at both places, and just like Lisa, has been working at diners most of her life. She started at the Stage and Blue Moon Diners in New York City before moving to Goshen. They both remember their days in the small diner, when lunchtime meant that the horsemen from the local trotting track would come in for a bite to eat. You knew it was lunchtime not by the smell of the food, but by the smell of the horsemen.

Both Shirley and Lisa are diner people. As Shirley says, they're not sitters, like people who work in offices, they're diner people, they need to be moving around. The customers, especially the regulars, are happy they're both there. They know that the Goshen Plaza Diner offers personalized service, just like a home away from home. Lisa and Shirley know what's going on in the lives of their regulars, and this, along with their homemade fare keeps the customers loyal to their diner. At breakfast, many people use the diner as a place to hold business meetings. At night, these same people can be seen eating with their families.

# CUP & SAUCER DINER

### 2001 PARAMOUNT

82 Boniface Dr. at Teds Dr., Pine Bush • (845) 744-5969

Pine Bush had been without a diner since 1989. In the next decade, the town's population increased by 25 percent. Dino Mavros knew that Pine Bush was ready for another diner. He bought a diner from Paramount and had it built across the street from a hotel and near some condos. Other businesses have since opened around the diner, obscuring its location from nearby Route 52.

The name Cup & Saucer Diner has dual meanings. The Pine Bush area is said to be second only to Roswell, New Mexico, in UFO sightings, the last on July 4, 1999. This reputation helped Dino come up with the motto for the diner, "food that's out of this world."

The day before the official grand opening in early 2001, Dino had a catered "blessing" party. In attendance were local dignitaries, the press, staff, friends, and family. The local Greek Orthodox priest, Father Steven, blessed the diner with fresh basil dipped in water, which he gently sprinkled over the entire party. Dino said, "I want to start the business in the right way, with a blessing."

Dino came to the United States from Chios Island in Greece, the same island that claims the poet Homer as its most famous son. Dino has been in the food business a good many years. He owned the Middletown Forum Diner at one time. Today he also owns the Yankee Clipper Diner in Beacon

Blessing at the Cup & Saucer Diner in Pine Bush.

and runs the Dino Mavros Company, a wholesale distributor of Greek and Italian foods.

The diner's interior is brightened by colorful recessed lighting and just as colorful plates and dishes. The goal at the Cup & Saucer is to provide a delightful and cheery atmosphere. Dino's son Steve and his wife Laura work at the diner, making sure everything is going smoothly. So far, the diner has been a successful addition to Pine Bush.

# DINER DIRECTORY

## BLOOMINGBURG

**Quickway Diner**
68 Rt. 17K
(845) 733-1012
*O'Mahony*

## DOWNSVILLE

**Downsville Diner**
18 Main St. (Rt. 206)
(607) 363-7678
*Kullman*

## ELLENVILLE

**209 Diner**
Rt. 209
(845) 210-1322
*1952 Silk City #5216*

## GOSHEN

**Goshen Plaza Diner**
Route 207 Goshen Plaza
(845) 294-7800
*1985 Paramount*

## GRAND GORGE

**Crossroads Diner**
Jct. of NY Rts. 30 and 23
(607) 588-8960
*1955 Fodero*
Closed.

## GREENWOOD LAKE

**Ashley's Pizzeria & Cafe**
75 Windemere Ave.
(845) 477-7118
*1940s Mountain View*

## HAINES FALLS

**Selena's Diner**
Rt. 23A
(518) 589-0438
*1959 Kullman*

## HANCOCK

**Circle E Diner**
97 E. Front St.
(607) 637-9905
*1985 DeRaffele*

## KERHONKSON

**Rainbow Diner**
6132 Rt. 209
(845) 626-4635
*1950s, remodeled.*

## LIBERTY

**Liberty Diner**
30 Sullivan Ave.
(845) 292-8973

**Munson Diner**
18 Lake St.
(845) 292-1144
*Late 1940s, Kullman*
Moved from Manhattan in 2005.

## LIVINGSTON MANOR

**Robin Hood Diner**
Old Rt. 17
(845) 434-9830
*1955 Silk City #5541*
Remodeled. Attached to a tavern.

## LOCH SHELDRAKE

**Hollywood Diner**
Rt. 52
*Kullman*
Closed.

## MIDDLETOWN

**Americana Diner**
420 Rt. 211
(845 ) 344-6060
Environmental.

**Colonial Diner**
8 Dolson Ave.
(845) 342-3500
*Manno*
Remodeled.

**Johnny D's Diner**
229 Rt. 211E
Closed.

## MONROE

**Monroe Diner**
1797 Rt. 17M
(845) 783-8916

## MONTICELLO

**Blue Horizon Diner**
Rt. 42N
(845) 796-2210
*1987 DeRaffele*

**Gager's Diner**
345 Broadway
*1950s Manno*
Remodeled. Closed.

**Miss Monticello Diner**
199 Broadway
(845) 791-8934
*1936 Silk City*
Remodeled by Manno 1972.

**Tilly's Diner**
5 Raceway Rd.
(845) 791-9849
*1940 O'Mahony*

## PARKSVILLE

**Sullivan Diner**
Rt. 17
*Circa 1948 Paramount*
Remodeled. Closed.

## PHOENICIA

**Diner**
Old Main St.
*Silk City*
Closed.

**Phoenicia Diner**
Rt. 28
(845) 688-9957
*Possibly a 1960s Fodero*

## PINE BUSH

**Cup & Saucer Diner**
82 Boniface Dr. (at Teds Dr.)
(845) 744-5969
*2001 Paramount*

## PLATT CLOVE

**Lin's Wood Shop**
Greene Co., Rt. 16
*O'Mahony or Mountain View*
Closed.

## PORT JERVIS

**Port Jervis Diner**
41 E. Main St.
(845) 856-7978
*Silk City*
Remodeled.

## ROSCOE

**Roscoe Diner**
Old Rt. 17
(607) 498-4405
*DeRaffele*
Several remodels.

## WALTON

**Papa's Family Diner**
209 Delaware St.
(607) 865-8050
*1992 Paramount*

## WESTBROOKVILLE

**Riviera or Fort Westbrookville Diner**
Rt. 209
*Master*
Closed.

## WURTSBORO

**Royal Diner**
Old Rt. 17
*Silk City/Erfed*
Closed.

# CENTRAL
# LEATHERSTOCKING

New York's Central Leatherstocking region is centered on the Mohawk Valley, west of the Capital District and between the Catskill and Adirondack Mountains. Its name refers to the Leatherstocking Tales, a series of novels about the New York frontier written in the early nineteenth century by James Fenimore Cooper. The main character in the books is known as Leatherstocking because he wore leather leggings like the local Iroquois Indians. This area was sparsely populated until the Erie Canal was completed in 1825. Villages such as Syracuse and Utica became industrial centers that grew even larger with the arrival of the railroad. Although the canal's importance faded in the twentieth century, its imprint on the region is still evident. The Erie Canal predetermined the location of population centers that eventually attracted many of the region's diners. Forty-four percent of operating diners are within two miles of the canal. Sixty-six percent of the diners are within a mile of the interstate highways that followed the path pioneered by the canal.

A few lunch wagons popped up in these cities before the turn of the twentieth century. Ned Kornblite had the Horseshoe Lunch in Binghamton, and Charles Clark and F. W. Steinbeck had wagons on the village square in Watertown. T. H. Buckley summered in Ogdensburg around the turn of the century. Buckley was good friends with an Ogdensburg minister. More than a few Adirondack villages had a White House Cafe. Buckley leased out White House Cafes in places like Carthage, Syracuse, Utica, Cortland, and Plattsburg, to name a few. Ephraim Hamel of Lynn, Massachusetts, also sent wagons to the region. In 1894, an Oswego newspaper announced that he had two wagons in Auburn, and was placing one in Oswego. Asa Fisk of Plattsburgh, who owned one of Hamel's Columbian Cafes, even invited Hamel to visit him in Plattsburgh. Cortland also had its own locally built lunch wagon. The Ellis Omnibus and Cab Company, which according to a *Carriage Monthly* magazine, built a lunch car in 1896. The first decade of the twentieth century seems to be the time when every village of any size got into the business. Busy villages like Gloversville started with a homemade wagon and the Queensboro Lunch known as "The Little Waldorf Astoria on Wheels," which was located right next to the Kingsborough Hotel. Even smaller vil-

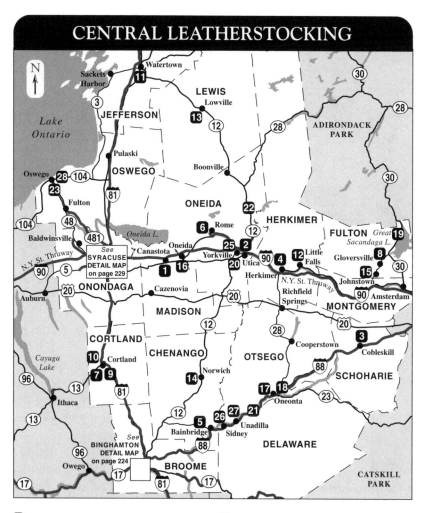

# CENTRAL LEATHERSTOCKING

N ↑

Watertown

Sackets Harbor ❶❶

LEWIS
Lowville

③

Lake Ontario

JEFFERSON

❶❸

⑫

㉘

ADIRONDACK PARK

Pulaski

Boonville

Oswego ㉘ ⑩④

OSWEGO

⑧①

Fulton

ONEIDA

㉒

HERKIMER

FULTON *Great Sacandaga L.* ❶❾

⑩④

㊽

Baldwinsville

Rome ⑫

㊷❶

*Oneida L.*

See SYRACUSE DETAIL MAP on page 229

Oneida

Canastota

㉕❷

Yorkville

Little Falls ❶❷

Gloversville ❽

⑨⓪④

㉙

Utica

Herkimer ❶❻

❷⓪

Johnstown ❶❺ ㉚

N.Y. St. Thruway

ONONDAGA

⑨⓪ ⑤

Cazenovia

Richfield Springs

Amsterdam ⑨⓪

Auburn ❷⓪

⑳

MONTGOMERY

❷⓪

MADISON

⑫

㉘

CORTLAND

Cooperstown

❸

Cobleskill

*Cayuga Lake*

❶⓪

Cortland

CHENANGO

OTSEGO

SCHOHARIE

㊶

❾

❼

Norwich ❶❹

⑧⑧

㊈❻

❶❸

⑧①

Ithaca

Oneonta ❷❸

❶❼❶❽

⑫

❺ ㉖㉗㉑

Unadilla

See BINGHAMTON DETAIL MAP on page 224

�96

Owego

❶❼

BROOME

⑧①

❶❼

Bainbridge Sidney ⑧⑧

DELAWARE

CATSKILL PARK

❶❼

N.Y. St. Thruway

**❶** Anne Marie's Family Diner: Canastota (MS)
**❷** Betty's Diner: Marcy (MS)
**❸** Colonial Diner: Cobleskill (E)
**❹** Crazy Otto's Empire Diner: Herkimer (MS)
**❺** Diner: West Bainbridge (BR)
**❻** Eddie's Paramount Diner: Rome (MS)
**❼** Frank & Mary's Diner: Cortland (R)
**❽** Gloversville Palace Diner: Gloversville (R)
**❾** Gracie Rachel's Diner: Cortland (EM)
**❿** Hyde's Diner: Cortland (R)
**⓫** Jen's Diner: Watertown (BR)
**⓬** Kristen's Café: Little Falls (R)
**⓭** Lloyds of Lowville: Lowville (BR)
**⓮** Millie's Diner: Norwich (BR)
**⓯** Miss Johnstown Diner: Johnstown (R)

**⓰** Morey's Diner: Oneida (BR)
**⓱** Nick's Diner: Oneonta (R)
**⓲** Neptune Diner: Oneonta (P)
**⓳** Northampton Diner: Northampton (R)
**⓴** Raspberry's Café & Creamery: New Hartford (E)
**㉑** Red Bear Café: Otego (E)
**㉒** Remsen Grill: Remsen (R)
**㉓** Ritz Diner: Oswego (R)
**㉔** Route 8 Diner: New Berlin (MS)
**㉕** Sophie's Chuckwagon (Bev's Place): Whitesboro (R)
**㉖** Trackside Dining: Sidney (R)
**㉗** Unadilla Diner: Unadilla (MS)
**㉘** Wade's Diner: Oswego (R)

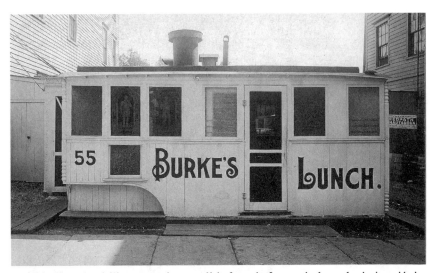

The White House Lunch Wagon started out on Main Street in Oneonta in front of a business block. When it was known as Burke's it was moved to a side street.

lages like Sidney (population 4,000) and Oxford (population 1,000) had lunch wagons somewhere in their main business district.

Norwich, on the old Chenango Canal, had three wagons, two in view of the park in the middle of the business district and one at the Ontario and Western Railroad (O&W) station about a quarter of a mile east. At a time when there were only 2,200 automobiles in America, almost every village of any size had a railroad station and quite often a lunch wagon.

By the mid 1920s, central New York saw an increase in diners thanks in part to the western New York diner builders of the time. The Mulholland Company constructed the Eat Shoppe in Oneonta and the Oneida Diner in Syracuse. Ward & Dickinson built diners for the Jack & Andy Diner chain in Utica, Dan's DeLuxe Diner in Cortland, and Robert Fulton's diner in Johnson City (which originally operated in Schenectady). Besides the titans, New Jersey–based O'Mahony and Tierney in New Rochelle, Ward & Dickinson supplied many of the diners in the region. If you were traveling in places like Fayetteville, Watertown, Pulaski, Malone, and Binghamton in the 1930s, you would have seen Ward dining cars.

Small diner chains, like Jack & Andy, were significant in the placement of diners in the central New York region. Two chains from New Jersey were perhaps the biggest players. The Bradley chain placed two cars in Oneonta, and was once reported to be placing a diner a month in places between New Jersey and Oneonta. A gentleman by the name of Harvey Bradley, perhaps related to the chain, ran two diners in Binghamton and Johnson City

# LUNCH LADIES

Lunch wagons were created to serve men who worked any shift of the day or night, or the businessman. They were never intended for the "fairer sex." So to find women running lunch wagons at the turn of the twentieth century was unusual. The *Plattsburgh Sentinel* picked up on the following story, noting a decided improvement in patronage, and declared these wagons, "all right."

Aug 27, 1901
*Oswego Daily Palladium*

Running a lunch wagon is a plan that some Syracuse women have adopted as a means of gaining a livelihood. Three are now in the business and all report plenty of patronage. The average number of customers for each from nine in the evening until seven in the morning is 200, and often 800 are served with coffee, pie and sandwiches. "What made me think of going into the business" said the proprietor of one of them the other night in reply to a Herald reporter, "Merely the fact that I knew it was paying other people fairly well and thought that I might be as lucky as they were. And I really have done better than I expected. The expense of a lunch wagon isn't very heavy and you don't not get returns from the money you put into it. I had to borrow money to start with, but I had it paid off and a little nest egg into the bargain at the end of six months. I never had any doubt that I would get on all right, so probably that's why I did."

HANOVER HISTORICAL CENTER

Bradley's Diner in Syracuse was a highly popular Ward & Dickinson diner. Ward & Dickinson made similar looking diners. This was their forty-foot model.

for a few years. The National Dining Company out of Bayonne, New Jersey, focused more on the Mohawk Valley. They had over twenty diners in locations like Little Falls, Herkimer, Utica, Rome, and Syracuse. In Syracuse, they had options on four more diners, but never acted on them. Another smaller chain was the Genesee Grill, which included two Bixlers and one Rochester Grills, two in Utica and one in Syracuse. Another chain, located solely in Syracuse was started by A. E. Cameron. The chain had at least five diners at its peak and lasted into the 1980s. One Bixler still remains from the chain, and is now known as Serpico's. The company was also known to have used at least one diner from Ward & Dickinson and Mulholland.

The National Dining Company did not use one standard brand of diners, though the majority were probably O'Mahonys. In the late 1930s, they replaced their Herkimer diner with a Sterling, built by J. B. Judkins of Merrimac, Massachusetts. Not since the early times of the lunch wagon was a New England–based company able to get diners into central New York. Judkins had a sales representative in Rochester, A. Tomborelli, who was able to place more than a few diners in central and western New York. Tomborelli was no stranger to this type of diner, as he had been a sales representative for Bixler a few years earlier. Bixler's shop foreman J. H. Shale was hired by Rochester Grills when Bixler closed shop.

Utica, Johnson City, Cortland, and Syracuse received Sterling diners. Some replaced older diners. Brassell's Diner replaced an early 1920s O'Ma-

Lloyds of Lowville has been in Lowville for a long time. It is a destination for locals and travelers alike. Its make is unknown.

BROOME COUNTY HISTORICAL SOCIETY

This Sterling diner was known as Sitar's Diner in 1949. It was located in downtown Johnson City before being moved outside of town.

hony called the Wilcroft Lunch in Utica. Danny's Diner in Binghamton actually did time at another location in Binghamton before replacing an older diner at its current location. Danny's was originally known as the A & L Sterling Diner, located on Front Street. An opening-day advertisement stated, "The comfortable seating capacity offers ample room and the instant service will appeal to the busy business people who have limited time for meals. This courteous and quick service is given on quick lunches, casual full-course dinners and after theater or dance snacks."

Another Sterling diner sat in the American Diner Museum's storage facility in Fall River, Massachusetts, for a few years. The Liberty Diner from Syracuse was saved in 2000. Built in 1938, it had done business in three different Syracuse locations. Frequent customer Kathy Stribley helped to save the historic landmark from demolition. Volunteers from the community and the museum came out in droves to help take the diner apart and it was moved away in pieces. Today, the diner is being restored by Tom Mertl in Mountain View, California.

Both Rochester Grills and the General Diner Co. began building sectional diners during the late 1930s. In 1939, Morris Whitehouse and Arthur Halladay formed General Diners. They built two diners in Watertown and decided on Oswego as a permanent location for their company in 1940. General Diners were very inexpensive, selling for $5,500 and up in 1940. After moving to Syracuse, the company closed in 1942. General sent diners

The Tinker Tavern Diner in Pulaski collapsed a few years ago after being closed for many years.

to Cortland, Utica, and at least two to Syracuse. They also sent the last new diners to the towns of Malone and Canton on the edge of the Adirondacks. Today, Jen's Diner in Watertown may be the last General Diner in existence, as well as the last diner in Watertown. With Jen's closed, and the recent demolition of a Rochester Grill known as the Victory Diner, Watertown may soon be without a diner.

Two Rochester Grills still remain in central New York. The JR Diner, now on Wolf Road in Syracuse, was formerly known as Griffeth's Swanky Diner and originally sat on East Fayette Street. It is open for breakfast and lunch and serves up delicious daily specials. The Broadway Diner in Endicott started in Johnson City, and today feels more like a restaurant, as the diner is encased in a larger building with an attached dining room. Norwich and Sidney both had Rochester Grills. Today, only a shell of the former Reed's Diner in Sidney exists. In 2004, the counter that had been brought back again after the diner served time as Dave's Hair Den, was removed. The Norwich diner was best known as Scarcella's. The Scarcella family replaced this diner with a late-model Silk City that was located outside of town. This diner was moved to Morrisville, and demolished in 2004.

Amazingly, with all the diners that were located in the city of Utica at one time, there is not one single diner to be found within the city limits now. Utica is not the only place in the region where diners have disappeared. Much has to do with an economic downturn which began in the 1960s, when many jobs were sent to the south to take advantage of cheaper labor.

Since the 1950s, when New Jersey builders were the only option, other diner builders have not made much of a dent in the region. Only Binghamton saw a mini boom in diners in the 1950s. Lewis Greene became a Mountain View sales representative and brought at least four diners to the southern tier, including a diner for himself and his wife Pearl known as the Red Robin. Today, that diner is located in downtown Johnson City. Vestal received a O'Mahony known as the Skylark, and a Kullman was moved from Elmira to the Vestal Highway. The Kullman, first known as the Village Chef, escaped demolition in 2002, only to be removed to New Hampshire. The Skylark, though, is open twenty-four hours, and is a favorite hangout for the late-night crowd, though it's a rare time of day when the diner is not busy.

A few more stainless-steel diners did find their way into the region. Unadilla is home to the only Master Diner in Central Leatherstocking. The diner was added to a homemade diner that resembled a Sterling Streamliner, and thrived in the days before I-88 was built. Unadilla is a small village located on Route 7, the main road between Binghamton and Albany. In Herkimer, another diner can be found on a state road that was once heavily traveled. Herkimer is bigger than Unadilla, and Route 5 serves as a much bigger commercial strip. The Empire Diner has survived a fire and two moves. This Mountain View was open twenty-four hours ten years ago. Since then, Herkimer has become saturated with generic chains. A new owner attempted

The Blue Beacon sat on the east side of Binghamton before being replaced by an on-site restaurant in 1984.

to bring this great-looking diner back to the forefront of Herkimer's culinary choices, but it closed up shop in the summer of 2006. It reopened in 2007 as Crazy Otto's Empire Diner.

Perhaps the most well known stainless-steel diner of the region is Doc's Little Gem Diner. This 1958 Fodero replaced an older diner at a different site for former owner Henry McCall. Francis "Doc" Good lamented the changing of the smoking laws in New York in 2003, but fortunately, the citizens of Syracuse still fill the seats in this diner. A minor fire in 2007 closed the diner for a few months. Doc's has since reopened, although is no longer open 24/7.

During the 1960s, the Skyliner Diner in downtown Cortland was moved south of town and joined with what may have been the last Silk City diner ever built. The diner complex was known as the Suburban Skyliner, with one diner being used as more of a gift shop than an actual diner. Unfortunately, the diners were consumed in a mysterious fire in 2005. Fire also destroyed a Sterling diner, which came to Cortland from Ithaca. While in Ithaca it was part of a short-lived chain of three diners known as the R&S before it moved onto U.S. Route 11. The diner was located halfway between Homer and Cortland. Here, it went by the name Midway and later the Riverside Diner before it closed in 1990. There are two diners left in Cortland today, both extremely remodeled. Hyde's Diner may be a Ward & Dickinson and Frank & Mary's Diner may be a General diner.

Like the Riverside Diner, the Remsen Grill in Remsen is mentioned in Will Anderson's book *Lost Diners and Roadside Restaurants of New England and New York*. The diner was originally Ted's Diner in North Utica, which replaced an older Ward & Dickinson at that location. In North Utica, Ted's

The Suburban Skyliner just south of Cortland was two similar Silk City diners placed together. One diner started in downtown Cortland while the other was a gift from the company.

Today, the former Ruth's Diner in Remsen looks nothing like it does in this picture.

was set up to catch travelers coming into Utica from every direction but south, as east–west Route 5 was aligned just north of the diner. In 1959, Ted Camesano sold Ted's and the new owner moved the diner into the foothills of the Adirondacks, onto a four-lane highway that went from the western Adirondacks over to Watertown. First known as Ruth's Diner in Remsen, this Fodero also went by the name of the OK Corral before changing to its current name in 2005.

The Route 8 Diner is a Kullman that sits just north of New Berlin. In the 1970s, this blue vertical-fluted diner was moved from the southside of Oneonta, where it may have been known as the 3-D Diner. During the last five years it has had multiple owners, and it is now closed and again for sale. The diner's interior is yellow with light blue tiles on the floor and counter base, with the original booths still extant.

Around 1960, Kullman manufactured the Midway II Diner, south of Cortland. Close to where the Suburban Skyliners once did business, this boxy diner, now known as Gracie Rachel's Diner, has large windows above small, blue tiles and circles similar to the burnished once found on some Paramount diners. Inside, the diner has six booths, and ten to fifteen stools.

Central Leatherstocking has only five environmental diners. Cobleskill's first diner is a mirror-finished DeRaffele, seemingly with no name, that sits in front of a motel. At one time it was known as the Mountain View Diner, but today the sign is gone. New Hartford, a suburb of Utica, is home to Raspberry's Café and Creamery, a popular Swingle diner formerly called the Hartford Queen. Binghamton is definitely a diner city, and even though Danny's Diner is the last of the classic diners left in the city, there are two environmental diners, The Red Oak and The Spot, operating on Route 11.

The Midway near Cortland is a unique looking Kullman diner, built during the period when stainless steel was being phased out as a popular choice for a diner's exterior.

The Red Oak is in a more urban setting and The Spot, a twenty-four-hour diner is closer to Broome County Community College. The former I-88 Diner in Otego was once the popular Neptune Diner on the south side of Oneonta. The diner was so popular that the owners were able to buy a new diner just sixteen years after opening the first. The diner originally had wooden shingles on the mansard roof, but they have been replaced by shiny red panels.

The current Neptune Diner in Oneonta is a central New York rarity. It is the only postmodern diner in the region, and the westernmost postmodern diner in New York State. Kullman built this diner in 2000, and it features a horseshoe counter/bar and a large fish tank that separates the main dining room from a conference room. While the prices are higher than a typical diner in the region, it still outdraws the neighboring Denny's each night, and both places are open twenty-four hours.

# DINER DRIVES

### ONEONTA–BINGHAMTON–VESTAL

This diner drive starts in Oneonta, the City of the Hills, and ends outside of Binghamton. Much of it follows Route 7, the main road between Binghamton and Schenectady/Albany. West from Oneonta, Route 7 follows the Susquehanna River valley, passing through small villages before heading over hills outside of Harpursville. In Port Crane, the highway meets the Chenango River, which flows into the Susquehanna in downtown Binghamton. Here, our drive leaves Route 7 and takes Route 17C, which was the road to the factory towns of Johnson City and Endicott, named after the Endicott Johnson Company, a shoe and leather manufacturer. The trip ends in suburban Vestal, on Route 434 (old Route 17) that once connected the Southern Tier communities of Binghamton, Elmira, and beyond.

The Neptune Diner is on Oneonta's south side commercial strip along Route 23. The 2000 Kullman is open twenty-four hours a day and sports a great neon sign that welcomes visitors at night. Route 7 passes through downtown Oneonta, where two diners once did business, and continues into the west end of town, where Nick's Diner sits across from the former Wagars ice cream plant. This barrel-roof diner has been remodeled with an addition at one end. Nick's is open for breakfast and lunch and served locals and travelers in its setting until I-88 took away many passing long-distance travelers.

Speaking of I-88, the former Neptune Diner sits just off of exit 12 near Otego. This 1984 environmental diner once had a wood shingled mansard roof but has gone through a succession of owners since being moved to its current site from the south side of Oneonta. In 2005, Randy Garbin of *Roadside* magazine reported that this diner was going to be moved to Owego, west of Binghamton. This never materialized, and instead, the diner was reopened under the name Red Bear Cafe. The Red Bear has since closed, and the building is again vacant.

Taking exit 11 off I-88, get back onto Route 7 and into Unadilla, home of the Unadilla Diner, a 1955 Master. Unfortunately, the diner has been

The Neptune Diner in Oneonta replaced an environmental diner. The diner features a large fish tank in the wall and a horseshoe counter.

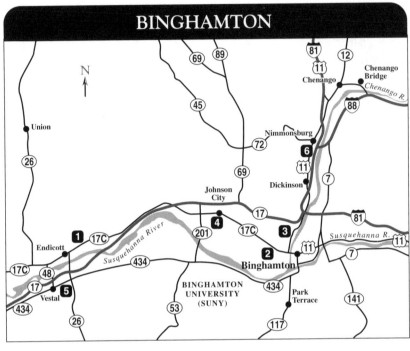

# BINGHAMTON

1 Broadway Diner: Endicott (BR)
2 Danny's Diner: Binghamton (BR)
3 Red Oak Restaurant: Binghamton (E)

4 Red Robin Diner: Johnson City (MS)
5 Skylark Diner: Vestal (R)
6 Spot Restaurant: Binghamton (E)

closed more than it has been open in the past six years. Linda Corter, one of the last owners, did a good job of serving good food, but was not able to make a go of it in this tiny, quaint community.

Take I-88 to exit 2 and follow Route 12A, turn south on 12A and join U.S. Route 11 south. Travel about one mile on Route 11S to get to the Spot Diner/Restaurant, a 1970s Kullman Mediterranean diner. Continue south on U.S. Route 11 2.7 miles into the residential outskirts of Binghamton and the environmental Red Oak Restaurant, a 1971 Swingle, appears on the right. Follow U.S. Route 11 south and turn right onto Route 17C, also known as Main Street, to get to Danny's Diner (less than a mile). At this Sterling diner the food is cooked right in front of you on the grill. The Red Robin is a mile and a half farther west on Route 17C (Main Street) in Johnson City, where it has operated since it was moved from Binghamton in 1958. Widely recognized as the subject of a painting by John Baeder, the Red Robin has a unique interior arrangement. When a customer sits at the counter, they are actually facing the road out front.

The Spot, as it is affectionately known as, is a classic environmental diner in Binghamton. Built by Kullman, it shows how each company made similar looking environmental diners.

Continue west on Route 17C to Route 33 (Hooper Road). Turn right, then make a left on Watson Boulevard. You'll come to the Broadway Diner in Endwell, a Rochester Grills that began business as the B & E Diner in Johnson City. Remodeling and an addition make this building unrecognizable as a factory-built diner from the outside.

Continue on Watson Boulevard and take a left on McKinley Avenue (Route 26). Cross the Susquehanna River and get off on the Vestal Parkway (Route 434). Go west on the parkway, and you will reach the final diner on this tour, the Skylark Diner in Vestal. Situated in front of a hotel of the same name, this 1956 O'Mahony is open twenty-four hours a day. The diner lost its stainless steel in a remodeling and has colonial décor inside.

## MOHAWK VALLEY

This drive meanders through the Mohawk Valley from the shores of Great Sacandaga Lake through Utica and Rome to Syracuse, mostly following Route 5. Start in Northville, once the site of a popular amusement park that operated on the lake at the end of a trolley line. The Alhambra Restaurant called Northville home before it was torn down in the 1970s, but the Northampton Diner is still in business about four miles south on Route 30 in Northampton. From the outside, it looks nothing like a diner, but once you get inside, you'll see a 1938 O'Mahony in excellent shape. Originally in Glens Falls, the diner was moved sometime in the 1960s and sat idle for ten years. It is now run by the Morehouse family.

South of Mayfield Route 30A splits off Route 30 and connects the old leather towns of Gloversville, and Johnstown. Mayfield was once home to a trolley diner. The city of Gloversville has seen better days, as you can tell by the gorgeous homes and the ornate but shuttered buildings of its downtown. A 1924 O'Mahony, the Gloversville Palace Diner, sits at the southern end of the business district on South Main Street. Take Route 29A (Fulton Street) west off Route 30A. It has a brick front, but a patron seated at the counter will still be surrounded by the ambiance of the 1920s. Even more amazing than the age of this diner, is the fact that it has only had two owners, the current one being Tony Sena, who makes sure that everyone who enters is warmly welcomed.

Four miles south, the Miss Johnstown Diner, on East Main Street in Johnstown, is the first place I ever saw hot gravy poured over macaroni salad. It turns out that this is a local tradition. This Ward & Dickinson diner had its front wall removed to add tables, causing it to be barely recognizable as one of theirs. Typical of diners that still have their wheels visible in the basement, it often gets misidentified as a trolley car.

Turning west on Route 67, the drive winds through Amish Country and rejoins Route 5 near St. Johnsville, once home to a classic stainless-steel diner that was the Empire and then Swank's, named after the last owner, DeForest Swank. Go west on Route 5 to Little Falls, our next destination. The site of the first lock on the Mohawk River was once home to two 1920s diners, but today only one exists. The current diner, Kristen's Cafe, is an

Crazy Otto's Empire Diner is a great looking Mountain View diner. This is the third location for Empire in Herkimer.

O'Mahony with original stools and not much else. The gem of this trip is eight miles west in our next town.

Well known for its nearby diamond mines, Herkimer is home to Crazy Otto's Empire Diner, which sits facing the main thoroughfare at the end of the old main street. At night, its classic neon sign is a photographer's dream. In fact, it was featured in photographer Robert O. Williams's book *Hometown Diners*.

After following Route 5 through the north side of Utica, merge onto Route 49, which becomes River Road. This was once the main artery to Rome before the bypass was built in 2004. Along the road, Betty's Diner, a classic Silk City Diner in Marcy, seems to be holding on well with apparently dedicated patrons. The diner started out in Frankfort and moved to Utica's north side for a few years before moving to its current location.

Continuing west on River Road and turn left on Route 291, then left on Route 69, you come to Bev's Place in Whitesboro. This was the 125th Silk City diner, built in 1945. Bev's proclaims that the diner serves "all old fashioned cooking, just like grandma's." The diner itself originally sat on South Street in Utica and was called Smiley's Diner. Today the diner has been remodeled on the inside with black and white checkerboard flooring.

From Bev's, travel to Rome via Route 69. Rome was once home to four diners, including a lunch wagon that stayed unaltered into the 1960s. Eddie's Paramount Diner is located at 414 West Dominick Street in downtown Rome. The 1941 O'Mahony is very much original on the inside.

Drive west fifteen miles on Route 365 past Turning Stone, and head into downtown Oneida. Only one of the three original diners in Oneida exist today. This Ward & Dickinson was only days away from ending up in the scrap heap before former cop Lynn Morey stepped in. He spent five years restoring the diner, taking layer upon layer of paint off on the inside. Above the counter, Ward & Dickinson's slogan—"they're built to last"—is etched in wood. Open only for breakfast, Morey's Diner sits almost hidden off Main Street (Route 46) on Phelps Street, near the restored Kallet Theater (now the Kallet Civic Center).

Route 5 goes west to Canastota, home of the International Boxing Hall of Fame. For visitors, Anne Marie's Family Diner is a little tough to find. It is at 517 North Main Street, one block west of the main road through town. This late-model Silk City came from North Syracuse where it was known as the Pelican Diner. Ann Marie's Family Diner hopes to resurrect the popularity that this diner had in the 1990s when it first moved to town. Bill Younis, whose family has been involved in many central New York diners brought this diner to Canastota and named it the Canastota Dinerant.

Originally the Pelican Diner in North Syracuse, Bill Younis had it moved to Canastota.

From here, Route 5 continues about fifteen miles westward into Syracuse, passing the eastern suburbs of Fayetteville and DeWitt. Go north on Route 257 (North Manlius Street) in Fayetteville for about two miles and turn right on Manlius Center Road (Route 290). Go about three and a half miles and then turn right on Bridge Street (still Route 290). Turn left on East Manlius Street (East Syracuse) to reach the Redwood Diner at 121. The Redwood is a remodeled Ward & Dickinson that still shows some of its original details.

Continue on Manlius Street, which joins James Street as it heads into Syracuse. Just like Erie Boulevard, which parallels it to the south, this street once had many diners. Anne Marie's Diner may have once called James Street home, as well as the former Tinker Tavern Diner.

Turn right on Grant Boulevard from James Street and follow it to Wolf Street (Route 11). Take a right onto Wolf and Serpico's Diner will be on your left at 913. This Bixler is a former Cameron's of Syracuse Diner and was then Stella's, which moved into a built-on-site restaurant closer to the nearby mall. Serpico's and JR Diner, which is located at 1208 Wolf Street, are both sectional-built diners. The JR Diner, a remodeled Rochester Grills, started out as Griffeth's Swanky Diner. This Greek-owned diner has fresh food and is probably best known for its lunch specials.

Heading back downtown on Route 11, pass under the interstate and take a right onto East Water Street to find the Miss Syracuse Diner. The first owners of the diner were Stephen and Anna Petrunick, who ran the diner for about forty years. Then Ralph De Priore ran the diner for five years. In 2000, Charlie Roman saved the diner from being demolished and turned into a parking lot. Along with his partner Brian Casey, he had the diner restored and reopened. At this writing, the diner is closed and for rent.

Continue west and take a right onto North Clinton Street and a left on West Genesee Street (Route 5). After a mile, turn right on North Geddes Street, drive under the interstate, and take a left on Spencer Street to get to Doc's Little Gem at 832 Spencer. A Syracuse institution, Doc's is like stepping back in time to 1957. Fortunately for fans of diners, this is just before the time when diners were starting to lose their stainless steel. When Mario

1 Doc's Little Gem Diner (MS)
2 JR Diner (R)
3 Miss Syracuse Diner (BR)
4 Redwood Diner: East Syracuse (R)

5 Serpico's Diner (BR)
6 West Side Diner (R)
7 Valley Diner (R)

Doc's Little Gem is a popular destination in Syracuse.

Biasi bought the diner in 1982 there was a foot of water in the basement. He quickly did some remodeling, being careful to leave the original facade intact, along with the faded and worn countertop. Doc Good bought the diner from Mario in October 1997 and has owned it since. In 2001, he was chosen Restaurateur of the Year by the Central New York Chapter of the New York State Restaurant Association.

# EDDIE'S PARAMOUNT DINER
## 1940 O'MAHONY
414 West Dominick St., Rome • (315) 336-9581

Rome once had five diners, and at least four were O'Mahonys. Eddie's Paramount is the only one left today. Charles Ottaway bought the terra cotta O'Mahony in 1940. At this time, diners were only about a year away from being predominantly clad in stainless steel. This historic nugget offers an opportunity to study the progression of O'Mahony dining cars from 1938 to 1941 by comparing the interior stylings of the Northampton Diner (1938) with Eddie's Paramount (1941). Note that both diners have transom windows in their monitor ceilings. This is a style that many diner manufacturers had already lost, and O'Mahony was about to move on to newer styles. The Miss Rome, which opened on June 2, 1940, featured only four transom windows on its exterior.

The next comparison is the ceilings. The Northampton Diner has a painted metal ceiling with storage room in the ceiling at each end of the diner, finished in wood. Eddie's has a ceiling covered with Formica, with rolling curves at each end of the ceiling. By 1940s, Formica was taking its place as a predominant feature in diners.

Both backbars have stainless steel on the walls, but the menu board at Eddie's consists of stainless-steel trim, while the Northampton is predominantly constructed with wood.

The interior at Eddie's Paramount Diner in Rome shows an original 1941 O'Mahony.

The Long family has run Eddie's since 1968. The diner's few previous ownership changes came with interesting circumstances, including one owner who lost the diner in a poker game. The current owner, Edward Long Sr. made the deal to purchase the diner one night in a bar. All he had with him was $500 and one of his friends.

Everyone in the Long family has worked in the diner at one time or another. Son Edward Jr., who has been working at the diner twenty-four years, started working at age thirteen. Today, he still works in the kitchen. At Eddie's Paramount, it seems to be the norm to have an employee with more than twenty years under their belt.

With their daily specials, locals know what to expect each day. For example, on Thursday, the Longs cook seventy pounds of roast beef in their kitchen. And it wouldn't be a family run diner without homemade pies, and these keep the locals coming.

# GLOVERSVILLE PALACE DINER
### 1923 O'MAHONY
62 S. Main St., Gloversville • (518) 725-9056

Often, diners that last only twenty or thirty years have had more than ten owners. The Palace Diner has been in business for eighty-four years with only two owners. Al Main and Carlton Clute bought the O'Mahony lunch car in 1923 for $4,000. Main left the partnership to run the Miss Gloversville Diner, leaving Carlton to run the Palace, which he did for the next fifty years. Around 1944, Carlton hired twelve-year-old Tony Sena. Sixty-four years later, he owns the place, having bought it in 1973.

Tony is not the only person who has been coming to the Palace for sixty years. Come in any morning and you can find customers who have been patronizing the diner for just as long. And for even longer than that, the meat has been coming from Bowman's Meat Market, whose owner is also a regular breakfast customer of the diner.

This 1923 O'Mahony originally had a row of stools along the counter, and along its front wall. In the 1930s the front wall was removed, and the diner was expanded to allow room for a few tables. The original tile floor is still there in the diner part, showing the exact location of the original door. In the 1950s, new equipment was added to the diner, and in the 1990s, the current enclosed porch was added. But, if you sit at the counter today, you can still get a real feel for what it must have felt like to be in one of these

Although the diner has been expanded, this view still evokes the feeling of a 1920s diner.

diners in the 1920s. Many people think of stainless steel and booths when they hear the word diner, but at the Palace patrons get to feel what diners were like before those elements became customary.

Something that has not changed is the food. Tony Sena Jr. now works the grill, and he knows his customers just as well as his parents did. But Tony Sr. still does much of the cooking in the back. He says that 99 percent of the food is homemade. On a typical day, you'll find him making soups from scratch, meatloaf, or possibly the diner's popular pasta fagioli. Perhaps this is why the Morehouses from the Northampton Diner stop into the Palace when they are in Gloversville.

Tony remembers a Monday in 1948 when Carlton raised the price of coffee from 5 to 10 cents. He says that the customers protested by going down the street to the B&L Diner for two weeks before they came back. Gloversville was home to six diners in the 1940s, but today, the Palace is the only one. With the population of Gloversville nearly cut in half since the heyday of the leather factories, the Palace still shines with its dedicated and stable ownership.

# NORTHAMPTON DINER

### 1938 O'MAHONY

1205 State Hwy. 30, Northampton • (518) 863-2567

The Northampton Diner proclaims itself as the "home of Sacandaga's most famous pancake," but it is so much more to its customers. Like any good family-run diner, the customers are more like family. Also, when you walk into the pristine 1938 O'Mahony, you are guaranteed to be waited on by a family member.

The diner started out in Glens Falls as the Miss Glens Falls Diner. The diner was moved to the Northville area in the 1950s and sat unopened for ten years. In 1965, Florence Wilson had the diner moved to its current location. Before the Morehouses bought the diner in 1988, it was known as the Dun Dozin Diner.

It all started when Harold Morehouse wanted to open an ice cream stand. Instead, he got a diner. Everyone he knew told him he would never make it in this diner, but he proved them wrong. At the beginning, Harold was still working at General Electric. This left it to daughter Darlene and her mother to run the diner. The diner proved so popular that Harold quit his job six months later and talked his daughter Chrissy into leaving hers. Today, Harold has retired from the diner, leaving his daughters, Chrissy Yorks and Darlene Smith in charge. At any time when the diner is open at

Roadside Fans creator Glenn Wells is shown inside this pristine 1938 O'Mahony.

least one of them are there, making sure the customers are happy and everything is running smoothly.

The Morehouses have been successful with good home-cooked food and good family help. Their only non-family employee, Angie, has been with then since 1988 and has become just like family. The diner is closed on Mondays. The diner is also only open for dinner on Thursday and Friday until 6:45. Haddock fish fries are served on Fridays. The chili is homemade, as are the salads, and strawberry shortcake, just to name some of the more popular items. But what about those pancakes? Everyone loves these pancakes, and every stack comes with a smiley face unless it's raining; then you just might get a frowning face.

# SKYLARK DINER
## 1956 O'MAHONY
248 Vestal Pkwy. E., Vestal • (607) 785-9795

Vestal's Skylark Diner celebrated its fiftieth year in 2006, all under the same family. What started with Orval and Gladys Stevens running other diners has turned into an institution. The Skylark is a classic twenty-four-hour roadside diner. All the desserts are homemade, and all the food is served quickly and at very affordable prices. Greg Stevens, their grandson and current manager of the Skylark, says that the cooks they have now are incredible, the best that he has seen. Three generations work at the diner and some employees have been there more than twenty years.

Orval Stevens started out as a salesman for H. J. Heinz. He called on area diners as part of his job and soon realized he wanted one of his own. He ran the Blue Beacon Diner for a year in 1954, changing the name to Steven's Junior Diner. Orville and Gladys bought a Sterling diner in Westover that was originally located in downtown Johnson City; it became known as Walter's Diner in honor of their son. A year later, with a partner, they bought a new diner and placed it in Vestal, then a small village on Route 17. Walter's Diner declined when the state widened the road in front of the diner. As business slowed, they moved their seasoned cook Harold

Fulmer to the larger and busier Skylark. Here is where he prepared the specials for both places. Walter's eventually closed around 1970.

Gladys loves the diner business. She lived in a house right behind Walter's Diner, and remembers her sons having their friends over, and calling down for their meals from the diner. Today, she still comes to the Skylark for dinner each weekday night. Besides the food, many of the customers come back for the 10 percent senior discount offered every day.

Greg has been running the Skylark since 2002, a job that he happened to fall into. He remembers having to stand on crates to do the dishes as a youngster, but he never envisioned himself staying in the business. In 2000, he returned from a job fair at the local mall, dressed in a shirt and tie, to have lunch at the diner. His father Walter said, "I have a job for you," adding, "I need some place to eat when I get old." Gradually, Greg took over more and more of the business. He started out with jobs like scheduling the help and took over the entire operation in 2002. Today, he says that he really enjoys his job. His duties change depending on what is needed, but he enjoys most of the customers who have become friends and part of an extended family. Sometimes, when there are only four of five parties in the diner, and everyone knows one another, it feels like being in someone's home kitchen.

The diner has seen a few changes over the years. Orval started running the diner from the beginning, buying out his partner shortly after opening up. In 1961, Gladys and Orval's son, Walter, opened up the Skylark Motel behind the diner and ran that with his wife until 1971 when they took over the diner. In 1961 they added the back dining room and removed the stainless steel which had tarnished. That room served as a bar until 1984, when they decided to go twenty-four hours and focus on the diner business.

# DINER DIRECTORY

## BINGHAMTON

**Danny's Diner**
151 Main St.
(607) 724-9873
*1939 Sterling #396*

**Red Oak Restaurant**
305 Upper Front St. (U.S. Rt. 11)
(607) 722-0440
*1971 Swingle*

**Spot Diner**
1062 Upper Front St. (U.S. Rt. 11)
(607) 723-8149
*1977 Kullman*

## CANASTOTA

**Anne Marie's Family Diner**
517 N. Main St.
(315) 697-8191
*1958 Silk City #5808.*
Originally the Canastota Dinerante.

## COBLESKILL

**Colonial Diner**
1009 E. Main St.
(518) 234-2808
*1980s DeRaffele*
Formerly the Mountain View Diner.

## CORTLAND

**Frank & Mary's Diner**
10 Port Watson St.
(607) 756-2014
*General Diners*
Remodeled.

**Gracie Rachel's Diner**
3821 U.S. Rt. 11
(607) 756-6088
*Kullman*
Formerly the Midway II Diner.

**Hyde's Diner**
157 Homer Ave.
(607) 753-8521
*Probably by Ward & Dickinson*
Remodeled.

## EAST SYRACUSE

**Redwood Diner**
121 E. Manlius St.
(315) 437-5790
*Ward & Dickinson*
Remodeled.

## ENDICOTT

**Broadway Diner**
3140 Watson Blvd.
(607) 658-1002
*Rochester Grills*
Remodeled. Formerly B & E Diner
in Johnson City.

## GLOVERSVILLE

**Gloversville Palace Diner**
62 S. Main St.
(518) 725-9056
*1923 O'Mahony*

## HERKIMER

**Crazy Otto's Empire Diner**
100 W. Albany St. (near the corner
of Rt. 5 and N. Washington Street)
(315) 866-8801
*1951 Mountain View*

## JOHNSON CITY

**Red Robin Diner**
268 Main St..
*1952 Mountain View #281*

## JOHNSTOWN

**Miss Johnstown Diner**
28 1/2 E. Main St.
(518) 762-1994
*Ward & Dickinson*
Remodeled.

## LITTLE FALLS

**Kristen's Cafe**
28 W. Main St.
(315) 823-4354
*1920s O'Mahony*

## LOWVILLE

**Lloyd's of Lowville**
7405 S. State St.
(315) 376-7037

## MARCY

**Betty's Diner**
9585 River Rd.
(315) 732-9300
*1951 Silk City #51112*

## MASSENA

**Spanky's**
3 N. Main St.
(315) 847-1216
Remodeled.

## NEW BERLIN

**Route 8 Diner**
5079 State Hwy. 8
(607) 847-8975
*1948 Kullman*

## NEW HARTFORD

**Raspberry's Cafe and Creamery**
4784 Commercial Dr.
(315) 736-0312
*1978 Paramount*
Formerly the Hartford Queen.

## NORTHAMPTON

**Northampton Diner**
1205 State Hwy. 30
(518) 863-2567
*1938 O'Mahony*
Remodeled. Originally in Glens Falls.

## NORWICH

**Millie's Diner**
26 E. Main St.
(607) 334-7933
1920s.

## OGDENSBURG

**Phillips Diner**
415 Ford St.
(315) 393-9738
*Ward & Dickinson*
Remodeled.

## ONEIDA

**Morey's Diner**
Phelps St.
*Ward & Dickinson*

## ONEONTA

**Neptune Diner**
5001 State Hwy. 23
(607) 432-8820
*2000 Kullman*

**Nick's Diner**
220 Chestnut St.
(607) 431-1951
*Possibly a 1928 O'Mahony*
Remodeled.

## OSWEGO

**Ritz Diner**
361 W. 1st St.
(315) 342-0947
Remodeled.
Formerly in Syracuse as
Grimlow's Diner.

**Wade's Diner**
176 E. 9th St.
(315) 343-6429
*Ward & Dickinson*
Remodeled.

## OTEGO

**Red Bear Cafe**
Exit 12 off I-88
*1985 Paramount*
Formerly Neptune Diner in
Oneonta. Closed.

While Morey's Diner in Oneida looks remodeled on the outside, owner Lynn Morey did an incredible job restoring the interior of this Ward & Dickinson.

## REMSEN

**Remsen Grill**
Rt. 12
(315) 831-8831
*Fodero*
Remodeled. Formerly Ted's Diner
in North Utica.

## ROME

**Eddie's Paramount Diner**
414 West Dominick St.
(315) 336-9581
*1941 O'Mahony*

## SIDNEY

**Trackside Dining**
88 E. Main St.
(607) 563-3737
*Rochester Grills*
Remodeled. Formerly Sidney Diner
and Reed's Diner.

## SYRACUSE

**Doc's Little Gem Diner**
832 Spencer St.
(315) 422-1686
*1957 Fodero*

**JR Diner**
1208 Wolf St.
(315) 472-2267
*Rochester Grills*
Remodeled. Formerly Griffeth's
Swanky Diner

**Miss Syracuse Diner**
258 E. Water St.
(315) 477-9769
*Bixler*
Remodeled.

**Serpico's Diner**
913 Wolf St.
(315) 422- 6410
*Bixler*
Last of Cameron's Syracuse chain.

**Valley Diner**
4710 S. Salina St.
(315) 492-8415
*Possibly by Ward & Dickinson*
Remodeled.

**West Side Diner**
900 Erie Blvd. W.
*Ward & Dickinson*
Remodeled. Closed.

**UNADILLA**

**Unadilla Diner**
57 Main St.
*1955 Master.*
Closed.

**VESTAL**

**Skylark Diner**
248 Vestal Pkwy. E.
(607) 785-9795
*1956 O'Mahony*

**WATERTOWN**

**Jen's Diner**
455 Court St.
*1940 General Diners*
Closed.

**WHITESBORO**

**Bev's Place**
372 Oriskany Blvd.
(315) 736-2499
*1945 Silk City #45125*
Formerly Smiley's Diner in Utica,
then Augie's Diner and Sophie's
Chuck Wagon at current location.

# WESTERN
# NEW YORK

This chapter includes two diverse regions, reflecting the lack of diners in the western half of the state. There are only twenty-seven diners in this twenty-county region, or an average of 1.3 diners per county. Only the Adirondacks have less. But what western New York, including the Finger Lakes region, does have is a unique assortment of diners for people who don't mind traveling. This assortment of diners is enhanced by the history of diner manufacturers, eight of which operated in the region. Forty-six percent of the diners in the region are the only representative of their particular make in the region, and two are the last remaining examples by their manufacturers in the world.

Before the region got its manufacturing fame, New England lunch wagon builder T. H. Buckley got the exclusive contract for the 1901 Pan-American Exposition in Buffalo. He supplied twenty-five kiosks of his own patented design and brought numerous lunch wagons to the city beyond the confines of the exposition. Buckley tried to get R. H. Hanna, who ran a wagon for him in Plattsburg, to run the kiosks in Buffalo. Hanna declined the offer. After the event in Buffalo was over, he decided to sell the lunch wagons instead of bringing them back to Worcester, Massachusetts. One was bought by J. Corwin "Crab" Miles. Miles was known as Olean's "Midnight Mayor," running a lunch wagon parked outside city hall every night. Robert L. Ripley portrayed this lunch wagon in his *Believe It or Not* cartoon as "the oldest lunch wagon in the country still drawn by horses." The end came on Christmas Eve in 1937, when Crab Miles decided it was time to retire.

Grapes are the common denominator in Western New York. The Lake Erie region is known for Concord grapes and the Finger Lakes for its wine grapes. Grapes, particularly the Concord grape, played a role in bringing the first diner manufacturer to western New York.

In the book *Welch's Grape Juice: From Corporation to Co-operative*, William Chaznof notes that Dr. Charles E. Welch had an "ever-roving mind" for different industries. Daniel Zilka, director of the American Diner Museum, believes that Welch was well aware of the lunch wagon industry. His family lived in Vineland, New Jersey, where diner manufacturer Jerry O'Mahony vacationed and the two became acquainted. It may be coincidence, but in

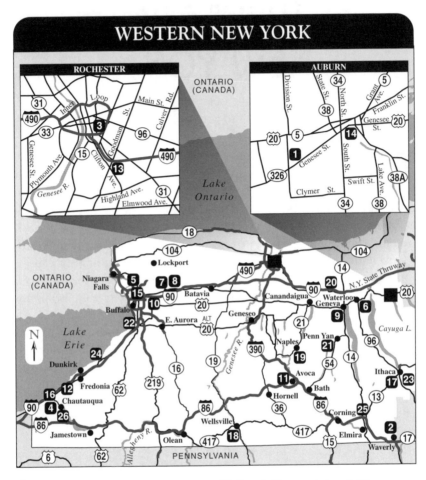

1 Auburn Diner: Auburn (R)
2 Beauty Shop: Waverly (R)
3 Bill Gray's Skyliner Diner: Rochester (MS)
4 Bonars Restaurant: Mayville (R)
5 Coffee Crossing: North Tonawanda (R)
6 Connie's Diner: Waterloo (EM)
7 Diner: Clarence (R)
8 Diner: Clarence (R)
9 Diner: Geneva (BR)
10 50's Diner: Depew (MS)
11 Grandma's Kitchen: Avoca (MS)
12 Green Arch Restaurant: Brocton (R)
13 Highland Park Diner: Rochester (MS)

14 Hunter's Dinerant: Auburn (MS)
15 Lake Effect Diner: Buffalo (MS)
16 Main Diner: Westfield (BR)
17 Manos Diner: Ithaca (E)
18 Modern Diner: Wellsville (R)
19 Naples Diner: Naples (R)
20 Newark Diner: Newark (BR)
21 Penn Yan Diner: Penn Yan (BR)
22 Rainbow Diner: Woodlawn (R)
23 State Diner: Ithaca (R)
24 Steve's Diner: Silver Creek (BR)
25 Sullivan's Diner: Horseheads (MS)
26 Tasty Acre of Chautauqua: Chautauqua (R)

1912, Welch bought the Closson Lunch Wagon Company and moved it from Glens Falls to Westfield. The company lasted about four years before going bankrupt. The idea of building lunch wagons may have been inspired by Earl Richardson, who already had a homemade wagon in Silver Creek. Richardson was from Westfield and, according to the story, he brought his homemade lunch wagon to Silver Creek's Old Home Days in 1909, and met with so much success that he decided to stay. Richardson started building lunch cars in 1921, and it is he who started the boom of dining car building in western New York. Other lunch car building companies and individuals followed, like Peter Schneider, Mulholland, Modern, Goodell, Dr. J. J. Sharp, Guy Russell, and Ward & Dickinson.

In addition to selling their own diners, Mulholland contracted with the Dunkirk Dining Car Company to sell diners for them. Dunkirk set up a demonstration car in Marion, Ohio. Robert McKendrick, who also worked for Ward & Dickinson as a salesman, was a manager at the Marion location. At one time, Dunkirk had six salesman looking for locations for their diners. One of them was Wallace Gillson, who either worked for Mulholland directly, or the Dunkirk Dining Car Company. He sold thirty-two diners for the company before being laid off at the onset of the Great Depression.

CLARENCE HISTORICAL SOCIETY

Employees of the Liberty Dining Car Company in Clarence building diners.

Probably built by J. J. Sharpe, this design in East Aurora resembled the crossover period between diners and lunch wagons.

A couple of years after Taylor's Lunch, J. J. Sharpe built this diner for Silver Creek resident Larry Bader. It was in Medina, Ohio.

Then he worked with his parents who ran a Mulholland in Olean known as the State Diner. His parents bought their diner in 1925, quite possibly through their son. Clem and Bessie Gillson had experience cooking for P. T. Barnum in Rochester. In 1972, William Dascomb bought the property and razed the diner. All that is left is one set of the wheels that the diner was brought into town on.

Wheels beneath a stationary diner may seem to be an unusual thing. But the laws in New York State at the time allowed a diner to be taxed if it was built without wheels. So there was a strong incentive for the owner to keep the delivery wheels attached even after the diner was set on its foundation.

Ward & Dickinson is the most well known of the western New York companies, and easily built the most diners. What was once thought to be the last diner built by Ward & Dickinson now sits in Silver Creek, restored in part to the efforts of chief of police and village historian Louis Pelletter. Although the diner was moved twice in its life, it stayed the closest to its original home of any Ward & Dickinson. The diner started out within sight of the factory, and was owned by John Lown, who ran another diner in Ithaca. Later, it was moved to the edge of town on Route 5 at Steve's Truck Stop. Today, Steve's Diner serves as a community meeting place. A double-wide model sent to State College, Pennsylvania, in 1940 is now presumed to be the last Ward & Dickinson built.

HISTORICAL SOCIETY OF DUNKIRK

This unique diner was built by Mulholland. It is now operated as the Green Arch Restaurant in Brocton and has been extensively remodeled.

Louis Pelletter spearheaded the restoration of one of the last Ward & Dickinson diners built. It stands in Silver Creek as a monument to the company.

This Bixler diner, the Auburn Diner, was almost destroyed in a fire. The current owner, Steve Bianco, restored it and put it back to work.

Booth service had become more important by the 1930s, stimulating the market for sectional diners wide enough to have a row of booths parallel to the counter. Mulholland built their diners in three-foot sections, ten feet wide, and shipped the diners in one piece. Bixler also built these sectional diners at their Norwalk, Ohio, factory. However, they shipped them in four-foot sections, putting the diners together on the site. The former

This old O'Mahoney is the last remaining diner in North Tonawanda. After years of being vacant, the diner opened as the Coffee Crossing in 2008.

Patti's Lakeview Diner, a Bixler saved for preservation by the city of Geneva, sits in storage after being moved to make way for a hotel. The last owner of the diner, Patti Guererri, restored the diner in the 1990s after it had been covered over by past owners.

As Bixler's business faded in 1935, others tried to build sectional diners. Rochester Grills and Sterling were both significant suppliers of diners to western New York. Although Sterling was located in Merrimac, Massachusetts, they had an effective sales representative in Rochester, which helped to bring at least ten Sterling diners to the city, including more than a few of their famous streamliners. Not one of these Sterlings is extant in Rochester, the last being the Rail Diner, a Sterling dinette that was moved to Alpena, Michigan, in the 1990s. Rochester Grills was a less prominent builder, but three survive. All three diners are outside of the region, but are easily within driving distance. One is a florist shop in Bradford, Pennsylvania, and the other two are in Endwell and Syracuse.

Besides building diners that looked similar to Bixlers, Rochester Grills also built sandwich grills. They advertised these as being all-steel and fully insulated, and the grills measured fifteen feet by twenty-five feet. The Red Dome at State and Church Streets was one of Rochester Grills' sandwich shops that stayed in Rochester. Joseph Entress, a locally known developer in Rochester, built at least one diner in the city—Herbert's Diner—in 1938. That diner looked strikingly similar to a Rochester Grills.

Western New York has only twenty-seven diners, representing sixteen unique builders. The ages of the diners range from the 1924 Penn Yan Diner built by Earl Richardson to the 1977 Manos Diner in Ithaca, built by Swingle. There are two severely remodeled Ward & Dickinson diners in Wellsville and Naples and two O'Mahony diners in North Tonawanda and Auburn. The owner of the former 412 Diner in North Towanda offered one year of free rent to anyone wanting to reopen this 1920s barrel-roof diner. The Auburn O'Mahony, known as the Hunter Dinerant, replaced a Ward & Dickinson that had replaced an even older Ward & Dickinson. The diner sits cantilevered over the Owasco Creek on Genesee Street, the main business route through the city. This 1951 O'Mahony has ceramic tiles in vertical lines between the stainless steel. The diner has seen a succession of owners since the 1970s, but might be back on the road to prosperity.

## RESEARCHING DINERS

Besides being a great resource of current diners in upstate New York, www.nydiners.com is also dedicated to documenting diners that were built in upstate New York. The primary focus started on New York, but quickly included New York diners located in other states. Ward & Dickinson sent at least eight diners to Michigan and the Richardson Company moved from Silver Creek to Dayton, Ohio, in 1926, in an attempt to capture the market in that region.

Many Ohio villages and cities received a Richardson diner built in Chautauqua County. Richardson sent cars to Ravenna, Conneaut, and Bryan. The little village of Wellington had a rare Goodell up to 2002. The diner was saved and moved to Towanda, Pennsylvania, where it is undergoing restoration. Gordon Tindall, who expertly restored a Tierney Diner first known as the Lackawanna Trail Diner, is doing the same to this Goodell diner. The Dunkirk Dining Car Company, which sold Mulhollands, had a demonstration car in Marion, Ohio.

There is so much history out there that has either been forgotten or will shortly become forgotten. Ward & Dickinson displayed a diner at the Minnesota State Fair in 1926. Did it help to sell diners in Minnesota? Apparently not. Ward & Dickinson had built 233 diners by 1932, how many did they build before they closed shop? And where did they all go? Then there were the companies that liked to call their diners sectional restaurants: Bixler, Rochester Grills, and General. The company that started this movement over a century ago was the Closson Lunch Wagon Company.

If you're interested in more diner history, visit www.nydiners.com. This site also encourages you to share your own history and help preserve a diner's memory.

This diner in Avoca is for sale; someone bought the caboose seen here and moved it away.

The region's three Silk City diners date to 1940, 1948, and 1955. Sullivan's Diner is the oldest of the three. Originally called Vic's Diner, it was the last diner out of Elmira, a city that once had eight diners, including an O'Mahony, Bixler, Kullman, Ward & Dickinson, and a Sterling streamliner. The diner was moved to its current site in Horseheads in 1974, where it was run faithfully by Arthur and Fran Sullivan until early 2006.

The second Silk City diner sits in Avoca, on Route 415. This road was once the main thoroughfare from Rochester to Corning and south into Pennsylvania and beyond. This changed in the late 1970s when I-390 was built to connect Rochester with the Southern Tier's Route 17. The traffic that gave the diner much of its business was siphoned onto the interstate, and now the diner is closed and for sale at the time of this writing. It sits across from the Caboose Motel, which features a string of five cabooses that you can stay in. At one time the diner itself had a caboose attached to it, but the railcar was recently sold. The diner has been on this location since it was first bought from Silk City in 1948. It is unique because the bathrooms are located inside of the diner, and take up a space that could have accommodated two more booths.

Depew is now considered an eastern suburb of Buffalo. At one time, Depew and Lancaster were distinct villages outside of Buffalo. The former Roberts Diner in Depew is now known as the 50's Diner. This 1955 Silk City originally cost $42,000 and $2,900 for the vestibule. When Peter Sciolino bought the diner in 1966, he kept the name. His daughter, who started working at the diner when she was twelve, still works there, even though Peter has since retired and sold the diner. Besides their home-cooked food, they are known for their Hi-Boy, a triple decker hamburger.

Outside the 50's Diner in Depew.

The Lake Effect Diner, named for Buffalo's snowy winter weather, is on Main Street near the University at Buffalo's south campus. This Mountain View diner came from Wayne, Pennsylvania, where it last did business as a Chinese restaurant. It was moved to Buffalo with the help of the American Diner Museum. Owner Tucker Curtin placed it next to his Steer Restaurant & Saloon, in the University Heights District of Buffalo. Tucker uses his two restaurants to help revive the neighborhood that surrounds the University at Buffalo's south campus.

Buffalo used to have many more diners. Its proximity to the diner manufacturers in the 1920s helped to bring in about two dozen diners. When the economy deteriorated in upstate New York, Buffalo went along for the ride. Beginning in the 1950s, diners were closed up and leveled one by one. Some neighborhoods couldn't support a diner anymore, others had become too dangerous for them. Owners retired, and no one was willing to take over a marginal diner. In addition, many of the diners built in western New York were not built to handle larger crowds—they sat only twenty to thirty people—so many potential owners saw no way to make a profit.

An article that made the national news in March, 1975, tells the whole story of the economic decline. Louis Muscato, who was running the Hinman Diner, a Liberty dining car in the north part of Buffalo, decided to lower the price of coffee from his normal 15 cents to 5 cents for any unemployed customer. He said, "How can I afford not to do something to let the guys who have been customers for years know that I want somehow to share in and perhaps ease their troubles."

From 1927 to 1931, Clarence was home to the Liberty Dining Car Company. Charles Ward founded the company after he left Ward & Dickinson. Two Liberty diners survive. One is located on Route 5 in Clarence, but it is currently closed. The other is still serving food in Milford, New Hampshire.

At one time, Buffalo was home to at least three Liberty Diners, each costing $7,500. Charles Ward was also able to place Liberty dining cars in Attica, Gowanda (replacing a homemade diner built by the owner's son-in-law Peter Schneider), and in Depew, close to the current 50's Diner.

Clarence is also home to another diner, also closed, which was last used as an antiques store. The diner is, at the time of this writing, for sale. What makes this shell of a diner so interesting is that no one knows who built it. It is possible that the same person who built the still-standing State Diner in Conneaut, Ohio, also built this diner. Both diners have a barrel roof, with a flat beveled section at each end.

Two diners sit almost side-by-side south of Buffalo in Woodlawn. The current Woodlawn Diner is an on-site diner, but it replaced an authentic diner that was either a Ward & Dickinson or a Sharpe/National diner. Inside you will find a counter and booths, the classic diner setup, along with pictures of the original diner being removed. While J. J. Sharpe did become the only barrel-roof diner builder in Silver Creek, at one time he also built lunch cars with monitor roofs.

Two buildings north on Route 5 is the closed Rainbow Diner, built by the Master Diner Company. Its history is unknown, but it has been closed for more than twenty years. At one time, this tiny community had three din-

This diner in Clarence has been gutted and last did business as an antiques store. Its maker is unknown.

ers. Bell's Diner was run by Sidney and Isabel Schweikert, and the Wood-lawn Diner was run by Mary Schweikert.

Bell's Diner likely moved to Woodlawn from Buffalo's Bailey Street. A picture of the diner hangs on the wall in the current Woodlawn Diner. This picture shows a closeup of what seems to be a Richardson-built diner.

At one time in Silver Creek's history, there were four lunch cars set up to catch a mix of locals and visitors traveling on Route 5 and U.S. Route 20, the main road from New York and New England westward. One diner was only run for a year by Walter Plum at his ostrich and alligator farm. This zoo only lasted a few years in Silver Creek, as the animals became difficult to maintain in the winter months. Another car located in town was later moved to Wesleyville, Pennsylvania. (This was actually the fourth diner built by Ward & Dickinson, and it was sold back to the company by Roy Payne, who originally ran it in Silver Creek.) Payne went on to run diners for Ward & Dickinson in places like Batavia and Kane, Pennsylvania. J. J. Sharpe, who is said to have built a diner a year, built one for Miss Florence Clute in Silver Creek in 1927. Miss Clute married Howard Centner, and the diner became known as Centner's Diner up until 1945.

Fredonia had a Ward & Dickinson that replaced an older lunch car, possibly a Closson or early Richardson. The town also has a trolley car that was once used as a diner. Former owner Richard DeJohn bought the place in 1967 when it was known as the Park Diner. He later sold the diner to his brother, but not before remodeling the interior. Today, it is known as

The Rainbow Diner in Woodlawn has not been a working diner for at least twenty years.

CATHERINE GAETANO

Clarence Harrison Jr., the owner's son, making change. The photo was taken in November 1948 inside Barney's Diner in Franklinville.

DeJohn's Italian Spaghetti House. Unfortunately, Fredonia's diner history is marred by fires. One diner had a fire less than a year after reopening from a previous fire.

Although centers of the lunch car manufacturing boom of the 1920s, neither Silver Creek nor Dunkirk have a working diner today. At least eight diners once called these two places home, including Sharps, Richardsons, Ward & Dickinsons, and Mulhollands. The Dunkirk Diner was relocated in 1955 to nearby Portland. Unfortunately, with the opening of the New York State Thruway, the diner never reopened. Mulholland mostly built monitor-roof cars, although at least one barrel-roof diner was constructed. That diner still exists in nearby Brocton, though it has been remodeled and is missing its original booths. Although tiny Brocton had a much smaller population than the 5,000 needed to support a diner in the 1930s, the town had two. Its location on U.S. Route 20, a major transcontinental highway made up the difference, bringing a steady stream of long-distance travelers. Brockton's Mulholland Diner, now the Green Arch, is open for breakfast, lunch, and dinner.

One diner in Dunkirk, unable to turn a profit across from the very popular Cease Lunch Car, was sold to Bert Maggio, who moved it to a campground on U.S. Route 20 just outside of Westfield. The famous Kendall Diner also got a new lease on life. Vintage postcards illustrate how the busi-

The first Kendall Diner is shown here, with an added on dining room. When the Kendall Company traded this in, the old diner possibly went to Irving.

ness changed over time. It originally sat on a section of U.S. Route 20, just west of Silver Creek. When they first opened, they were surrounded by vineyards, so the owners gave a pint of grapes to everyone who bought gas at their adjoining station. The vineyards were eventually cleared away to make room for forty-eight tourist cottages (one for each state.) This first diner was a typical thirty-foot by ten-foot Ward & Dickinson. It was later enlarged with the addition of a dining room. The last postcard printed shows a large Ward & Dickinson, five windows wide. It is believed that it is the only one this wide that Ward & Dickinson built. As talks about the New York State Thruway started and this section of U.S. Route 20 was bypassed, this diner, along with the cabins, were sold. The diner was moved to Fredonia, to a section of U.S. Route 20 where exit 59 off I-90 is located. The diner was remodeled by the Sorge Diner Company in 1946 and renamed the Friendly Diner.

The Main Diner down the road in Westfield is another Ward & Dickinson, and has been a town mainstay since the 1930s. Recently the diner had their classic "Main Diner" neon sign restored. Westfield's diner history is complex, with diners coming and going regularly.

The Closson Lunch Wagon factory was located in Westfield between 1913 and 1917, and placed one of their wagons in town. A Ward & Dickinson called the Starlite Diner did business just outside of town at one of the many tourist camps on U.S. Route 20. It is possible that this is the diner that came from Dunkirk. Diner historian John Shoaf turned up a another mystery on Portage Street—a barrel roof building the size of a lunch wagon that is now used as a house. Its history remains unknown.

## DYNORS AND DINORS

In northwestern Pennsylvania and eastern Ohio, you may find variations in the spelling of the word diner. It has been said in these areas that when you go out to eat, you are a "diner," but you eat in a "dinor." Jamestown, New York, was home to yet another variation, "dynor." The original dynor was a trolley car converted into a lunch wagon in 1925. It was later known as Pickup's Dynor and then the Cherry Dynor, before it was removed from service in the 1940s. Another dynor was the Red Top, but it had reverted back to diner by 1952. Other 1930s and 1940s diners used the dinor spelling, but the variation was not used east of Olean or west of Mansfield, Ohio. Some diners still today use the "dinor" variation, the most famous being the Lawrence Park Dinor in Lawrence Park, Pennsylvania, a suburb of Erie.

After World War II, Charles Sorge, a Silver Creek carpenter, started building diners resembling the Ward & Dickinson models in 1947. Sorge probably built five diners. The local newspaper in Oil City, Pennsylvania, reported that two of them ended up there. The last known Sorge, Bonars Restaurant, though quite remodeled, is located in the Chautaqua Lake town of Mayville. The interior has a tile wall base and unpainted stainless-steel ceiling panels, possibly the only original part of the diner.

The owners of Pratt's Diner in Rochester pose for this picture taken by a Ward & Dickinson sales representative in the 1930s.

Many villages bypassed by I-86 once had diners. Falconer had two, one of which was a Richardson. Randolph had a Sharpe. The diner had many owners before Sam Abbott bought it. The diner was closed during World Ward II, but had a grand reopening celebration after the war's end. Salamanca had a couple of diners. One was run by Lloyd Blanding, who quickly bought out his partner Montford Fox. After about ten years running this diner, he moved to Watertown to run a new Ward & Dickinson. Olean had a Rochester Grills, Mulholland, and a Modern and, on the outskirts of town, a stainless steel O'Mahony. While it's possible that Pickup's Diner in downtown Olean was built by Mulholland, the owner's son, Jim Pickup, said his father Estes had invested in the Modern Dining Car Company, which leads to the possibility that the diner is a Modern. As to how Pickup's came to Olean from its original location in Brooklyn, Jim likes this story the best. "With the mob ruling the Brooklyn area, telling you with whom you would do business, no one wanted to buy [or move] that diner." Estes finally found a company that went in at night, "jacked it up, transported it to the freight yard, and loaded it on a flat car to ship it to Olean." The Pickups retired in 1969 and business faded shortly thereafter.

Olean had two other notable lunch cars. The Miles "Crab" Corwin lunch wagon, previously mentioned is by far the most famous. The lunch wagon was cited for breaking parking rules many times, but it was such an institution, a place where many a politician would meet and eat, so the laws were often overlooked. The other was the Truman's Lunch Car, built by Truman W. Kreamer on a truck chassis.

Route 417 east from Olean slices through western New York's oil country. In the late 1800s, places like Bolivar and Wellsville were known as prime areas to speculate for oil. The town of Richburg swelled to over 10,000 practically overnight when oil was discovered in 1881. As the Richburg oil boom subsided a year later, most of the population moved on. Over time, however, diners moved in to serve the remaining population. Bolivar was home to a Richardson diner that started out in Wellsville. While in Bolivar it did business as Walker's and then Abbott's Diner, run by Sam Abbott. One of the funnier stories from the diner concerns a state trooper who stopped in for some pie. The trooper said, "Give me a piece of pie and step on it," which is exactly what the counterman did. The trooper, not amused in the least, grabbed the cook, pulled him over the counter, and handcuffed him to the footrail on the customer's side. The diner called Bolivar home until 1988, when it was razed.

Wellsville has the Modern Diner, a remodeled Ward that was probably moved to town from another location around 1938. Until about ten years ago, there was an old O'Mahony barrel-roof diner in town known as Cross's Diner.

Corning does not have a single diner anymore. The glass city started out with a few lunch wagons, but as few as three diners. Stanton's Diner was probably the best known of them. It was a Silk City diner that replaced an older lunch car. Vernon and Maude Harvey, who are said to have run diners in as many as five locations, also ran a diner in Corning for at least a year. Before ending up in Amsterdam, the couple ran diners in Silver Creek and Corry, Pennsylvania. There was also a Ward & Dickinson on Route 17 in Corning that was replaced by a Montgomery Wards.

Two of Elmira's three diners were destroyed by the 1972 flood spawned by Hurricane Agnes. Schanaker's Diner, a Sterling Streamliner, was evicted from its downtown location in 1967 because of urban renewal, but the owners had plans to reopen. Unfortunately, the flood swept the diner down the Chemung River, and it was deemed unsalvagable. The nearby Colonial Diner was also destroyed by the flood, but a third downtown diner, the Mayfair, survived. The Mayfair was a very long Kullman, possibly lengthened by the company during a remodeling. The diner was moved to Route 17 in Vestal in the 1960s, where its name changed to Village Chef.

The last diner to leave Elmira was Vic's Diner. It was bought by Arthur and Frances Sullivan and is now Sullivan's Diner in Horseheads. The Agnes flood hit Vic's as well, and stickers inside the diner shows just how high the water got. Other diners to call Elmira home included the Elmira and Lokken.

East of Elmira, Waverly is the home of the state's only Valentine diner, now used by a hair stylist. Valentines were distributed through a Long Island company known as National Diner. Very little of its original features remain

Shortly before the diner was razed, it seemed clear that the time was near for this Ward & Dickinson in LeRoy.

The shrubs that surrounded Sullivan's Diner in Horseheads have finally been removed, allowing for great photos of this Silk City.

intact. The former Mel's Diner sits on downtown Waverly's main street. Waverly briefly had an early Ward & Dickinson that was moved to Binghamton by William Caple.

Bath had a Goodell diner known as the Court House Diner, but a fire destroyed it in the 1970s. Bath also had a few lunch wagons.

Ithaca has a diner that might make metropolitan college students feel right at home. Manos Diner is the only Swingle left in western New York, and the westernmost environmental in the state. (Jay's Diner in Rochester, another Swingle, used to hold this record, but it was leveled for an on-site diner.) Downtown Ithaca used to be home to a few diners, including one owned by Harry Potter. The current State Diner on State Street has been in Ithaca since the 1930s. The diner appears to be a remodeled Sterling. The ceiling is covered with tiny ceramic tiles, like one might see on a bathroom floor. The first reference to a diner at this location was in 1937 when L. Gerald Rich and Kenneth Hardenbrook had a chain of three diners, two of which were built by Sterling. One of their Sterlings was moved up to the Cortland area.

LARRY CULTRERA

The only Valentine known to exist in New York state, now a beauty salon in Waverly.

Lunch wagons and diners have long served the Cornell campus in Ithaca. Even today, there is a version of a lunch wagon that goes around campus. In the nineteenth century, Ephraim Hamel brought a lunch wagon in Ithaca, giving a license to run the place to Robert and Amanda Love. The Loves subsequently bought the wagon from Hamel, with the understanding that Hamel would not maintain a wagon in Ithaca, or sell one to another party. The Loves forgot to mention this to their attorney when he drew up the contract and Hamel placed another lunch wagon in Ithaca. The Loves sued Hamel and won, but the decision was reversed on appeal. *The New York Times* reported on May 21, 1901, "Judgment for the plaintiffs has been reversed by the Third Appellate Division, the court holding that the oral agreement in regard to maintaining another lunch wagon was not a collateral and independent agreement, and that oral evidence of such agreement was inadmissible, as it tended to vary the written contract."

Penn Yan has the only known Richardson in existence. Just a block off the main drag on East Elm Street, this small diner is the jewel of Penn Yan. Rochester is home to the Highland Park Diner, the last diner built by the

## LINDA GOTTWALD

Linda Gottwald grew up in Baltimore, but lived much of her adult life in Rochester. She loved to take pictures of diners and roadside places and had a knack for making the ordinary look extraordinary. She worked with inner-city youth and taught them to take pictures of subjects from their daily lives. Sadly, however, Linda was stricken with cancer.

The Highland Park Diner was Linda's favorite, and a frequent subject of her photographs. Before Linda passed away in October 2004, her friend Susan Levinson helped set up Linda Gottwald Day at the diner. The

Linda Gottwald Day at the Highland Park Diner in Rochester: Glenn Wells, Michael Engle, Sally Broadbent, Linda Gottwald, and Steven Boksenbaum.

owner at the time, Bob Malley, agreed to donate a percentage of that day's profits to a fund for Linda.

Linda's photography is highly valued. Collectors of diner ephemera cherish notecards that she created featuring her work.

The back building blends in well with this 1939 Sterling diner in Newark. The Newark Diner is the last surviving Sterling in western New York and still has the original glass built into the counter.

Orleans Dining Car Company. But don't go to these diners just for their style, go there to eat! Both diners have fantastic cooks who serve some of the best homemade food in western New York.

The Newark Diner is the last Sterling diner in Western New York. It retains its original glass-top counter. The locals and owners still talk about the time the diner was featured in the soap opera *General Hospital*.

Newark was also home to a Richardson diner, first owned by George Dickinson. Dickinson sold it to his son-in-law Walter Dennis and moved to Albion, where he ran a Ward & Dickinson called the Albion Diner, located in the center of town. The Albion was replaced with a newer, forty-foot Ward & Dickinson around 1930. Dishwasher Ralph Eibl remembers when the diner got an electric dishwasher and his pay got cut from $10 to $8 a week. Dickinson became known around Albion as "Little Dick from Silver Creek (pronounced "crick")." By 1940, he had retired, moved back to Silver Creek, and sold the diner to Walter Chatfield.

Albion was also home to the Liberty Diner, quite possibly built by the Liberty Dining Car Company. Libertys were so similar to Ward & Dickinsons that it is hard to tell the difference. Another Ward & Dickinson, known as Skip's Diner, operated in nearby Medina.

# PENN YAN DINER
## 1925 RICHARDSON
131 E. Elm St., Penn Yan • (315) 536-6004

In a village best known for its location on Keuka Lake sits a true gem of a diner less than a block off the main drag. This is the last known diner built by Earl Richardson of Silver Creek. Although a newspaper article originally stated that this was a Galion dining car, no information has ever been found that verifies a Galion Dining Car Company even existed. The best that anyone can guess is that Richardson may have had a model of lunch car that he named the "Galion."

In 1925, Alfred Smith, Mather Morse, William Walstrum, and E. B. Richardson came to Penn Yan to build a kitchen under the diner. Up until the 1940s, when there was a fire in the kitchen, the diner was supplied by a kitchen that was built under the diner. After the fire, a kitchen was built on the back of the diner, along with an additional dining room, perpendicular to the dining car. This provided room for five more tables.

The diner has had multiple owners. The first were Byron and Lena Legters and Carol Bond from Silver Creek, who claimed that chicken pies were their specialty. The next owner was Mrs. Richardson who had her son Douglas King manage the diner. After that, it went to Odell Jones, who is

Diners built in the 1920s did not have much space, as evidenced by this view.

said to have remodeled the diner. He sold the diner to John Quenan, who in turn sold the diner to the current owner, Lyman Beecher.

For the past twenty-six years, Lyman Beecher has been operating the Penn Yan. Humorous signs hang on the walls, such as "There will be a $5 charge

The crew at the Penn Yan Diner: Willy, Cindy, Lyman.

for whining" and "All visitors bring happiness, some by coming, others by going." Lyman says most of the signs were there when he bought the diner, but occasionally a customer will bring in a new one. During the day, Lyman is in the back of this yellow-and-lime-green-colored diner, prepping for the lunch and dinner crowd. Cindy Bechard, who has been there for seventeen years, takes care of the cooking and waiting. Her sister, Heidi Catlin, has been there for twenty-six years, but only works on Saturdays. Heidi and her husband run a hardware store in the nearby town of Rushville.

Cindy can not think of a better job. The customers are like family to her, and they have a great time visiting with her. When it comes to the food, it's just as good. Each day, there are one or two specials. Some of the perennial favorites are the turkey on Thursdays and the creamed codfish on Friday. Make sure you save room for dessert—Lyman makes all the pies himself.

After twenty-six years, Lyman is ready to hang up the spatula. Hopefully he will pass his recipes on to the next owner, especially the one for his popular French silk pie.

# MANOS DINER
### 1977 SWINGLE
357 Elmira Rd., Ithaca • (607) 273-1173

If the Manos Diner was in the New York City metropolitan area, it would be one of many environmental diners, but in central New York State, it is a rarity. James and Helen Manos came from Des Moines, Iowa, in 1962 and bought an old wooden building, known as Hoyt's Trailer Park and Diner. At this time, Elmira Road was only two lanes wide with few businesses. Even when the Manos's son Bill bought a new Swingle diner in 1977 to replace the original, the area was still not well developed. The family, however, correctly assumed the road would become a major commercial strip.

The Manos is a stock model Mediterranean diner with a mansard roof. One end of the diner is taken up by the Ichabod Restaurant and Lounge, where cocktails are served, alone or with meals. Bill buys only choice meats, and unlike many other diners of the same size, the Manos does not offer specials. Bill says the focus is on consistently good home-cooked food.

In 1987, Bill opened a second Manos Diner in Elmira, putting Chris Carvell in charge as manager. Chris had originally worked for Bill at the Ithaca Manos and decided he wanted to move back to his home town of Elmira and run a diner there. Chris later went on to work for Kullman Industries. Bill's daughter Eleni, suggested she should replace Chris and has been running the Elmira diner since 2001. Bill says that since his daughter has been running the diner, he hardly knows what goes on there anymore, she does such a good job.

# LAKE EFFECT DINER
## 1955 MOUNTAIN VIEW #446
3165 Main St. (Rt. 5), Buffalo • (716) 833-1952

Many factors led to the Lake Effect Diner finding its way to Buffalo's University Heights district from Wayne, Pennsylvania. Erin and Tucker Curtin owned the Steer Restaurant in Buffalo, but Tucker always liked diners. They found a diner for sale on the American Diner Museum Web site. It was a Mountain View, last run as a Chinese takeout, and it needed to be removed from its location. So they moved the diner up to Buffalo and restored it. The

The Lake Effect in its previous life as China Buddha in Wayne, Pennsylvania.

interior color scheme is now gray and pink, with new booths and yellow highlights. The yellow on the inside complements the silver and yellow on the exterior.

The diner has twenty-two flavors of milkshakes, and on Tuesdays the milkshakes are two for one. If you walk into the diner at 10 P.M. on Tuesday night, it seems like everyone orders a milkshake. The diner also offers freshly squeezed orange juice from a machine with transparent casing that allows patrons to watch the juice being made right behind the counter. And then there is the Blizzard Plate, Buffalo's answer to the garbage plate. The cook makes a meal of whatever he wants to put on a plate, such as turkey and roast beef and whatever else is on hand, all covered with gravy.

Just like Rochester's Highland Park Diner, the Lake Effect has become a place local residents show off with pride. Stop in at lunch, and you'll see a mix of businessmen, students, workers on their lunch breaks, or regulars with friends from out of town. The Weather Channel liked the diner so much they used it as a background during one of the heavy snowstorms that hits the city yearly, an appropriate compliment to its name.

On a wall outside of the main diner are photographs and articles about the diner's history—its life in Wayne, its move to Buffalo, and its opening as the Lake Effect. Some customers remember eating at the diner when it was in Wayne.

# HIGHLAND PARK DINER

**1948 ORLEANS**

906 Clinton Ave. S., Rochester • (716) 641-5040

There has been a restaurant on the site of the Highland Park Diner for much of the twentieth century. The original street car diner was replaced by a Sterling dinette on February 22, 1940. This diner proved to be too small, and in 1948 it was moved to Ridge Road to allow a brand new, larger diner to take its place. That diner came from the Orleans Dining Car Company of Albion and was called Dauphin's Superior Diner. Dauphin's did business until 1972 when it became an Off Track Betting (OTB) location.

The diner was gutted in the conversion. The diner was brought the diner back to its original splendor by Bob Malley, who bought the building in 1985. It now has a yellow ceiling and walls with green booths and a black counter. The outside is yellow, with some classic neon.

Bob and his son Jim updated the typical diner menu to make it healthier. They wanted a menu that was also interesting, featuring gourmet foods made from scratch. The Empire Diner in Manhattan, a gem in its own right, was an inspiration. Jim says the first five years were a blur. People were surprised that a diner could serve such good food. Their apple pie earned recognition in *Conde Nast Traveler*, which basically said this is the best pie in the country. The news of the restoration and opening made the Associated Press, and brought customers from all over the globe. There are a few catchy signs around the diner like, "Keep your kitchen clean, Eat at the Highland Park Diner," and "Good food is not cheap. Cheap food is not good." Despite these truisms, the prices at the Highland Park are comparable to many other diners.

Bob and Jim Malley like the idea that the diner is across the street from an operating movie theater. They worked closely with the theater to entice people to come to the Highland Park neighborhood for dinner and a movie. In 1993, the Malleys also bought the former Mountain Top Diner, which sat on Route 15 north of Williamsport, Pennsylvania. Bob received a call telling him that the diner needed to be moved within a week. He had planned to move the diner to the corner of Culver and University, but when the land deal fell through, he ended up selling it to the Strong Museum in Rochester. Today it is operated for the museum by Bill Gray's Restaurant, a small local chain that started in Webster as a roadside stand.

Bob Malley is now retired, and his son Jim runs the Mercury Poster Shop not too far from the diner. The good news is that not much has changed at the diner. Ti Lee still manages the place for the new owner, Van Zissis. The food is still the same high quality food, and the place is just as friendly.

# DINER DIRECTORY

## AUBURN

**Auburn Diner**
64 Columbus St.
(315) 253-7375
*Bixler*

**Hunter Dinerant**
18 Genesee St.
(315) 255-3578
*1951 O'Mahony*

## AVOCA

**Grandma's Kitchen**
8621 Rt. 415
*1948 Silk City*
Closed.

## BROCTON

**Green Arch Restaurant**
41 W. Main St.
(716) 792-9526
*1931 Mulholland*
Remodeled.

## BUFFALO

**Lake Effect Diner**
3165 Main St. (Rt. 5)
(716) 833-1952
*1955 Mountain View #446*

## CHAUTAUQUA

**Tasty Acre of Chautauqua**
In front of the Chautauqua Institution
(716) 357-2232
*Possibly by Ward & Dickinson*
Remodeled.

## CLARENCE

**Diner**
10939 Main St. (Rt. 5)
Closed.

**Mazio's Pizza**
10837 Main St. (Rt. 5)
*Liberty*
Remodeled. Closed.

## DEPEW

**50's Diner**
(716) 683-9248
*1954 Silk City #5425*
Formerly Robert's Diner.

## GENEVA

**Patti's Lakeview Diner**
*Bixler*
In storage.

This O'Mahony diner is actually cantilevered over the Owasco Creek that cuts through downtown Auburn.

## HORSEHEADS

**Sullivan's Diner**
59 Old Ithaca Rd.
(607) 796-9950
*1940 Silk City #4075*

## ITHACA

**Manos Diner**
357 Elmira Rd.
(607) 273-1173
*1977 Swingle*

**State Diner**
428 W. State St.
(607) 272-6189
*Possibly by Sterling*
Remodeled.

## MAYVILLE

**Bonars Restaurant**
7 Chautauqua St.
(716) 753-3887
*1949 Sorge*

## NAPLES

**Naples Diner**
139 S. Main St.
(716) 374-5420
*Ward & Dickinson*
Remodeled.

## NEWARK

**Newark Diner**
246 E. Union St.
(315) 331-2270
*1939 Sterling #397*

## NORTH TONAWANDA

**Coffee Crossing**
412 Oliver St.
(716) 692-8427
*Possibly a 1920s O'Mahony*

Bob Malley tried to open the Skyliner up in Rochester, but ran into problems with the city. He then decided to sell it to the Strong Museum. Note the fake building in the background.

## PENN YAN

**Penn Yan Diner**
131 E. Elm St.
(315) 536-6004
*1925 Richardson*

## ROCHESTER

**Bill Gray's Skyliner Diner**
1 Manhattan Sq. at Strong Museum
(585) 232-5284
*1956 Fodero*

**Highland Park Diner**
906 Clinton Ave. S.
(716) 641-5040
*1948 Orleans*

## SILVER CREEK

**Steve's Diner**
172 Central Ave.
*1938 Ward & Dickinson* (Ward & Dickinson Museum)
Open by appointment.

Connie's Diner in Waterloo is a rare 1965 Manno. The inside has lots of 1950s memorabilia and packs customers with good food at low prices.

## WATERLOO

**Connie's Diner**
205 E. Main St.
(315) 539-9556
*1965 Manno*

## WAVERLY

**Terry's Styling Salon**
226 Broad St.
*Valentine*
Closed.

## WELLSVILLE

**Modern Diner**
73 N. Main St.
(585) 593-9842
*Ward & Dickinson*
Remodeled.

## WESTFIELD

**Main Diner**
40 E. Main St.
(716) 326-4351
*Ward & Dickinson*

## WOODLAWN

**Rainbow Diner**
3196 Hamburg Tpk. (Rt. 5)
*Master*
Closed.

**Woodlawn Diner**
3200 Lake Shore Rd.
(716) 822-8449
On-site replacement. Replaced an old lunch car.

# Further Reading

Anderson, Will. *Lost Diners and Roadside Restaurants of New England and New York.* Utica, NY: North Country Books, 2001.

———. *Where Have You Gone, Starlight Cafe: America's Golden Era Roadside Restaurants.* Portland, ME: Anderson and Sons, 1998.

———. *Mid-Atlantic Roadside Delights.* Portland, ME: Anderson and Sons, 1991.

Baeder, John. *Diners.* Rev. and updated ed. New York: Harry N. Abrams, 1995.

Boyle, Tish. *Diner Desserts.* San Francisco: Chronicle Books, 2000.

Butko, Brian, and Sarah Butko. *Roadside Attractions: Cool Cafés, Souvenir Stands, Route 66 Relics, & Other Road Trip Fun.* Mechanicsburg, PA: Stackpole Books, 2007.

Butko, Brian, and Kevin Patrick. *Diners of Pennsylvania.* Mechanicsburg, PA: Stackpole Books, 1999.

Everett, Linda. *Retro Diner: Comfort Food from the American Roadside.* Portland, OR: Collector's Press, 2002.

Garbin, Randy. *More Retro Diner: A Second Helping of Roadside Recipes.* Portland, OR: Collectors Press, 2005.

———. *Diners of New England.* Mechanicsburg, PA: Stackpole Books, 2005.

Gutman, Richard J. S. *The Worcester Lunch Car Company.* Mount Pleasant, SC: Arcadia, 2004.

———. *American Diner: Then and Now.* Baltimore: Johns Hopkins University Press, 2000.

Kaplan, Donald, and Alan Bellink. *Diners of the Northeast.* Stockbridge, MA: Berkshire Traveller Press, 1980.

Kittel, Gerd. *Diners: People and Places.* New York: Thames and Hudson, 1998.

Liebs, Chester. *Main Street to Miracle Mile: American Roadside Architecture.* Baltimore: Johns Hopkins University Press, 1995.

Monti, Mario. *A Directory of Diners.* 3rd ed. New York: Self-published, 2004.

Offitzer, Karen. *Diners.* New York: MetroBooks, 1997.

Williams, Robert O. *Hometown Diners.* New York: Harry N. Abrams, 1999.

Witzel, Michael Karl. *The American Diner.* Osceola, WI: MBI Publishing, 1999.

# Acknowledgments

Thanks to Stackpole Books for the opportunity to write this book. Also thanks to Gordon Tindall at the Broome County Historical Society, Vince Martonis at Hanover History Center, Clarence Historical Society, Chenango County Historian, Dunkirk Historical Society, Albany County Hall of Records, American Diner Museum, City of Buffalo Office of Permits, Daniel Zilka, Richard Gutman, Louis F. Pelletier, Tom Tryinski, Ron Dylewski, Gregg Anderson, Glenn Wells, Colin Strayer, Gary Thomas, Randy Garbin, Larry Cultrera, Linda Schiele, City of Buffalo Office of Permits, William Rhodes, Connie and Margaret Hoffman, Richard and Francis Engle, John Koutouzis, Kathy Stribley, Susan Levinson, Don Huelett, Don Rittner, Dave Waller, William Preston Gates, James Malley, Clark Fegraus, Catherine Gaetano, Tom Prebble, Dave Faulkner, Wally Day, Harvey Kaplan, Forgotten NY, every employee of the western New York lunch wagon and diner builders, many libraries that have local history sections, and all the owners of the featured diners—they're great people! And anyone else whose name I may have forgotten.

*ME*

Thanks to those whose knowledge and inspiration made this book possible: Will Anderson, John Baeder, Wallace W. Broege, Brian Butko, Phil DeRaffele, Peter Genovese, John Gilman, Robert Heide, Steven Izenour, Edwin Kruse, Susan Levinson, Chester Liebs, Joe Manning, Kevin Patrick, Ron Saari, Michael Stern, and Robert O. Williams. Special thanks to Lucille Monti, who accompanied us on those long diner trips and took detailed notes describing the exterior and interior architecture of the featured diners.

*MM*

# Index